INTERSECTIONS: WOMEN ON LAW, MEDICINE AND TECHNOLOGY

Titles in the Series:

A Patient's Right to Know: Information Disclosure, the Doctor and the Law
Sheila A.M. McLean, University of Glasgow

New Reproductive Techniques: A Legal Perspective
Douglas J. Cusine, University of Aberdeen

Medico-Legal Aspects of Reproduction and Parenthood
J.K. Mason, University of Edinburgh

Law Reform and Human Reproduction
Edited by *Sheila A.M. McLean*, University of Glasgow

Legal and Ethical Issues in the Management of the Dementing Elderly
Mary Gilhooly, University of Glasgow

Legal Issues in Human Reproduction
Edited by *Sheila A.M. McLean*, University of Glasgow

Mental Illness: Prejudice, Discrimination and the Law
Tom Campbell, Australian National University, Canberra and
Chris Heginbotham, Riverside Mental Health Trust, London

Pregnancy at Work
Noreen Burrows, University of Glasgow

Changing People: The Law and Ethics of Behaviour Modification
Alexander McCall Smith, University of Edinburgh

Health Resources and the Law: Who Gets What and Why
Robert G. Lee, Cardiff Law School and *Frances H. Miller*, University of Boston

Surrogacy and the Moral Economy
Derek Morgan, Cardiff Law School

Family Planning Practice and the Law
Kenneth McK. Norrie, University of Strathclyde

Mental Health Law in Context: Doctors' Orders?
Michael Cavadino, University of Sheffield

Artificial Reproduction and Reproductive Rights
Athena Liu, University of Hong Kong

Medicine, Law and Social Change
Leanna Darvall, La Trobe University

Abortion Regimes
Kerry A. Petersen, La Trobe University

Human In Vitro Fertilization: A Case Study in the Regulation of Medical Innovation
Jennifer Gunning, Agricultural and Food Research Council and
Veronica English, Human Fertilisation and Embryology Authority

Law Reform and Medical Injury Litigation
Edited by *Sheila A.M. McLean*, University of Glasgow

Legal Issues in Obstetrics
Vivienne Harpwood, Cardiff Law School

Competence to Consent to Medical Treatment
John Devereux, Griffith University

Death, Dying and the Law
Edited by *Sheila A.M. McLean*, University of Glasgow

The Contractual Reallocation of Procreative Resources and Parental Rights: The Natural Endowment Critique
William Joseph Wagner, The Catholic University of America

Clinical Resource Allocation
Christopher Heginbotham, Riverside Mental Health Trust, London and
Peter Mumford, King's Fund College, London

Designer Babies
Robert Lee, Cardiff Law School and *Derek Morgan*, Cardiff Law School

Contemporary Legal Issues in Law, Medicine and Ethics
Edited by *Sheila A.M. McLean*, University of Glasgow

All titles are provisional

INTERSECTIONS: WOMEN ON LAW, MEDICINE AND TECHNOLOGY

Edited by
KERRY PETERSEN

Routledge
Taylor & Francis Group
LONDON AND NEW YORK

First published 1997 by Dartmouth and Ashgate Publishing

Reissued 2018 by Routledge
2 Park Square, Milton Park, Abingdon, Oxon, OX14 4RN
711 Third Avenue, New York, NY 10017, USA

Routledge is an imprint of the Taylor & Francis Group, an informa business

A Library of Congress record exists under LC control number: 97006072

Typeset by Manton Typesetters, 5-7 Eastfield Road, Louth, Lincolnshire LN11 7AJ, UK.

ISBN 13: 978-1-138-35134-9 (hbk)
ISBN 13: 978-0-429-43535-5 (ebk)

Contents

List of Contributors

Belinda Bennett is a lecturer in the Faculty of Law, University of Sydney.

Alison Britton is a research fellow in medical law in the School of Law, University of Glasgow.

R. Alta Charo is an Associate Professor of Law and Medical Ethics, University of Wisconsin Schools of Law and Medicine.

Leanna Darvall is a senior lecturer in the School of Law and Legal Studies, La Trobe University, Melbourne.

Sarah Elliston is a lecturer in medical law in the School of Law, University of Glasgow.

Philippa Gannon is a lecturer in the School of Law, University of Glasgow.

Melinda Jones is a senior lecturer in the Faculty of Law, University of New South Wales, Sydney.

Sheila McLean is the International Bar Association Professor of Law and Ethics in Medicine, School of Law, University of Glasgow.

Lee Ann Marks is a lecturer in the School of Law and Legal Studies, La Trobe University, Melbourne.

Wendy Mitchinson is a Professor of History, Department of History, University of Waterloo.

Kerry Petersen is a senior research fellow, School of Law, University of Glasgow.

Sharyn L. Roach Anleu is an Associate Professor in sociology at the Flinders University of South Australia.

Preface

Modern society is in a state of turmoil and transition. Political, social and technological changes are challenging the foundations of social institutions and forcing a re-evaluation of many cherished and established human values. The expansion of medical power and the growing threats to human rights being unleashed by scientific advances such as reproductive technologies, life-sustaining technologies and the new genetic knowledge have the capacity to affect every human being and demands a reappraisal of medical practices, philosophical principles and legal structures. Medical work cannot be viewed in isolation from social and legal contexts as it intersects many boundaries and has important consequences for individuals and society as a whole. The central aim of this book is to dissect medical power and examine alternative approaches to current practices as a means of reframing the issues and establishing principled foundations for the future. A major goal underlying this discussion is to achieve a balance between the competing goals of public interest and human rights.

The contributors to this book provide insights, explanations and critiques of past and present medical practices from the disciplines of history, sociology and law. In some cases, they point to the future. The chapters are written by women who add their distinctive intellectual perspectives to this myriad of complex social, legal and ethical questions. This book adds an international dimension to the debate as the contributors are from Australia, Canada, the United Kingdom and the United States; although specific laws and medical practices may vary from country to country, the underlying fundamental principles and human rights issues affect us all.

I would like to acknowledge the Editorial Board of Law in Context and the editor, Chris Arup, for permitting me to reprint five chapters in this book which were previously published in *Law and Medicine: A Special Issue of Law and Context* (1994). I am also grateful to Belinda Bennett, Alta Charo, Leanna Darvall, Sheila McLean and Sharyn Roach Anleu for undertaking the task of updating and rewriting the earlier versions of these chapters. I would also like to thank Alison Britton,

Sarah Elliston, Philippa Gannon, Lindy Jones, Lee Ann Marks and Wendy Mitchinson for their contributions and assistance in bringing this collection together. It is hard to imagine editing an international book without E-mail and fax machines. In this instance advances in technology have been most welcome.

I would like to extend my appreciation to the Scottish Higher Education Funding Council and the Law School at the University of Glasgow for appointing me as a Senior Research Fellow and giving me the opportunity to pursue projects such as this one. It has been a pleasure working with the members of the medical law unit in the Law School. I would like to express a very warm thank you to Sheila McLean, the International Bar Association Professor of Law and Ethics in Medicine, for welcoming me as a member of the medical law team and for facilitating and assisting in the production of this book. And for being such a hospitable Glaswegian. Thanks to my other colleagues on the medical law team: Alison Britton, Sarah Elliston and Philippa Gannon. As ever, my mother in Australia has given me encouragement and support.

It has been a pleasure to publish another book with Dartmouth and I would like to pay a very special tribute to John Irwin, who readily took on the idea of publishing this collection of essays.

Kerry Petersen
University of Glasgow
Samhair, Scotland 1996

To four special little Australians: Laura, Alexander, Lawrence and Isabella Petersen – with love and hope.

1 Hippocrates: Dead or Alive?[1]

ALISON BRITTON

The Life so short, the art so long to learn, the chance soon gone, experience deceptive and judgement difficult.[2]

Modern writers increasingly express dissatisfaction with the Hippocratic Oath. In particular, critics point to its inability to serve any useful purpose within medical practice today (Clements, 1992, pp.367–90; Monmeyer, 1995, pp.13–24). One reason for this may well be tensions between increasing clinical capacity and the expectations that are generated as a result. Given these tensions, does the Hippocratic Oath serve any useful purpose when doctors are faced with an ethical dilemma? This chapter will address the question whether or not the ethical dilemmas confronting the modern physician can or should be resolved by reference to the Hippocratic Oath, or whether a better resolution could be achieved by a broader reference to societal ethics.

First, the chapter provides a brief history of medical ethics, paying particular attention to the development of the Hippocratic Oath. An examination will then be made of the Oath's place in respect of contemporary concepts of health and healing and the doctor's professional role.

A Brief History of Medical Ethics

The evolution of medical ethics cannot be viewed as a neatly packaged set of principles. Instead their development has been protracted and piecemeal. Unsurprisingly, issues have been debated within the context and influences of the particular period of time in which they arose. In other words, ethics need time to develop, they need to be thought about, written down and debated (Richter, 1994, p.44), but, more importantly, such protracted development provides them with a flexibility so essential if they are to withstand pressures which are contextual or transient. A central feature of the argument in this chapter will be to suggest that the Hippocratic Oath, even if it took time to develop, was as much a creature of its time as it was an ethical position which continues to have relevance.

Throughout the centuries, medicine has been practised with an air of mystery surrounding it. The assumption was that some special understanding was required to practise medicine. Therefore its practice was limited to groups of people to whom this knowledge was passed down from generation to generation or to those who were educated in the formal sense. In other words, its development was sufficiently institutionalized to allow information and knowledge to be passed on. Influenced by culture and time, throughout history different groups of people have been seen as having this special knowledge. Healing could come in many forms and from different sources, such as witch doctors, who often relied on basic superstition, priests, who employed an arguably more developed superstition in the form of religion, and philosophers whose medical practice often reflected quite sophisticated philosophic reasoning. At various times, these groups were all seen as purveyors of medicine. Even the monarchy were included in this elite group. Jonathan Miller refers to the supernatural abilities of the 'royal touch', a practice which continued in England and France for more than 700 years, where the patient only had to come into contact with the monarch to be healed (Miller, 1980, p.59).[3]

The influences of these three main groups varied. Witch doctors, for example, were often called to ward off evil spirits or encourage good ones. 'Cures' for inclement weather or a potion to ensure victory in combat would also be within their ambit. The powerful influence of religion meant that illness could also be construed as a punishment from God for committing a 'sin'. Priests, already enjoying great reverence and status, were turned to for a 'cure', and perceived as having a supernatural medical ability. Also holy water or revered artefacts were seen as having healing properties. Even today, when faced with ill-health or awareness of mortality, many people turn to God or his representatives for help either in this life or the next. However, in contemporary western societies, the person to whom the individual will most likely look for healing or reassurance in ill-health will be the doctor, either in conjunction with, or without, God. The expansion of the role of the doctor and of orthodox medicine may be seen as a kind of contemporary parallel of the historical gaining of power and authority of religion and its priests.

Hellenic medicine took a completely different approach. Whereas magic and priestly practices were primarily based on instinct and observations of nature, Hellenic medicine was developed within the framework of the Greek philosophic schools. Instinct still prevailed but it was coupled with scientific enquiry, observation, discussion and analysis.

The Hippocratic Oath

As Richter says, 'To make people believe in something makes them ten times more powerful' (Richter, 1994, p.15). Unlike many other forms of regulation and rules, an oath can be seen as a very individual and personal thing. It is possible to be unaware of or to disregard many regulations, but one actually 'takes' an oath. Therefore it would be difficult to deny knowledge of its contents once it has been taken. An oath, therefore, has undeniable symbolism in developing a professional ethic. Adhering to its provisions may create a sense of unity; it may reassure the individual that a benchmark exists. It can also unify groups and raise their prestige in society. Richter suggests its importance is even more widespread, suggesting that 'An oath is a sort of handshake in a network, which is the structure for future society' (ibid.).

It is by no means clear when the Hippocratic Oath was composed, but it would not be unreasonable to suggest that it evolved at a time when the priests in the Greek medicine temples were losing their position of authority over their patients. People were questioning their supposed expertise and certainly it would be wrong to assume that early Greek medicine had any great sophistication. The practice of medicine in ancient Greece was diverse and expertise varied both in breadth and depth. The physician could be a trained master craftsman or simply a novice (Cowley *et al.*, 1992, p.1475). Homer provides a good account of ancient Greek medical practices and the *Iliad* highlights the fact that religion and magic were still influential (Richter, 1994, pp.19–21) so there were plenty of charlatans offering magical cures and potions. Furthermore, for people who were studying the general arts, medicine was an integral part of those studies. In short, many people felt they had medical knowledge, at least to a certain extent, and were willing to use it. Greek medicine was therefore a relatively uncertain affair; the practitioners' competence could have been limited or skilled and their methods were varied and practices unregulated. So, around 400 BC, the time was right for an extended family of about seven doctors to transform medicine into a 'modern science' and the family name of Hippocrates became one of the most famous in history (Richter, 1994, pp.19–21).

The Hippocrates we tend to associate with the Oath was born on the Greek island of Cos around 460 BC. He was the second in the line of seven doctors and was apparently small, ugly and bald-headed, with a big nose.[4] What he lacked in stature he made up for in bravery, going to Athens during the plague in 430 BC. Like many of the early physicians, it is thought that Hippocrates travelled widely, dying in Thessalia in 377 BC (Richter, 1994, p.20). Research has shown that the famous Oath which is attributed to Hippocrates was not in fact solely his work but encompassed a wide range of doctrines, styles and ideas, written by many individuals over at least 150 years (King, 1971, pp.39–40). Although the Hippocratic school became the most well known, it was certainly not the only one. Large schools developed in a Greek settlement in Asia Minor and the island of Sicily, and there is evidence of smaller schools in Rhodes and Cyrene (Cowley *et al.*, 1992, p.1475).

The following, oft-quoted phrase may be attributable to Hippocrates himself: 'as to disease, make a habit of two things – *to help or at least to do no harm*'. This originated from the book of *Epidemics*, one of four that Hippocrates probably contributed to the 'Corpus Hippocraticum' which comprises about 70 such books. *Epidemics* provides descriptions of typhus, diphtheria and Hippocrates' first-hand evidence of the plague. He also wrote about epilepsy and the relationship between environment and health (Richter, 1994, p.21). The Hippocratic corpus as a whole describes the Hippocratean traditions and was probably one of the first attempts to lay down principles of medical ethics. It is interesting that, from the 70 books that were written, the Oath is the best known and most enduring part of the work.

In 1943, Ludwig Edelstein carried out a detailed analysis of the Hippocratic Oath and concluded that it was heavily influenced by the Pythagorean school of philosophy. Hippocrates' philosophy of his daily experiences of life are contained in the book of *Aphorisms*. The first aphorism, and perhaps the best known, is set out at the beginning of this chapter. The writings and the perceptions of the Pythagorean school, for example the way in which they viewed illness and disease, were very influential on the contents of the Oath. All the writings were based on the notion that the universe was made up of four basic elements: wetness, dryness, warmth and cold. Furthermore, the Greeks thought that humankind was a replica of the universe, so, logically, these basic elements would be replicated within the human body. They were represented by fluids or 'humours', namely, blood, phlegm, yellow bile and black bile. An equal proportion of these four humours would ensure good health and, similarly, excesses either way would result in a recognizable disease (Miller, 1980, pp.185, 225–6).

That the Hippocratic school shifted the balance from the strong influences of the priests to the more structured and reasoned influences of the Greek philosophers can be demonstrated in the following three ways. First, the Hippocratic physician took a realistic approach as to what could actually be done for a patient. In the early stages of medical ethics, the concern was that the public was given a realistic prognosis of what could be done for them. There was, no doubt, some self-interest here, as it would not do to see the medical profession killing off more people than it cured, and explaining limitations in advance would doubtless keep a check on the expectations of patients. In contrast, modern society seems to have high expectations of medicine. Patients and doctors both anticipate that the practice of medicine will involve some active intervention. There is, however, nothing in the Hippocratic Oath which promotes such tampering. Indeed, Hippocrates observed that doctors should do their best not to kill their patients with treatment and that, with decent hygiene and a sensible diet, most people get better anyway. As Gaarder explains, 'The most essential safeguards against sickness, according to the Hippocratic medical tradition, were moderation and a heathy lifestyle. When sickness occurs, it is a sign that nature has gone off course because of physical or mental imbalance'(Gaarder, 1996, p.47). This is consistent with the Pythagorean school of philosophy, which considered that most illness could be attributed to opulent living. Considering the excessive eating and drinking that many of the wealthy Greeks enjoyed, this observation may well have been based on fact. It is also not incompatible with the 'natural balance' argument of the four basic elements. This approach to dietetics was a critical feature of the original Oath, but is one which appears to have lost favour over the centuries, with the advent of technological medicine.

Secondly, and related to the above, the Hippocratic corpus was a 'struggle for respectability' (Cowley, *et al.*, 1992, p.1475):

> While conscious of his limited capabilities, the Hippocratic physician was undoubtedly committed to the restoration of health and the alleviation of suffering. Beyond such general standards, however, the corpus suggested that the medical community was largely unregulated, and that physician conduct varied widely. The practice of medicine lacked any enforceable rules of conduct. (Ibid., p.1476)

Thus the primary purpose of the medical ethic during Hippocratic times was to raise the standard of medical practice and exclude those who used less competent or more dubious methods.

Thirdly, the Hippocratean school debunked the notion that illness was a punishment for sin. Instead, it was regarded as a natural biological event and this promoted a more realistic attitude towards illness and death.

Dark Ages – Nineteenth Century

The Middle Ages saw a return of priestly influence. Communities developed and grew, but all too often good diet and hygiene were inadequate to support such growth. Disease therefore spread quickly and, given its large scale, medicine was unequal to the task. As there was little hope of cure, people turned to the Church to help them prepare for death. Medical practice did not therefore change much during this time. If anything, these circumstances made physicians even more reluctant to interfere. Not only were they probably more acutely aware of their professional limitations, but they feared for their own lives. However, the seventeenth century witnessed the eclipse of religious domination and the ascendancy of medical potential. Kafka describes this beautifully: 'That's the way they are, the people in my district. Always asking the impossible of their doctor. They have lost the old faith; the priest sits at home and picks the vestments to pieces one by one; but the doctor, with his sensitive surgical hand, is expected to do everything'(Underwood, 1995, p.186).

It is around this time that a further change takes place. In an attempt to reconcile the new thinking with the old, religious influences and Hippocratic traditions seemed to merge. This is not surprising, given that many provisions of the Oath can be found reflected within the Christian teachings, for example the contents of the Ten Commandments. The overall result was, however, a strict adherence to the principles of the Hippocratic Oath, in particular to those concerning the sanctity of life, but without the realism that accompanied the original thoughts and writings. Cowley *et al.* sum up this period: 'Moral theologians gave considerable attention to the ascendance of the medical profession, and continued to extol the sanctity of life. Within the medical community, the codified and christianised ethical principles of Hippocrates were firmly established and religiously followed' (Cowley *et al.*, 1992, p.1479). Once established, these principles of medical ethics were consolidated and survived successfully and relatively unquestioned until the mid-twentieth century.

In the late Middle Ages the clergy ceased to practise medicine on the instructions of Pope Honorius III and professional guilds for those practising medicine were established. The status of physicians had therefore been improved, but medical knowledge had not (Margotta, 1996, p.66).

Modern Times

It is suggested that Hippocratean traditions disappeared for some time and re-emerged fairly recently into western cultures. Other writers (Miller, 1980, ch. 2; King, 1971, ch. 1) have substantiated the view that current medical practice and ethics have a fairly recent past, probably dating from around the seventeenth century. But it is suggested that medical developments within the past 50 years have presented the most serious challenge yet to the Hippocratic Oath. Other commentators have identified a more precise time scale. For example, Clements suggests that 1969–70 heralded this move, referring to it as the 'Medical Ethics Discontinuity' (Clements, 1992, p.367).

There are many theories on why this occurred. What does seem clear is that, as more choices in people's lives became available, individuals wished to have a more active say in the making of those choices rather than leaving decisions to be made by others. Medical decisions are perhaps but one example of this. For instance, a further milestone was the legal recognition of values such as autonomy, as evidenced by the early twentieth-century decision in *Schloendorff* v. *Society of New York Hospital*, leading to the development of doctrines like informed consent. Once rooted within the public consciousness, discussions of these principles and doctrines became more intense.

The changes cannot, however, be solely attributed to legal developments, and it is possible to identify other factors which changed the fabric of society. The twentieth century has witnessed radical political and social change. Two world wars have had a profound effect on people's lives, bringing with them rapid advances in technology. Whilst some developments, such as the jet engine, were viewed positively, others, such as the limitless power of nuclear weaponry, made people wary. Similar reactions occurred with respect to medical technologies. Refinements in plastic surgery were of special benefit to fighter pilots and crews who had been badly burned, but not all medical developments were used to such benefit: for example, the legacy of the 'eugenics' policies of Hitler and his Nazi euthanasia programme is still one of the main arguments used against legalizing medical assistance to end life. However, there is no empirical evidence which would allow a conclusion as to which of these forces proved to be the most significant in modifying ethical codes.

As a general consequence, people became generally more distrustful of authority (Clements, 1992, pp.374–5) and certainly more questioning and less passive, at the same time as they were becoming better educated. More specifically, the examples of the negative application of medical knowledge left people in little doubt that what was now medically possible could be used with both positive and negative effect, and trust in those practising medicine was seriously eroded. In an effort to buttress the Oath and salvage the standing of the medical profession, the World Medical Association drew up the Declaration of Geneva in 1947. This declaration emphasized that the medical profession was to act in the service of humanity and the last obligation in the declaration provides that: 'I will maintain the utmost respect for human life from the time of conception; even under threat, I will not use my medical knowledge contrary to the laws of humanity' (Declaration of Geneva, as amended at Sydney, 1968). This was probably the first serious attempt to ensure the continuity of the Hippocratic Oath since its conception and brought respect for humanity back to the forefront of medical (and social) ethics.

Changing Concepts of Health

There can be no doubt that medical advances changed the approach of individuals and doctors to the practice of medicine, but seemed to leave the Hippocratic Oath relatively unscathed. Doctors still took the Oath (or a modern equivalent) on graduation, and turned to its terms for resolution of ethical dilemmas and as a foundation of 'good' practice.

But much had changed. Advances in medicine shifted the focus from survival to issues of prevention and quality of life. Social and political change generated different expectations of life itself and of medicine. The ethos of medicine was, unsurprisingly, affected by its new capacities. Progress removed constraints, with advances in microscopy, anaesthesia and microbiology being particularly important. Miller reinforces this when he observes: 'some of the most important advances in medicine have been the result of identifying and forestalling some of the agents responsible for the pathological changes ... the recognition of the role of micro-organisms, for instance, and their control by asepsis and antibodies' (Miller, 1980, p.103; see also King, 1971, p.32).

These developments served to overcome the age old problems of sanitation and sepsis. Freed from these threats to health and well-being, survival was not the struggle that it had once been. When combined with the breakthroughs of immunization and the isolation of penicillin in 1940, western civilizations had reached the stage where there was a greater concern about the *quality* of survival than ever before. As Callahan notes, 'the most potent social impact of medical advancement is the way it reshapes our notions of what it is to have a life' (Callahan, 1990, p.25). As medicine showed what it could do, the Hippocratic tradition of non-intervention was replaced by a new imperative – a medical imperative to do everything possible to increase a person's longevity. Expectations increased and medicine and those who practised it knew no limits. As Callahan notes:

> Medicine and healthcare have ... entered a new stage of their history, one where the successes of medicine and not its failures alas – in the way they interact with our values – have been the main source of our

> problems. That success has raised expectations beyond a sustainable point, addicted the system to an unending search for new and usually expensive technological solutions (many of them occasioned by earlier technological solutions). (Ibid., p.23)

In transforming the practice of medicine from one of minimalist involvement to one which mandates increased intervention, it is arguable that scientific advances have already reduced the relevance of the Hippocratic Oath. It is indisputable that much of the Hippocratic tradition was founded on what medicine actually could do. Although there are some values expressed in the Oath which may be described as universal, there is a close link between capacity and the guidance given to doctors about what should be done. The Oath was composed in the light of what was socially acceptable and medically possible at the time it was written. Technology and knowledge have advanced since Hippocrates, at some times more rapidly than others, but these changes have posed a challenge to some of the specific commitments in the Oath. The general commitments of the Oath can be found in most modern statements of medical ethics but many of its specific provisions have already been overtaken.

Our expectations of what medicine can do seem to have increased not only in depth but also in breadth. For example, over the past 50 years, what is regarded as being a matter of 'health' has expanded dramatically. Improved techniques for birth, assistance in procreation, the resculpting of our perceived physical imperfections, preventive screening processes and ultimately seeking a perfect or at least a controlled death have all been crammed into the category of health care. The World Health Organisation (WHO) has taken this even further. WHO defined health as being: 'a state of complete physical, mental and social well-being and not merely the absence of disease or infirmity'. This definition was drawn up just after the Second World War, when policies sought to emphasize a more positive future, not only for the individual, but also for a stable, more peaceful world. Social stability was seen as an integral part of the world at peace as well as being part of an overall healing process. In turn, attainment of peace would help to promote good health for the individual so that he or she would have a positive role to play in the new world vision. Callahan comments on:

> the political tendency to define all social problems, from war to crime in the streets, as health problems; the blurring of lines of responsibility between and among the professions, and then between the medical profession and the political order; and the implicit denial of human freedom that results when failures to achieve social well-being are defined as forms of 'sickness' somehow to be treated by medical means. The WHO definition replaced the traditional definition of health as

> bodily integrity and wholeness with a far more ambitious one, that of individual well-being more generally. (Callahan, 1990, p.36)

Such definitions tend to result in more and more aspects of our lives being viewed from a medical perspective so that, when something goes wrong, we have become increasingly dependent upon the medical profession to correct it. This tends to create unrealistic expectations of those who have to tend to, and try to 'cure', the ever-lengthening list of what constitutes a 'medical' condition. It also leads to an increasing imbalance of power in the relationship between doctor and patient. This in itself does not actually suggest that the Oath cannot be followed either pragmatically or philosophically, but, because the scope of 'health' and the potential of medicine have altered so dramatically, it may provide a reason to address the question of the Oath's contemporary relevance.

The Professional Ethic

> as to disease, make a habit of two things – *to help, or at least to do no harm*. (Jones, 1923, p.165)

One of the cornerstones of modern medical ethics is the principle of beneficence (including non-maleficence). Beneficence applies almost exclusively to the doctor's daily professional actions, such as preserving life, restoring health and the relief of suffering. Non-maleficence refers to its traditional corollary: first do no harm. Beauchamp and Childress suggest that principles of beneficence potentially demand more than those of non-maleficence, because beneficence involves a positive action to help others. In comparison, principles of non-maleficence tend to be negative prohibitions on action. Thus the positive principles override the negative ones (Beauchamp and Childress, 1994, pp.262–3).

It is these positive perceptions of restoring, preserving and healing that have come under the most scrutiny and, arguably, attack in the last 30 or so years. Nonetheless, contemporary formulations have much in common with the general terms of the Hippocratic Oath. For example, each contains an equivalent to the exhortation to 'do no harm', the obligation of confidentiality and so on. However, whilst the general commitments may remain valid, there are some specific provisions which may be subject to reinterpretation in the light of changing values and increased knowledge. In what is usually referred to as the 'ethical section' of the Hippocratic Oath, three major 'do nots' have been challenged: first, the performing of surgery, second, performing abortion and, third, providing assistance to end life.

Surgery is now a specialist and respected branch of medical practice, yet it was ruled out by the terms of the Hippocratic Oath. There may be a number of reasons for this prohibition, but one very plausible explanation may be that, in the absence of modern capacities, surgery was simply too dangerous to contemplate. In other words, the basis for the prohibition was just as likely to be found in pragmatics as in ethics. The fact that modern medicine has chosen to ignore this prohibition lends weight to this suggestion. However, it also lends credibility to the challenge discussed in this chapter to the fundamental value of the Oath itself.

Equally, the Oath's prohibition on pregnancy termination may have had both a pragmatic and an ethical basis. The ethics, however, have been overtaken by reassessment over the years, so that abortion is now an accepted (even if not universally welcomed) aspect of medical practice.[5] Thus doctors are selectively interpreting the Oath and, by so doing, are acknowledging that its specific provisions in particular, may have had temporal rather than eternal validity. However, one final taboo remains, namely the prohibition on assisting in the death of a patient. Because this remains generally outlawed, and given what has been said about the inadequacies of the Oath in confronting modern values, it is worth spending a little time on this issue before reaching a conclusion as to whether or not the Oath is a genuine set of principles, valued for all time, to which the modern practitioner may look with confidence for a resolution of ethical problems or for sound guidance about what he or she should and should not do.

Hippocrates, Ethics and the End of Life

The debate about third party involvement in the end of life has a long history and is still to be resolved in most countries. The arguments for and against euthanasia and assisted suicide are many, wide-ranging and deeply felt. It is not, therefore, the intention here to cover them all; rather, this section will concentrate on one of the main objections which is usually accompanied by a direct appeal to the contents of the Hippocratic Oath. This objection relates to the general provision of 'at least do no harm' (*Epidemics*, Jones, 1923, p.165) and, more specifically, to the statement, 'I will neither give a deadly drug to anyone if asked for it, nor will I make a suggestion to this effect.'

With regard to the general provision, Beauchamp and Childress note that the phrase did not in fact originate from the Hippocratic corpus and suggest that the statement 'at least, do no harm' is a 'strained translation of a single Hippocratic passage' (Beauchamp and Childress, 1994, p.189). Nonetheless, every modern statement includes this as a fundamental tenet of medical ethics. Whether or not this provision directly emanates from the Hippocratic Oath, it is one with which most people would find it difficult to argue. As a basis for the good practice of medicine, it is probably generally accepted as being both useful and morally appropriate. However, merely to accept this statement as a mantra is to ignore the fact that it tells us nothing about what is meant by 'harm'. Even in its more positive rendering, that is a positive obligation to act beneficently by doing good, there is no definition of what is 'good'. Thus we may accept the general proposition, but we must analyse it for content and context before it actually constrains or permits certain behaviour.

In any event, the obligations of beneficence and non-maleficence *can* be found in the Hippocratic Oath: for example, 'I will use treatment to help the sick according to my ability and judgement, but I will never use it to injure or wrong them.' There is no evidence, however, in this passage of the Oath to suggest that doctors had to treat their patients and save their lives, whatever the consequences. Rather, they were not to injure or wrong them. The Hippocratic writings illustrate the duty of medicine quite clearly: 'In general terms it is to do away with the sufferings of the sick, to lessen the violence of their diseases, and to refuse to treat those who are overmastered by their diseases, realising that in such cases medicine is powerless' (Jones, 1959, p.193). The emphasis in this quotation is on not injuring or causing harm, but, as has already been noted, harm is not a rigid concept and what constitutes harm is something which is not solely definable according to what Hippocrates thought. Present-day patients and society have an interest in contributing to its definition.

With regard to the second, more specific, provision, it is well established that Greek and Roman physicians, even those who were Hippocratic, often supplied their patients with the means to commit suicide despite the injunction against assistance in suicide embodied in the Hippocratic Oath. In other words, even in its earliest times, the Oath was not universally adhered to. Now this does not mean that it *should not* have been, but it does suggest that the apparently absolute nature of this provision was not accepted even at the time it was written.

It is, of course, also worth bearing in mind that, for the doctor in Greek and Roman times, and indeed for many years afterwards, there was only one question – whether or not the patient would live. The practice of assisting in the death of those patients who would not live was the doctor's only 'remedy'. The modern doctor, however, faces a much wider range of options and a much more complex set of ethical considerations. Modern medicine can keep people alive who would otherwise have died; it can salvage the nearly dead; it can maintain insensate existence; it can alleviate much pain. In other words, the true ethical dilemma for the modern doctor is the extent to which what can be done blunts the edges of a desire for death, by rendering a request for assistance in dying less intelligible. In many ways, this may have resulted in the development of practices which are as much based on sophistry as they are on fundamental principles.

Margaret Battin makes an interesting comparison. She notes the Oath's clear prohibition, 'of the then current practice among mainstream Greek physicians of providing euthanatic drugs on request to patients they could not cure and The American Medical Association's 1973 policy statement that the physician is always morally prohibited from killing patients but is not morally bound to preserve life in all cases' (Battin, 1994, p.16). She suggests that this comparison actually shows the same categorical assertion: that is, that even if a physician may sometimes allow a patient to die, the physician must never kill.

However, this assertion rests on the philosophically dubious distinction between acts and omissions which has also been challenged in some recent legal decisions.[6] What is clear is that, whether or not death comes about because it is permitted or because it is actively assisted, it is not uniformly able to be characterized as a 'harm'. If this is the case, unless the distinction between moral responsibility for an act and an omission can be rehabilitated, and in the circumstances of the doctor–patient relationship this seems most unlikely, there is no absolute prohibition in Hippocrates' general statement on assisting death. But, of course, Hippocrates then became much more specific, referring directly to the doctor's obligation not to offer active assistance to die. This aversion to active involvement has continued, largely untouched, through the centuries, and although there may be many other arguments which could be brought into play to strengthen it, the doctor's first resort is to appeal to the Hippocratic prohibition as the source for his or her antipathy to change in this area. Given what has already been said about the durability of the Oath, this too is worthy of consideration.

In the late nineteenth century, the term 'euthanasia' first appeared as 'the new cure for incurables' (Tollemache, 1873, pp.218–30). Euthanasia continues to be at the forefront of debate and in the UK there have been several unsuccessful attempts to have its practice legalized. In the meantime, technological advances have allowed assistance in ending life to occur by other methods, for example switching off life support machines, withholding or withdrawing treatment and respecting advance directives, all of which are now deemed acceptable practices in certain conditions.

Doctors, therefore, can be seen to be participating in death, albeit passively, something that they could not have done in Hippocratic times because the vehicles for doing so were not there. This mirrors to an extent the points made earlier about the performing of surgery or abortions. The Oath addressed a specific culture, a specific time, a specific school of thought and a specific set of capacities. If this is accepted, then the selectivity of adherence to the rules can be challenged, on two counts. First, if the Oath was heavily dependent on practicalities, then its status as a fundamental ethical code may be challenged. Second, if doctors are prepared to dismiss some parts of the code, then a convincing rationale is needed for holding on to other parts of it. In fact, keeping someone alive against their wishes, without dignity and often with considerable suffering, may be seen by many as a far greater harm than assisting in death.

Hippocrates and the Doctor

Most people desire good health and there is no doubt that its promotion was within the aims of the Hippocratic Oath. The fact that health is such a precious commodity may be one of the reasons why the Hippocratic Oath has survived and allowed doctors' decision making to go relatively unquestioned. As Daryl Koehn notes: 'the goodness of health explains our willingness to accord doctors authority. If health is something we all desire as a good in itself, and as something of instrumental benefit to all of us as members of the community, then the physician's power to further health is also good' (Koehn, 1994, p.76).

The 'good' of health, therefore, stands in direct contrast to the 'bad' of ill-health. As guardians of health, doctors therefore command our respect. Their reliance on the beneficence/non-maleficence constraints derived from the Hippocratic Oath is therefore given additional support by the individual's desires and wishes. Arguably, also, the preference for health over ill-health serves to reinforce the status of the doctor, further elevating the power of the code to which he or she proclaims loyalty.

Of course, problems arise when health cannot be achieved. What happens to the professional's role and the Oath then? The Hippocratean writers seemed to be relatively untroubled by this and the *Prognostic* suggests:

> Now to restore every patient to health is impossible. To do so would have been better even than forecasting the future. But as a matter of fact men do die, some immediately after calling [the physician] in ... It is necessary, therefore to learn the natures of such diseases, ... and to

> learn how to forecast them. For in this way you will justly win respect and be an able physician. (Cowley *et al.*, 1992, p.1476, quoting the *Prognostic*)

Unfortunately, time and circumstances have reshaped the early and more modest role of the physician into the now familiar, often paternalistic, one. No physician can give eternal life to a patient, even with modern advances in medicine. But the expectations of the modern patient place a heavy burden upon a doctor and, while dealing with the pressures of these expectations, they must also try to ascertain what can reasonably be accomplished for any particular patient. While realizing that good health is a highly desirable thing, it is equally important to accept that its achievement may not be realizable in all circumstances. Monmeyer addresses this point and suggests that, rather than regarding healing as a 'goal' of medical practice, perhaps it would be more appropriate to regard it instead as an 'ideal'. Although he suggests that it should be something 'to be striven for' (Monmeyer, 1995, p.19), the ideal should not be an absolute one, for ideals are often impossible to achieve. As he says:

> Ideals are important in medicine, as they are elsewhere in life. Their importance lies in inspiring us to a higher level of commitment to moral practice than we might otherwise be capable of achieving. But there is a down side to ideals as well, and that is if they are too unrealistic, too impossible of attainment, they will distort our perception of what is morally acceptable practice. (Ibid.)

The greatest danger, Monmeyer feels, is that we will become cynical when medical practice falls short of an ideal. It is time to put away outmoded phrases such as 'doctor knows best' and to make decisions that may not be 'just what the doctor ordered'. This conclusion requires, of course, the acceptance of a shift in the balance of power between a doctor and patient, and also mandates acceptance that medicine is not a discipline with one goal or outcome. As Koehn notes:

> Some doctors, like members of other professions, are obsessed with controlling and manipulating their environment. It is equally fair to say that some patients share in this obsession. The Hippocratic Oath would not forbid the giving of deadly drugs and abortifacients upon demand if it did not foresee that people would pressure physicians to assist them in committing suicide or aborting a fetus. The Oath prohibits these two activities in particular because these practices have a great potential for luring the doctor away from healing. (Koehn, 1994, p.123)

The Message of the Hippocratic Oath

The Oath should be viewed as having two separate but related parts. The first is the covenant which sets out the duties of the pupil towards the teacher, the duties of the pupil to the teacher's family and the pupil's obligations relating to newly aquired medical knowledge. The second is what is generally seen as the ethical code which sets out a number of rules which have to be observed when treating a patient.

As to the general content of the Oath itself, there is no shortage of critics. James Rachels, for example, refers to the Oath as an 'historical relic' (Rachels, 1986, p.119). Beauchamp and Childress suggest that 'the Hippocratic tradition – the starting point in medical ethics for centuries – has turned out to be a limited and generally unreliable basis for medical ethics' (Beauchamp and Childress, 1994, p.25).

Not only is the Oath limited, but parts of it are phrased in a very generalized fashion, so its applicability, and therefore usefulness, in many situations is vague and uncertain. On the other hand, it could be said that the generality of these provisions is also one of its strengths. The fact that they are vague rather than precise has facilitated a breadth of interpretation which has allowed it to span 2500 years. Where the Oath is specific, however, as in the examples highlighted above, its relevance to the changing face of society and medicine is more in doubt. Its major weakness therefore lies in being overly proscriptive in specifics and in permitting doctors to use it as a shield when their personal beliefs fall foul of what their patients actually want. Recourse to the Hippocratic tradition is sometimes merely a smokescreen which, unless questioned, seems to offer the ideal way of dressing personal prejudice in the cloak of ethical respectability. In any event, as Edelstein points out, the Oath represents only the ancient ideal of the physician (Edelstein, 1943, p.4).

When provisions are inadequate or unclear the usual practice is to try to interpret what is meant by them. Arguably, then, when difficult and complex decisions have to be made on the borders of medical and professional ethics, they are sometimes made practically easier by a selective interpretation of the Hippocratic Oath's provisions. For example, it may be a relief to deflect decisions concerning assistance with death by stating that the Oath clearly prohibits such practices, but as Monmeyer notes there are other provisions in the Oath that now seem to be conveniently ignored. In addition to those mentioned earlier, these also include the positive requirements of sharing one's wealth with one's teacher, passing on skills to the sons of one's teacher and honouring a variety of Greek gods and goddesses (Monmeyer, 1995, p.18).

The extent to which interpretation is selective is in itself interesting and presumably says something about what doctors think is important, but not necessarily what their patients think is important. Beauchamp and Childress highlight the problems of interpretation:

> From the time of Hippocrates, physicians have generated codes without scrutiny or acceptance by patients and the public. These codes have rarely appealed to more general ethical standards or to a source of moral authority beyond the traditions and judgements of physicians. In some cases, the special rules in codes for professionals seem to conflict with and even override more general norms. The pursuit of professional norms in these circumstances may do more to protect the profession's interests than to introduce an impartial and comprehensive moral viewpoint. Other rules have traditionally been expressed in abstract formulations that dispense vague moral advice open to competing interpretations. (Beauchamp and Childress, 1994, p.8)

Other commentators point to the negative phrasing of the Oath's provisions; for example, the number of 'will nots' that it contains. Edelstein refers to the influence of the Pythagorean school on the content and style of the Oath. He suggests that this philosophy taught that it was not only what one was allowed to do that was important but also what one was not allowed to do (Edelstein, 1943, p.22). He explains their manifesto: 'Right living is brought about not only, not even primarily, through positive actions, but rather through avoidance of those steps that are dangerous, through the repression of insatiable desires which if left to themselves would cause damage' (ibid.).

It is often overlooked that the Pythagorean school was in the minority in its opinions and teachings, but that its influence endured in large part because it was so compatible with Christian teachings. More recently, another commentator has studied the provisions of the Hippocratic Oath. Richter analyses the original version of the Oath and breaks this analysis down into ten sections. His findings are reproduced in Table 1.1. He concludes: 'If we are allowed to deduce priority from sequence and text size, we see Hippocrates' main concern is the relation to his colleagues, teachers and pupils. The relation to the patient is given second priority' (Richter, 1994, p. 23).

This is entirely in line with what has already been suggested. Doctors' use of the Hippocratic Oath disguises the fact that, at best, it was a professional agreement designed to lend credibility to the wisdom and teachings of one particular school of medical thought. Admittedly, it also contained some 'ethical' prohibitions, but these may have had as much (if not more) to do with the agenda of the time they were written as with any timeless moral commitment. The Oath was not intended to confer any legal obligation, nor perhaps was it foreseen that it would still be referred to in current practice.

Table 1.1 Analysis of the original Hippocratic Oath

Statement	% of text	Effective status	Do (+) or do not (–)	Contents
1	10	obsolete	+	Call on the help of Olympic gods
2	25	unclear	+/–	Take care of teachers and their children, select pupils
3	8	modern	+	Only cure the patients, never harm
4	7	unclear	–	Never kill, no euthanasia
5	5	unclear	–	No abortion allowed
6	5	modern	+	Clean living style
7	5	obsolete	–	Operations
8	10	modern	–	No unethical profit
9	10	modern	–	Keeping secrets
10	15	modern	+/–	Honour and punishment

Source: Richter (1994, p.23).

Rather, it sought to 'stir up the conscience of the individual' (Edelstein, 1943, p.62). In contemporary medical practice, a wide and complex range of decisions calls for answers unfettered by the provisions of an Oath never intended for such a purpose.

Conclusions

In looking at the history of medical ethics, and in particular the development of the Hippocratic Oath, if we are persuaded by Edelstein's argument, the Oath originated from a group representing only a small section of Greek opinion. That the Oath was not accepted by all ancient physicians is clear, since philosophic, historical and medical documents provide evidence of the violation of almost all of its provisions. This can be demonstrated in the landmark decision of the United States Supreme Court, where Edelstein's interpretation was noted with approval (*Roe* v. *Wade*, at pp.131–2; see also Petersen, 1993, p.14).

Moreover, the intention of the Oath was to regulate the practice of medicine and to try and secure a high standard within that practice. The ancient physicians were aware of their limitations and this may have led the Hippocratic writers to reduce the chances of harming their patients by prohibiting the most risky procedures on pragmatic and perhaps self-seeking grounds rather than on the basis of a vision of a medical ethic which would endure throughout the centuries. The Oath, therefore, may realistically be described as of no more contemporary significance than oaths of allegiance to monarchs or countries which have also changed with the reality of social and political forces.

Since the Oath was conceived, increasing medical knowledge and intervention have replaced the elementary practice of medicine which it was designed to control. The simple faith in the healing powers of the doctor has been replaced by the interest of an educated and informed public in the basis of medical decisions, their efficacy and their relevance. The traditional faith invested in doctors has been replaced by a more realistic awareness of their limitations. Yet, despite this, as the controller of health, and given the armoury at the disposal of the modern doctor, the pragmatic approach to the doctor's capacities has been superseded by an often unrealistic optimism about what medicine can achieve. This has not only been perpetuated by the medical profession, but patients too are generally happy to endorse such optimism.

In industrialized countries, where good diet and hygiene have been secured, more and more emphasis has been placed upon the importance of longevity and, although the restoration, preservation and promotion of health are good and positive things, an absolute commitment to healing may create unrealistic expectations, mandate unwanted technological intervention and impose an onerous burden on the doctor.

Previous experience suggests that doctors appear to adapt to reformulations of the Oath and changing legal conditions without losing their professional integrity. The question still to be answered is whether or not there is any reason to suppose that they cannot continue to do so. In fact, as this chapter has shown, many (if not a majority of) Hippocratic writings have been dismissed over the centuries as being outdated, either technically or ethically. No contemporary doctor would look to the writings of the Hippocratic school for technical information, any more than they should expect an Oath which was designed for one purpose and for one time to meet the problems confronting the contemporary physician. That doctors nonetheless continue to do the latter is a matter for legitimate concern, since it seems to disguise prejudice rather than to encourage evaluation of the commitment made. It is not *in se* ethical merely to be able to point to a specific provision which endorses our preconceived idea of what is 'right', and this is particularly so when the authority purportedly derived from this is only appealed to when no other argument can be found.

This is not to say that there is nothing in the Oath of contemporary relevance. In its general commitment to doing good, the Oath has been echoed even in the most modern statements of medical ethics. As Battin says, 'What is central to the Oath and cannot be deleted without altering its essential character is the requirement that the physician shall come "for the benefit of the sick"' (Battin, 1994, p.219). In fact, this is virtually all that realistically remains of the Oath and, arguably, the fact that it has been taken into account throughout the centuries shows two things: first, that the Oath had a meaningful role to play in the development of what is now known as medical ethics, and second, that its contemporary value is so significantly reduced by modern ethics that the constant appeal to it is little more than a shield to avoid confronting the difficult dilemmas which face the modern doctor. Just as no modern doctor would envisage swearing allegiance to Greek gods and goddesses, so too he or she ought to question the occasionally blind assumption that what is contained in the ethical component of the Oath is cast in stone.

The modern doctor confronts dilemmas unthought of in the time of Hippocrates. Medicine today also generates problems from within its own capacities. Those parts of the Oath which remain relevant might reasonably be said to reflect nothing more than a general commitment to do the best for your patient, an idea which in itself could and should have developed with or without Hippocrates, as it has in other professions. For the rest, the Oath is primarily of historical interest. If calling the Oath into play caused no actual or potential harm, we might be satisfied with its constant reiteration today. However, as in the examples of the prohibition on performing surgery or that on assisting in death, where adherence to its strictest terms leaves a serious gap between contemporary ethics and historical cant, we would do well to remember that the Oath, as an ethical framework, is fundamentally flawed. Not only was it never intended to become the apotheosis of ethical dogma, it was constrained by having to answer the kinds of questions which were asked in those early days.

These limitations suggest that medicine would do well to adhere to the principles underlying all professions, which roughly equate to doing good and doing no harm, but to divorce itself from the specifics of any code which neither sought to be, nor could be, a genuine guide for modern medicine. It has been all too easy for clinicians to avoid respecting their patients by calling into use a code which has a symbolic strength. However, as has been seen, values have changed. Modern codes of medical ethics stress, for example, the rights of patients – something which Hippocrates never mentions. If modern doctors are to act ethically, they can neither choose selectively to interpret an ancient Oath nor ignore their responsibility to analyse the content and shape of their current obligations to their patients. The source of this responsibility, and the answer to the dilemmas raised by it, lies not in misguided adherence to a code of dubious value, but rather in an intelligent discourse on what is meant by doing good or doing no harm.

As attitudes to, and interpetation of, these concepts change, so too must the doctor. There is nothing absolute about these concepts, just as there is nothing constant in the gods people worship. The spectacle of the doctor who ignores most of the Hippocratic Oath while at the same time claiming adherence to its principles (when they suit) is as unedifying as it is detrimental to respecting and caring for patients.

Notes

1 I am grateful to Professor Sheila A.M. McLean and Dr Kerry Petersen for their invaluable comments and support on this chapter.
2 Hippocrates, *Aphorisms I*, translated in R. Margotta, *The Hamlyn History of Medicine*, London: Hamlyn, 1996.
3 This practice of the royal touch continued until the eighteenth century; apparently, William of Orange was the last king to practise it.
4 As described by Plato in Richter (1994, pp.19–21).
5 See, for example, the Abortion Act 1967 UK, as amended.
6 *Compassion in Dying* v. *Washington*; *Quill* v. *Vacco*.

Bibliography

Battin, M. Pabst (1994), *The Least Worst Death: Essays in Bioethics on the End of Life*, New York: Oxford University Press.
Beauchamp, T.L. and J.S. Childress (1994), *Principles of Biomedical Ethics*, 4th edn, New York: Oxford University Press.
Callahan, D. (1990), *What Kind of Life: The Limits of Medical Progress*, New York: Simon & Schuster.
Clements, C.D. (1992), 'Systems Ethics and the History of Medical Ethics', *Psychiatric Quarterly*, **63**, 367–90.
Cowley, L. *et al.* (1992), 'Care of the dying: An ethical and historical perspective', *Critical Care Medicine*, **20**, (10), 1473–82.
Edelstein, L. (1943), *The Hippocratic Oath*, Baltimore: Johns Hopkins Press.
Gaarder, J. (1996), *Sophie's World*, London: Phoenix.
Jones W.H.S. (tr.) (1923), 'Epidemics 1:11', *Hippocrates*, Vol. 1, Cambridge, Mass.: Harvard University Press.
Jones W.H.S. (tr.) (1959), 'Hippocrates: The Art', *Hippocrates*, Vol. 2, Cambridge, Mass.: Harvard University Press.
King, L.S. (1971), *A History of Medicine*, London: Penguin Books.
Koehn, D. (1994), *The Ground of Professional Ethics*, London and New York: Routledge.
Margotta, R. (1996), *The Hamlyn History of Medicine*, London: Hamlyn.
Miller, J. (1980), *The Body in Question*, London: Bookclub Associates.
Monmeyer, R. (1995), 'Does Physician Assisted Suicide Violate the Integrity of Medicine?', *The Journal of Medicine and Philosophy*, **20**, 13–24.
Petersen, K. (1993), *Abortion Regimes*, Aldershot: Dartmouth.

Rachels, J. (1986), *At the End of Life: Euthanasia and Morality*, Oxford: Oxford University Press.
Richter, J.W. (1994), *The Hippocratic Oath Revisited*, Durham: Pentland Press.
Tollemache, L., 'The New Cure for Incurables', *Fortnightly Review*, **13**, (1873).
Underwood, J.A. (tr.) (1995), 'A Country Doctor', in *Franz Kafka Stories 1904–1924*, London: Abacus.
Weir, R.F. (1992), 'The Morality of Physician Assisted Suicide', *Law, Medicine and Healthcare*, **20**, 116–26.

Cases

Compassion in Dying v. *Washington*, 49F.3d 590, F.3d en banc. 9th Cir. 1996.
Quill v. *Vacco*, F.3d 2nd. Cir.1996 No. 95–7028.
Roe v. Wade 410 US 113 (1973).
Schloendorff v. *Society of New York Hospital*, 211 N.Y. 125,105 N.E 92 (1914).

I swear with Apollo, the healing god,
with Asclepios, Hygieia and Panaceia,
with all gods and goddesses, whom I call to be witnesses,
that I will follow this oath and promise
to the best of my knowledge and ability.

I will honour my teachers as my parents,
support them in their cost of living,
and help them, if they wish so,
if they would run into distress or debt.
To me his child will be equal to my own brother;
and, if they wish so, I will be their teacher without any reward.

I will admit my children and my teacher's children and the pupils,
who are accepted members of our medical society,
to hear my colleagues, but no other persons.

I will apply medicine to the best of my knowledge and ability,
for the treatment of the sick and never for injuring them.

I will not apply lethal medicine or give relevant information,
not even if asked to do so.

I will never apply methods to destroy growing life in a woman's womb.

I will keep my life and my arts clean and pure.

I will not operate to cure the illnesses of the stones and I will not join
persons who do perform these operations.

Whichever home I enter, I will only enter to help the sick;
I will never do any harm consciously,
and not abuse the situation by prohibited intercourse with man or
woman, either free or slave.

If I hear or see anything confidential, even beyond my profession,
in my contacts with people, I will keep it a secret.

May I be blessed in my life and in my arts and be honoured forever by
all fellow-men, if I do pay honest attention to this oath,
but I shall serve the counterpart, if I violate and forswear this oath.

Figure 1.1 The Hippocratic Oath

2 'It's Not Society That's the Problem, It's Women's Bodies': A Historical View of Medical Treatment of Women

WENDY MITCHINSON[1]

Introduction

Feminist critics are concerned about what they see as the 'medicalization' of women's bodies. They point to the new reproductive technologies and the promotion of hormone replacement therapy for older women as only the latest in a long line of examples. Using Canada as a case study and focusing on the first half of the twentieth century, this chapter examines the theme of medicalization from a historical perspective. In many respects, developments in Canadian medicine were quite typical of what was happening elsewhere in western society. Canadian medical students were taught from British and American textbooks; the medical press was constantly reprinting international articles; Canadian physicians easily kept up with the latest 'advances' and participated in developing some of them. At one level, western medicine was not bounded by geography; at another it was, for the context of the practice of medicine is always particular to the place. By keeping the focus on Canada, the general conclusions drawn can be said to be applicable to other western nations, but the specific nuances may remain particular to Canada.

What do we mean by medicalization? Can it simply be equated with the increasing willingness and ability of medical practitioners to intervene in the workings of the human body? While this is certainly an aspect of it, the meaning of the term is broader and more nebulous. Intervention is part of the context of western medicine and medicalization is part of the modern cultural context of western society.[2] It refers to the way in which various aspects of life have become the focus of medical attention. In the present day, it is difficult to conceive of few aspects of our lives that could not be medicalized; health and medicine have become so closely interwoven within western society that they are difficult to separate, and what does not impinge upon our health?

When feminists refer to the medicalization of women's bodies they are referring to the fact that physicians' attention has focused more on women's bodies than on men's. The consequence of this focus has been to 'problematize' the female body. There is a vast literature on this, both historical and contemporary[3] and a general consensus seems to exist as to the reasons for this problematizing. First, doctors who, until recently, were predominantly male, have tended to view the male body as the norm and the female body as other than the norm. The male body was the body which they knew and with which they were familiar. Deviations from that body – menstruation, childbirth, menopause – appeared suspect and prone to weakness. Second, women were (and are) at a disadvantage in society and this was reflected in medicine. This meant that, when a woman patient faced a male physician who saw her body as 'other', she was in a less powerful position than a male patient would have been; the societal context, in which both the physician and the female patient lived, invested men with status over women. Third, the tendency of physicians has been to generalize the problems of sick women to well women; that is, they have essentialized women.

What this chapter does is to probe how this was done and to draw some lessons from it. Since the focus of much of the historical literature has been on childbirth, I have chosen examples outside of it to illustrate the above. Almost any facet of a woman's life could have been selected; most physicians felt that, since the female body itself was problematic, any aspect of its experience was suitable for medical gaze. The three areas on which this chapter concentrates are puberty, sexuality and menopause. None is innately problematic for women; all can be termed 'natural'. The fact that all three became pathologized reveals the kind of sway physicians had; it also reveals the general receptiveness of the society to that problematizing.

A word of caution is needed before we begin. We have to be careful that we do not make physicians the 'enemy'. Many women supported and even demanded medical care that could be construed as interventionist. They looked to physicians for advice about various aspects of their lives and hence participated in the medicalization of them. In addition, not all physicians supported the direction in which medicine was going and some were quite supportive of their women patients. Nonetheless, there was a mainstream current within medicine that is reflected in what follows.

Puberty

While both men and women experienced puberty, most physicians deemed puberty in woman much more significant, characterized as it was by the onset of menstruation, which was both a visible manifestation and a sign of its complexity. Throughout the first half of the twentieth century, physicians viewed the reproductive system in women as that which dominated their health experience and dictated their social role in society. Before puberty, the system was quiescent. At puberty, however, it awakened and the latent differences between the two sexes became evident. In an attempt to understand the phenomenon, doctors in Canada gathered as much information on puberty as they could, believing that science advanced with the accumulation of such data. The information became significant in and of itself and imbued with meaning as a result. One of the aspects which fascinated physicians was when menstruation began. Statistics were collected from all parts of the globe and estimates made about the average age of onset. The concern for establishing an average age was part of a desire to delineate a physiological norm, a point at which to draw a line between normality and abnormality. Physicians assumed that too early menstruation could pose a problem, as could too late menstruation. Within the Canadian context, it was usually the latter which was of particular concern, given the investment that a young society had in the childbearing capabilities of its women citizens. At the turn of the century, estimates were that puberty in women began somewhere between the ages of 13 and 16.[4] By 1950, the average was 13 years, with the range being between 11 and 16.[5] While most women probably did begin to menstruate between those ages, not all did and it was with these women that physicians became concerned. For example, J.S. Fairbairn, author of the 1924 *Gynaecology with Obstetrics – A Text-Book for Students and Practitioners*, believed that 'delay in the onset of menstruation beyond the age of seventeen must be regarded as pathological and due either to general conditions, such as anaemia, malnutrition, or abnormal metabolic states, or to local conditions in the reproductive tract'.[6]

Although age of menstruation was significant and provided physicians with some 'hard' data on which to focus, what fascinated them most were the reasons for the variation in the age of menstruation between groups of women. What were the factors, for instance, that brought about early menstruation? It was unclear what physicians thought they would do with the information once they had agreed on what the factors were. If they hoped to use it as a way of distinguishing between what was healthy and what was not, they were disappointed. The factors leading to early menstruation were so various and the relationship between them so vague that determining them became more of an exercise in data gathering rather than illuminating the functioning of menstruation in women. For instance, there was seldom any attempt to prioritize or discuss which factors, and under what conditions, would be more influential than others in bringing about early (or late) menstruation.

In the twentieth century, two factors dominated the discussion: climate and race. Both of these had been of interest to nineteenth-century physicians as well.[7] There was a general consensus that young women living in warm climates matured at an earlier age than those living in colder climates.[8] It was also often noted that Jewish women menstruated early, as did 'Hindoo' women, oriental women and black women. Among the groups who menstruated later were mentioned Aryans, Slavs, gentiles and of course the women of the extreme north.[9] At times, the racial differences could have been seen as a reflection of climatic differences, but this was almost never mentioned. Neither were the reasons why climate and race were so influential – physicians simply stated the connection. Nonetheless, by stating them, physicians were drawing lines between groups of women based on how their bodies worked. Because they seemed fascinated by the extremes of early and late menstruation, there was a sense that these extremes were pushing the boundaries of normalcy. It was best to be, not at the extreme edges, but somewhere in the middle, where most Anglo-Saxon women were. The eventual emphasis on race over climate, by the 1930s,[10] gave precedence to nature over nurture, reflecting a deep-seated belief in the influence of heredity. This was surely of significance for a country such as Canada which was becoming more multiracial than it had been.

Physicians linked factors other than race and climate to age of menstruation as well. They believed young women in cities menstruated sooner than women living in the country.[11] Aspects of life associated with wealth such as sedentary habits or too much social life and luxury also contributed to an early menarche.[12] Emotionality led to early menstruation,[13] as did early mental stimulation.[14] Early sexual stimulation, at times associated with reading romantic novels or eating highly seasoned food, was also a factor.[15] In addition, class affected the age of menstruation. Working-class girls clearly could not lead the lives that wealthy girls did and thus they were seen as coming to menstruation at a later age. But at times the class dimension held moral overtones. For example, in 1907, J. Clifton Edgar reported one study that noted sexual excitement among 'hard-working factory girls ... where, in the nature of the work, there is a promiscuous mixing of sexes'.[16] And he was not alone in believing this.[17]

What are we to make of these differing factors? Only occasionally did physicians make moral judgements about them as in the case of sexuality. But when you look at the factors leading to early menstruation, the image they depict is of a young wealthy woman, living in the city, tempted and stimulated by its excitement, being able to afford to take advantage of that excitement. Her opposite was either the good, clean country girl or the overworked working-class girl who is unable to get enough food to eat. The moral was there for all to draw.

While the factors affecting age of puberty were of interest to physicians, their major focus was on the physical changes occurring. In women this was characterized by a rounding of the body, the development of breasts and the growth of genital hair. Such descriptions would seem to be straightforward, only varying in their specificity and detail over time. At other times, however, physicians endowed such changes with cultural meaning. According to G. Todd Gilliam, in 1907, puberty was when the girl 'takes on the lines and curves that distinguish the mature female from the male. The increased development of bust and hips and general fullness of contour add greatly to her attractiveness, and proclaim her "readiness" for motherhood'.[18] Three themes emerge from this quotation. First is the use of the male as the basis for comparison, the norm; puberty is when the female is distinguished from the male, not when the male is distinguished from the female. Second, Gilliam linked the physical changes to attractiveness; they were no longer neutral changes. Third, the changes announced what a woman's social role was to be and her 'readiness' for it.

Different physicians focused on different attributes which they saw emerging in young women at this time, perhaps saying more about what they found attractive in women than about the actual changes occurring in women themselves. But not all changes were positive. Emotionality was seen as a female characteristic and a negative one. The young women readers of the 1946 *Gynaecology for Nurses* would certainly have taken away a mixed message about puberty. The authors were very clear that menstruation was normal and that the activities of girls should not be curtailed during that time – a very up-to-date and open view. But then they warned mothers and educators that, 'while apparently overlooking the event, consideration must be given to the girl's irritability which must never be actually blamed on the menstrual period'. Thus the girl was not made to feel that menstruation was a problem, but the people around her were being warned that it was. What seems to have been occurring is that pubescent girls were being compared to some ideal, which apparently was a non-menstruating girl. In this way, menstruating girls were placed outside the accepted model of girlhood, even though menstruation was viewed by physicians as the central event of girlhood.[19]

If emotionality and even irritability were experienced by most young women during this time, as some believed, then emotionality and irritability should have been seen as the norm. But they were not. Physicians and others viewed these attributes in a negative way and so they turned those attributes into something about which to be concerned. There was a sense that young women were experiencing so many changes that they were simply not able to cope. The changes occurring in boys were not considered to be of the same degree and so physicians did not perceive male puberty as potentially problematic. What is interesting in this scenario is that other factors associated with female puberty would seem to have provided young women with the resources to withstand the pressures on them. For example, physicians generally agreed that girls matured both mentally and psychologically at an earlier age than boys. This could have led to the view that they were placed in a position to cope with the changes they were experiencing – it did not. Physicians saw women, as Canadians in general did, as less in command of their emotions than men.

Physicians perceived puberty in women as a limiting rather than a liberating experience.[20] The language physicians used to describe puberty and all the changes associated with it denote some kind of major turning point. The adjective most favoured in the early years was 'critical'.[21] Compared to what happened to men, the changes occurring in women were seen as more complex and numerous. The accuracy of this perception is not the issue; it was a perception shared by many in society. The point is that physicians saw these changes predominantly in a negative way; they viewed puberty as full of danger rather than possibilities.[22] The metaphors used to describe puberty made this clear. For example, W. Blair Bell, writing in *The Principles of Gynaecology*, described how the changes during puberty 'spread their shadow over the whole range' of a young woman's life.[23]

A major concern about puberty in girls was education and how the educational system undermined their health to the detriment of their future ability to have children.[24] The specific concern was that education demanded too much nutrition (blood) for the brain, leaving the rest of the body weakened.[25] Various solutions were proposed, to alter the educational system, making it less stressful for young women, or even to withdraw them from it altogether.[26] The Minister of Health for New Brunswick in 1919 believed that, between the ages of 14 and 16, education for girls needed to be gender-specific. Girls should be taught by a woman of 'high moral character' capable of teaching them 'domestic science' and 'personal hygiene and household sanitation'.[27] Such an education would clearly send home the message to young women that their bodies were a problem and that their destiny lay in domestic work.[28] J.A. Lindsay, in the 1930 *Dalhousie Review*, comforted himself that girls themselves offset the educational pressure by a decline in their ability to acquire knowledge for a period after the age of 12 and by experiencing a 'period of lassitude and dullness' between the ages of 16 and 17. In his words, 'Dame Nature [was] playing her profound game'.[29] Thus nature would protect women even if society was unwilling. In this context, physicians saw the ill-health or problems of pubescent girls as a social construct – the result of the modern educational system. This concern stemmed from the reality of compulsory education laws extending education further into the teen-age years than had been the case and the movement on the part of an increasingly significant minority of women into the universities.

In examining the way in which many physicians perceived female puberty, several themes have emerged. One is the tendency of the medical profession to use the male body as the basis of comparison for the female. In doing this, it caused women's bodies to become the other, somehow foreign, and at risk. Second, in trying to determine what the average age of puberty was, physicians were establishing what it should be. They were creating the vision of what a healthy pubescent girl was. This assumed that all women should be this way. Third, physicians were clearly influenced by the cultural mores of their time. It was not coincidental that white, middle-class, Anglo-Saxon women were seen to be the healthiest type of pubescent girl. It is not coincidental either that the attributes of a healthy puberty were those attributes society deemed suitable for women to have and that any suggestion of assertiveness was deemed abnormal and thus unhealthy. All this, however, was not presented as socially influenced but as scientific fact.

Sexuality

Similar themes also emerge in descriptions of sexuality in women. Generally, physicians preferred to discuss sexuality within the confines of a marital relationship, which they viewed as the culmination of a woman's life and ambition. So significant was marriage that some physicians saw it as a cure for what 'ailed' women.[30] Harry Sturgeon Crossen and Robert James Crossen, the authors of the 1936 *Diseases of Women*, suggested that amenorrhoea was sometimes a 'functional disturbance, which [would] probably soon disappear under the influence of a happy married life'. Crossen and Crossen also believed that marriage was helpful in treating neurotrophic dysmenorrhoea, as did the University of Western Ontario's Dr E.V. Shute. According to Shute, marriage offered women 'relaxation from the mental and physical tension of unsatisfactory single life'.[31] In this case, the social role of women impinged on the medical view. Woman's destiny was to marry and have children; a denial of that destiny could only be harmful. Thus the health of a single woman was deemed at risk and, in some cases, restoring her destiny became the prescription. For some physicians, not only could marriage with its sexual activity and resultant pregnancy cure disease, it could also prevent it.[32] Marriage and children were natural for women and what was natural had to be healthy.

The marital relationship that physicians deemed so beneficial for women was not one of equality between the sexes, except that each had their own sphere. A woman was to focus her attention on the home, her responsibility to care for it and to bear and raise her and her husband's children. Men, on the other hand, were responsible for the financial support of the family. This kind of separation was a continuation of the Victorian ideal. Where it differed was in the actual relationship between the two spouses. Although the husband and wife may have had their separate spheres, there was a strong emphasis, especially after the First World War, on marriage being based on love and mutuality.[33] While admirable in the ideal, in reality the mutuality often seemed more akin to the subordination of the wife to the husband. Dr A. Lapthorn Smith, in an early diatribe against higher education for women, made it clear that one of the problems of educated women was that they did not make good wives. He had difficulty envisioning a relationship where the wife was superior in education to the husband. The consequence for the woman was that either she did not marry or, if she did, she would have an unhappy marriage since her education would prevent her husband from assuming his true place as the head of the household.[34] This theme of subordination of the wife to the husband continued throughout the 1900 to 1950 period.[35] That some physicians took this to heart was evidenced in two articles published in the mid-to-late 1940s, detailing the relationship between a doctor and his spouse. Each article described the very special responsibility that a medical wife had to uphold the prestige of her husband in public. Their husbands' jobs were so demanding that the authors suggested that the wives cater to their husbands and not speak too familiarly of them in society. As one author ruefully suggested, the wife should refer to her husband as '"The Doctor" using a tone just one shade less reverent than you'd use to say "Mr. God"'.[36]

Physicians deemed marital sexuality healthy, but what did it entail? Doctors' advice to couples was clearly influenced by the way they perceived both male and female sexuality. In general, they used male sexuality as the standard by which to compare female sexuality. The irony of this is that they did so even when they did not see women's sexuality the same way – they recognized the female sexual drive, but saw it as a lesser version of what men experienced.[37] Despite this view, physicians were fascinated by the issue of woman's sexuality and discussed it in much more detail than men's. The latter was simply a given.

Women's sexuality was not a given. There was an ambivalence about its nature and confusion about whether there was even a standard by which to judge it, other than comparing it to men's. One possible reason for this was the dichotomy between what physicians observed and what they and others deemed socially acceptable. Thus sexuality in women was seen as natural but ...[38] For some physicians, it was not only nature which accounted for the female sex drive but also society and the pressures placed on women.[39] This mixture of nature and nurture created in the minds of many physicians an ambivalence so that the same physicians who might argue that the sex drives in the two sexes were quite similar could also argue elsewhere that this was not true of all women.[40] Physicians were perhaps hedging their bets; they did not feel they could generalize female sexuality to the same extent as male sexuality. What all did agree, however, was that marriage was the only venue in which those feelings should be expressed. Unmarried women would simply have to control their normal desires and pay the price for doing so mentally, physically and socially.[41] For example, Dr Percy Ryberg believed that 'there is good reason to believe that the seminal products of the male which are precipitated into the vagina have a beneficial effect upon the whole system of the woman'.[42]

While physicians believed that sexuality was a natural instinct experienced by women, they believed that the purpose of marriage was the procreation of children. Not surprisingly, the old notion of sexual satisfaction being conducive to conception, going back to Galen, continued well into the century.[43] Not all physicians subscribed to this theory but they did acknowledge that the concept was widespread, especially among women.[44] So persistent was this idea that some physicians seemed to give way and argued that while orgasm was not a necessary precondition for conception, it could aid it, 'since it more often insures that the spermatozoa will enter the cervix before being injured by the acidity of the normal vaginal secretion'.[45]

If most doctors still depicted sexuality as somehow different for men and women, many no longer saw those differences as fundamental.[46] The sex manuals and medical advice of the time emphasized the mutuality of the sex act and were quite explicit about this. Some addressed the importance of the bridal night and how it could determine the direction of the marriage. There was the assumption that the husband would take the sexual lead and the husband was warned not to be too hasty in the act of love and to ensure that his bride experienced pleasure, a significant responsibility when it is remembered that she was to have been a virgin.[47] In the case where it was the bride who was experienced and the groom who was not, one physician advised: 'She must in particular be very careful not to remind him in any way of her experience or she may take away some of his confidence in himself and his own sexual powers that is so necessary for most men'. He pointed out to the woman that she needed to teach her husband that the sexual act meant more than 'the satisfaction of his animal impulses', and that a 'responsibility rests upon her for the whole future of their married life; a responsibility that is almost as great as in the case of the man who marries a virgin'.[48]

Sexual advice manuals, more often than not written by physicians or with physicians in the role of expert advisers, were quite explicit in the twentieth century compared to what they had been in the nineteenth. Detailed descriptions of the 'normal' ways of making love were provided. In particular, the importance of arousal was stressed.[49] Women were warned that their appearance was very important if they wanted to keep their husbands interested in them. Women must take into account personal hygiene and not take their husband's interest for granted by going to bed in pins and curlers and wearing face cream.[50] Neither were men exempt from such warnings. Percy Ryberg, in his medical manual, cautioned men that one of the 'first things a man should be concerned with is the state of his underclothing, and this should be changed as often as required to insure cleanliness. A daily bath or shower may not be necessary, but the smell of male sweat and other body odours, especially the smell of feet, are not pleasant to a sensitive wife'.[51] By giving such advice, physicians made it medical. By giving such advice physicians were also creating the image of what normal and good sex was. There was an irony here, however. While physicians believed that both husband and wife were to enjoy the sexual act and to have mutual orgasms,[52] they also believed that this was not going to be easy. Such a concept seemed more an ideal than reality, for a reading of the medical literature suggests that doctors believed sexual maladjustments abounded.[53] And if maladjustments in the normal existed, even more serious were the perversions of the natural. Fellatio, cunnilingus and masturbation without consummation were considered as outside the boundaries of acceptability.[54]

In discussing female sexuality, physicians were clearly outside their area of expertise. They did not receive any specialized training in sexuality at medical school but, since they were familiar with the human body, they saw themselves as experts on all of its experiences – including sexuality. Any examination of their ideas reveals the degree to which they were socially constructed. Doctors perceived female sexuality in a way that would ensure that women conformed to the conventional gender roles accepted by society. Those roles determined their perception of sexuality in both sexes. This meant that women continued to be compared to men, that their sexuality had to be seen as something other than that of men. In all this, there was an attempt to fashion normative behaviour, to define the limits of acceptability which in turn could be redefined as the limits of healthy sexuality.

Menopause

This concern with what constituted a healthy experience can also be seen in medical views of menopause. As with puberty, physicians were interested in when menopause began. Most agreed that it occurred some time between the ages of 40–55, characterizing menopause before this date as early, although not necessarily abnormal. Indeed, in 1915, Dr Cleland, surgeon and gynaecologist to the Toronto Grace Hospital, pointed out that in his own records the age of menopausal women ranged from 26 to 56.[55] Because the range was so wide, physicians were fascinated by what factors would produce an early menopause as opposed to a late menopause. There was a sense that, if the factors were eliminated, all women's bodies would behave the same, indeed that all women's bodies should behave the same. What interested doctors in their listing of influences was the correlation between them and menopause. They did not seem interested in explaining how the connection worked. Indeed, their discussions were mainly a repeat of discussions on age of menstruation, with a few additional factors introduced. Puberty and menopause were the two critical periods of a woman's life, and not surprisingly, doctors saw the influences on each as similar if not, in some cases, identical. Climate was such a factor: if warm climate brought on early puberty then it brought on early menopause as well.[56] Affluence was also linked to age of menopause. Luxurious living delayed menopause,[57] as did city living and education.[58] Not a major focus, but mentioned, was hair colour, with menopause occurring later in brunettes than in blondes.[59] Race, too, was a factor; for example, the 1912 *A Text-Book of Diseases of Women* and the 1935 text, *Gynecology and Obstetrics*, noted that menopause came earlier in Jewish women than in non-Jewish women.[60] Dr Gibson, writing in the 1950 *Canadian Nurse*, also noted that race was a factor and that 'southern and oriental types' tended to experience an early menopause.[61]

Because the factors which could influence the onset of menstruation were similar to those affecting menopause, doctors linked the two phenomena and tried to suggest a connection between them. The most widely noted one was that an early puberty would lead to a late menopause.[62] A minority seemed to disagree, however, arguing that an early puberty went with an early menopause, or that the connection between the two was simply not clear.[63] The concentration on age of puberty and its effect on age of menopause is noteworthy for its lack of substance. Some commentators pointed to the apparent contradiction between early menstruation and late menopause but no-one seemed able to explain why this apparent contradiction was the norm. As they did with other factors, doctors simply stated it, as a truism. The correlations became the explanations.

Doctors did not spend a great deal of time discussing the age of menopause. What they did delineate in great detail, probably more than most women wanted, were the myriad of 'symptoms' that could accompany menopause. In the process, two general overviews of menopause emerged. The first was positive, although this was often couched in such a way as to suggest a certain ambivalence about it. There was a recognition that menopause did not have to be a negative experience but – and there was a but – this focus on the positive always seemed to be phrased in a muted way or in a way that took away from the assurance. For example, in the October 1914 issue of *The Canada Lancet*, the editors reprinted an article by Dr E. Giles, who was surgeon at the Chelsea Hospital for Women, in which he made it clear that 'Normally, the menopause is no more a critical period than is puberty [for those familiar with medical descriptions of puberty this was not exactly reassuring]; the cessation of menstruation should be as uneventful as its onset, but both epochs are liable to be associated with some functional disturbance'.[64] Others also seemed to take away from the positive by concentrating on the negative.[65] Some discussed the unfounded fears that women had about menopause, others the statistics of those women who did have problems. Whatever way they did it, seldom was it an unadulterated positive view of menopause. In the 1901 text edited by Dr Charles Reed, students were warned that during menopause a woman was forced to perceive that her charms, her youth were disappearing. It noted that one-third of her life was still before her, 'full of promise', but the promise of what? – 'of placid enjoyment'. Others referred to the 'placid contentment' to which a menopausal woman could look forward, assuring their readers that the death or disease rate among menopausal women was not greater than at any other period; that it was difficult to judge 'where the normal [menopause] ends and the abnormal begins'; that at the age of 40 woman had reached her 'zenith';[66] and that there were 'compensations' for what women were losing. Physicians advised women not to let the possibilities of what other women might be experiencing affect their own menopause. Of course, this was easier said than done; in the discussions of menopause, the emphasis was not on the women who were not experiencing difficulties but on those who were.

It should be clear that the positive view of menopause was severely flawed. Negativity reigned supreme. Physicians linked menopause to disease.[67] They associated it with a change of life which was seldom seen as positive. This change was connected with loss – loss of reproduction, loss of youth, loss of femininity, the giving up of dreams, the beginnings of old age and entering the 'ebbing stream of life'.[68] Indeed, the adjectives and words chosen in the general descriptions of menopause often denoted negativity. One of the favoured ways of describing what happened to the genitalia was through the use of the word 'atrophy'. Other words chosen to describe the same phenomenon were diminish, shrivel, shrink, destruction, loss of elasticity, obliterate and retrogression.[69] Doctors referred to it as the critical period, which is where the meaning of climacteric originates.[70] It was a period that necessitated 'management' and 'supervision'.[71] Many referred to it as the 'involutional period' and discussed the specific nature of 'involutional melancholia'.[72] The definition of 'involutional' is a 'retrograde change of the entire body or in a particular organ; the progressive degeneration occurring naturally with advancing age, resulting in shrivelling of organs or tissues'.[73] Menopause brought with it the growth of hair on the face, 'even the development of an imperfect beard or moustache', a harsher tone of voice or the loss of breast tone, leading to flaccidity.[74] Disturbances of the stomach and digestive system as well as weight gain, usually evoked by words such as 'fat' and 'stout,' were not uncommon.[75] A lack of well-being seemed to be prominent: sleeplessness, lack of energy, general weakness, dizziness and vague and specific pains.[76] Doctors also linked more serious health problems with the menopause – kidney disease, arthritis and cancers among others.[77]

As pointed out in a recent article on menopause, 'although there is a large body of research on symptoms of menopause, there is no consensus on what actually constitutes menopausal symptoms, their categories, the number of women who exhibit these symptoms'.[78] Certainly this was true in the past as well. There was a sense among some physicians that any problem experienced by women during the menopausal years was to be blamed on impending menopause, experiencing menopause or suffering from post-menopausal difficulties. Doctors tended to group change of life or familial changes in with menopause simply because they tended to occur at the same time. By this sleight of hand, societal pressures on women became linked to changes occurring in the female body and thus open to medical treatment and advice. Menopause gave physicians a cause for physical problems of women in the middle years and with the assignment of cause came fulfilment of one responsibility of a physician. The biological assignment of causation was the one with which physicians would be most familiar and with which they were most comfortable.[79] This may be why the symptom that they focused most on was the hot flushes or sweating which, after the discovery of the sex hormones, they connected with oestrogen loss.[80] This was the one symptom for which physicians were convinced there really were strong physiological explanations.[81]

If physicians were confident about the physical consequences of menopause, they were more ambivalent about the nervous repercussions. In 1906, J. Bland-Sutton and Arthur E. Giles, in their *The Diseases of Women: A Handbook for Students and Practitioners*, noted that most women underwent a 'nervous phenomenon'.[82] At first it is difficult to understand how to interpret 'nervous', for in the medical parlance of the time it had two meanings. The first simply referred to the physical nervous system of the body and the second, which was the one with which lay people would be familiar, referred to the mental state of the person. Bland-Sutton and Giles followed their 'nervous phenomenon' phrase with a list of attributes which could fit into one or the other category. What their listing does is to raise the possibility that all the reactions could fit into the mental category rather than the physical simply because it is not clear which goes with which. It raises the spectre of how real menopause and the problems that many women experienced were. It seems to reflect an ambivalence on the part of physicians themselves which few ever faced. This association of menopausal symptoms with nervous changes was constant throughout the century. For example, the most significant women's magazine of the day, *Chatelaine*, in April 1948 published a lead article entitled 'The Truth About Menopause'. The author they chose to write the article was Robert A. Cleghorn, assistant professor of psychiatry at McGill University and in 'charge of the experimental therapeutics laboratories at the Allan Memorial Institute of Psychiatry', an affiliation which was made quite prominent in the article.

Menopause was clearly not an experience to be anticipated with glee. It is no wonder that physicians often remarked that women approached menopause with apprehension, even though doctors tried to stress that this was not necessary. Yet, considering the medical material, women could not be faulted for becoming confused by the mixed messages being sent out by physicians. Physicians were reflecting, in their negative views of menopause, the negativity of society in general towards aging women. Women were esteemed for their childbearing role; when they could no longer perform that role they were not deemed useful or attractive. Recent studies have revealed that menopausal systems are very closely linked to culture.[83] This is equally true with respect to the way physicians viewed it. Menopause was a phenomenon not experienced by men[84] and so most physicians, who were male, saw it as problematic even when they could acknowledge that for most women it was not. But they did not see most women – they saw women who were coming to them with problems and hence physicians saw these problems as the norm.

Conclusions

This brief overview of medical attitudes towards puberty, sexuality and menopause reveals a profession which is willing to proffer advice on a vast range of issues which are not inherently medical; that is, all are 'normal' or average experiences. Certainly some women experienced problems with those average experiences, but the tendency of physicians was to generalize from those women to all women. This is reflected in the medical literature they wrote. While acknowledging the problem-free nature of puberty, sexuality and menopause for most women, the literature emphasized the problematic side. Women would go to physicians because they had something 'wrong' and so it was the physician's job to find out what that was. The 'normal' body was the baseline for trying to do this. At times, however, normalcy was more culturally than physiologically defined. Sometimes physicians could recognize this but, even when they did, they did not question it. Why should they? It was not their responsibility to change the system. They simply accepted it as they found it and occasionally suggested adjustments, as when they discussed women's education.

Physicians and others in society tended to use the male body as the standard of normalcy. This did not mean that they felt women should be like men – clearly they did not. Indeed, physicians seemed to revel in the differences between the two sexes and it was those differences which were emphasized. But the way in which physicians looked at women meant that the emphasis was on how women differed from men, not on how men differed from women. The view that women's bodies were more complex than men's simply reinforced this view and lent credence to the perception that, not only were women's bodies different, but they were also subject to more problems.

The tendency to generalize from a population of women with 'problems' to the wider population raises the issue of whether medicine is a science. Certainly, the rigour with which many of us endow science is often missing in medicine. As revealed in medical discussions of puberty and menopause, connections were made between specific variables and age of puberty or menopause, yet little explanation of those variables was offered. Correlations became causes. Neither did physicians discuss in any meaningful way the degree to which various factors worked as causes: was climate more significant than race and, if so, to what degree and why? What occurred was simply a long list of factors that might act as causes. Lastly, physicians provided opinions on many areas which seem outside the purview of medicine. They were able to do this because society let them. Canadians imbued physicians with expertise because they did not question the 'scientific' rigour of medicine. Doctors 'knew' the body better than most experts and experts were what were increasingly being demanded. Doctors did not hesitate to expand their area of influence by giving opinions on a wide range of issues and, the more they did, the more they were seen as knowledgeable. The cycle became self-generating. In recent years, that cycle has been partially broken as medicine has come under criticism and challenge to its way of working.

Notes

1 Research for this chapter has been funded by the Social Sciences and Humanities Research Council of Canada [SSHRC] and the Hannah Institute for the History of Medicine. The Program for Scholars and Artists in Residence, funded by the Rockefeller Foundation in 1994, and participation in a SSHRC Network grant 1993–96 provided me with the opportunity to develop many of the ideas in this chapter.

2 Western medicine has tended to be crisis-oriented, has viewed the body as a machine, and has had an interventionist orientation. See Thomas McKeown, 'A Sociological Approach to the History of Medicine', *Medical History*, **14**, October 1970, 342–51.

3 See John S. Haller Jr., 'Neurasthenia: The Medical Profession and the "New Woman" of the late Nineteenth Century', *New York State Journal of Medicine*, **LXXI**, 15 February 1971, 473–82; Janice Delaney, M.J. Lupton and Emily Toth, *The Curse: A Cultural History of Menstruation*, New York: Mentor, 1976; Judy Litoff, *American Midwives 1860 to the Present*, Westport, Conn.: Greenwood Press, 1978; Marjorie Tew, *Safer Childbirth: A Critical History of Maternity Care*, London: Chapman & Hall, 1990; Patricia Anne Vertinsky, *The Eternally Wounded Woman: Women, Doctors and Exercise in the Late Nineteenth Century*, Manchester: Manchester University Press, 1990; Elaine Showalter, *The Female Malady: Women, Madness and English Culture*, New York: Pantheon Books, 1985; Veronica Strong-Boag and Kathryn McPherson, 'The Confinement of Women: Childbirth and Hospitalization in Vancouver, 1919–1939', *BC Studies*, **69–70**, Spring–Summer, 1986, 142–75; Barbara Rothman, *In Labour: Women and Power in the Birthplace*, London: Junction Books, 1982; Katherine Arnup, Andrée Lévesque and Ruth Roach Pierson (eds), *Delivering Motherhood: Maternal Ideologies and Practices in the 19th and 20th Centuries*, London: Routledge, 1990; Paul Atkinson, 'Strong

Minds and Weak Bodies: Sports, Gymnastics and the Medicalization of Women's Education', *British Journal of Sports History (Great Britain)*, **2**, (1), 1985, 62–71; Barbara Ehrenreich and Deirdre English, *For Her Own Good: 150 Years of the Experts' Advice to Women*, Garden City, New York: Anchor Press, 1978; Barbara Ehrenreich, *Complaints and Disorders: The Sexual Politics of Sickness*, New York: Old Westbury, 1973; Stephen Kern, *Anatomy and Destiny: A Cultural History of the Human Body*, Indianapolis: Bobbs-Merrill, 1975; Frank Mort, *Dangerous Sexualities: Medico-Moral Politics in England Since 1830*, London: Routledge & Kegan Paul, 1987). This interpretation that medicine has problematized the female body is also reflected in studies of modern maternity and medical care. See Suzanne Aims, *Immaculate Deception: A New Look at Women and Childbirth in America*, Boston: San Francisco Book Co./Houghton Mifflin, 1975; Sandra Coney, *The Unfortunate Experiment: The Full Story Behind the Inquiry into Cervical Cancer Treatment*, Aukland: Penguin Books, 1988; Nancy Stoller Shaw, *Forced Labour: Maternity Care in the United States*, London: Pergamon Press, 1974; Doris B. Haire, *The Cultural Warping of Childbirth*, Milwaukee: International Childbirth Education Association, 1972; Zelda Abramson, 'Don't Ask Your Gynecologist If You Need a Hysterectomy...', *Healthsharing*, **11**, (3), June 1990, 12–16; Ruth Bleier, *Science and Gender: A Critique of Biology and Its Theories of Women*, New York: Pergamon Press, 1984; Gena Corea, *The Mother Machine: Reproductive Technologies from Artificial Insemination to Artificial Wombs*, Markham: Fitzhenry and Whiteside, 1985; Gena Corea, *The Invisible Epidemic: The Story of Women and Aids*, New York: Harper Perennial, 1992; Gena Corea, *The Hidden Malpractice: How American Medicine Mistreats Women*, New York: Harper Colophon Books, 1985; Dawn H. Currie and Valerie Raoul (eds), *The Anatomy of Gender: Women's Struggle for the Body*, Ottawa: Carleton University Press, 1991; Claudia Dreifus, *Seizing Our Bodies: The Politics of Women's Health*, New York: Random House, 1978; Nicole J. Grant, *The Selling of Contraception: The Dalkon Shield Case, Sexuality and Women's Anatomy*, Columbus, Ohio: Ohio State University Press, 1992; Emily Martin, 'The Egg and the Sperm: How Science Has Constructed a Romance Based on Stereotypical Male–Female Roles', *Signs*, **16**, (3), Spring 1991, 485–501; Robert Mendelsohn, *Male Practice: How Doctors Manipulate Women*, Chicago: Contemporary Books, 1981; Eileen Nechas and Denise Foley, *Unequal Treatment:What You Don't Know About How Women are Mistreated by the Medical Community*, New York: Simon & Schuster, 1994; Ann Oakley, *Women Confined: Towards a Sociology of Childbirth*, London: Martin Robertson, 1980; Janice Raymond, *Women as Wombs: Reproductive Technologies and the Battle Over Women's Freedom*, New York: Harper, 1993; Janice Raymond, 'Medicine as Patriarchal Religion', *The Journal of Medicine and Philosophy*, **7**, (2), 1982, 197–216; Robyn Rowland, *Living Laboratories: Women and Reproductive Technologies*, Bloomington: Indiana University Press, 1992; Diana Scully, *Men Who Control Women's Health: The Miseducation of Obstetrician–Gynecologists*, Boston, Mass.: Houghton Mifflin, 1980; Alexandra Dundas Todd, *Intimate Adversaries: Cultural Conflict Between Doctors and Women Patients*, Philadelphia: University of Pennsylvania Press, 1989.

4 Henry Garrigues, *A Text-book of the Diseases of Women*, Philadelphia, 1894, p.114. Such estimates reflected those made earlier in the century as well. See William Carpenter, *Principles of Human Physiology*, London, 1869, pp.832–3; William Tyler Smith, *The Modern Practice of Midwifery: A Course of Lectures on Obstetrics*, New York, 1858, p.86.

5 Arthur Hale Curtis and John William Huffman, *A Textbook of Gynecology*, Philadelphia and London: W.B. Saunders, 1951, p.101.

6 J.S. Fairbairn, *Gynaecology with Obstetrics – A Text-Book for Students and Practitioners*, London: Humphrey Milford, Oxford University Press, 1924, p.485.

7 Tyler Smith, *The Modern Practice of Midwifery*, p.86; Arthur W. Edis, *Diseases of Women: A Manual for Students and Practitioners*, Philadelphia, 1882, p.133.
8 E.C. Dudley, *The Principles and Practice of Gynecology for Students and Practitioners*, Philadelphia and New York: Lea & Febiger, 1908, p.24; Joseph B. DeLee, *The Principles and Practice of Obstetrics*, Philadelphia and London: W.B. Saunders, 1913, p.16; William P. Graves, *Gynecology*, Philadelphia and London: W.B. Saunders, 1929, p.30; R.W. Johnstone, *A Text-Book of Midwifery: For Students and Practitioners*, London: A. & C. Black, Ltd., 1934, p.37.
9 *Canadian Practitioner and Medical Review* (hereafter *CPMR*), **26**, 5, May 1901, 248; J. Clifton Edgar, *The Practice of Obstetrics ... for the Use of Students and Practitioners ...*, Philadelphia: P. Blakison's Son & Co., 1907, p.22; Barton Cooke Hirst, *A Text-Book of Obstetrics*, Philadelphia and London: W.B. Saunders, 1912, p.74; DeLee, *The Principles and Practice of Obstetrics*, p.16; Johnstone, *A Text-Book of Midwifery*, p.37; Fred Adair (ed.), *Obstetrics and Gynecology*, vol., I, Philadelphia: Lea & Febiger, 1940, p.489; Emil Novak, *Textbook of Gynecology*, Baltimore: The Williams & Wilkins Co., 1944, p.111; Archibald Donald Campbell and Mabel A. Shannon, *Gynecology for Nurses*, Philadelphia: F.A. David Co., 1946, p.23; Curtis and Huffman, *A Textbook of Gynecology*, p.101.
10 J.M. Munro Kerr, *Combined Textbook of Obstetrics and Gynaecology for Students and Medical Practitioners*, Edinburgh: E. & S. Livinstone, 1933, p.38; Johnstone, *A Text-Book of Midwifery*, p.37; Ten Teachers (Comyns Berkeley, eds), *Diseases of Women*, London: Edward Arnold & Co., 1935, p.54; Carl Davis (ed.), *Gynecology and Obstetrics*, vol. I, Hagerstown, Maryland: W.F. Prior Company Inc., 1935, ch. 2, p.3; Adair (ed.), *Obstetrics and Gynecology* vol, I, p.489; Henricus J. Stander, *Williams Obstetrics: A Textbook for the Use of Students and Practitioners*, New York: D. Appleton-Century Company, 1941, p.72; Novak, *Textbook of Gynecology*, p.111.
11 Hirst, *A Text-Book of Obstetrics*, p.74; DeLee, *The Principles and Practice of Obstetrics*, p.16; Harry Sturgeon Crossen and Robert James Crossen, *Diseases of Women*, St. Louis: The C.V. Mosby Company, 1930, p.828; Johnstone, *A Text-Book of Midwifery*, p.37; Davis (ed.), *Gynecology and Obstetrics*, vol. I, ch. 2, p.4; Adair (ed.), *Obstetrics and Gynecology*, vol. I, p.489; Ralph B. Winn, *Obstetrics and Gynecology*, vol. I, p.489; Ralph B. Winn (ed.), *Encyclopedia of Child Guidance*, New York: The Philosophical Library, 1943, p.334.
12 J. Bland-Sutton and Arthur E. Giles, *The Diseases of Women: A Handbook for Students and Practitioners*, London and New York: Rebman, 1906, p.14; Edgar, *The Practice of Obstetrics*, p.22; DeLee, *The Principles and Practice of Obstetrics*, p.16; Munro Kerr *et al.*, *Combined Textbook of Obstetrics and Gynaecology*, p.38; Johnstone, *A Text-Book of Midwifery*, p.37; Davis (ed.), *Gynecology and Obstetrics*, vol. I, ch. 2, p.4; Adair (ed.), *Obstetrics and Gynecology*, vol. I, p.489; Winn (ed.), *Encyclopedia of Child Guidance*, p.334; Novak, *Textbook of Gynecology*, p.111.
13 Bland-Sutton and Giles, *The Diseases of Women*, p.14.
14 Edgar, *The Practice of Obstetrics*, p.22; Munro Kerr *et al.*, *Combined Textbook of Obstetrics and Gynaecology*, p.38; Johnstone, *A Text-Book of Midwifery*, p.37.
15 Edgar, *The Practice of Obstetrics*, p.22; Winfield Scott Hall, *Sexual Knowledge*, Philadelphia: The International Bible House, 1913, pp.179–80; Davis (ed.), *Gynecology and Obstetrics* vol. I, ch. 2, p.4; Novak, *Textbook of Gynecology*, p.111; Hirst, *A Text-Book of Obstetrics*, p.74.
16 Edgar, *The Practice of Obstetrics*, p.22.
17 W. Blair Bell, 'Disorders of Function', in Thomas Watts Eden and Cuthbert Lockyer (eds), *The New System of Gynecology*, vol. I, Toronto: The Macmillan Company of Canada Ltd., 1917, p.297.
18 G. Todd Gilliam, *A Text-book of Practical Gynecology*, Philadelphia: F.A. Davis Company, 1907, p.62; see also Francis H.A. Marshall, *The Physiology of Reproduction*, London: Longmans, Green and Company, 1922, p.713.

19 Davis (ed.), *Gynecology and Obstetrics*, vol. I, ch. 2, p.2; Adair (ed.), *Obstetrics and Gynecology*, vol. I, p.490; Winn (ed.), *Encyclopedia of Child Guidance*, pp.335–6; Campbell and Shannon, *Gynecology for Nurses*, p.25; Marion Hilliard, *Women and Fatigue – A Woman Doctor's Answer*, Garden City, New York: Doubleday and Company, Inc., 1960, p.14.

20 Often it was seen as liberating for boys. See *Maclean's*, **59**, 1, December 1946, 12.

21 *CPMR*, **26**, (5), May, 1901, 247; *Maritime Medical News* (hereafter *MMN*), **14**, (12), December 1902, 437; *The Canada Lancet* (hereafter *CL*), **38**, (5), January 1905, 431–2; Gilliam, *A Text-book of Practical Gynecology*, p.4; Dudley, *The Principles and Practice of Gynecology*, p.22; *The Public Health Journal* (hereafter *PHJ*), **4**, (12), December 1913, 649; *PHJ*, **10**, (11), November 1919, 491; Davis (ed.), *Gynecology and Obstetrics* vol. I, ch. 2, p.5.

22 Elizabeth Lunbeck, 'A New Generation of Women: Progressive Psychiatrists and the Hypersexual Female', *Feminist Studies*, **13**, (3), Fall, 1987, 517.

23 W. Blair Bell, *The Principles of Gynaecology*, London: Longmans, Green and Co., 1910, p.68.

24 Crossen and Crossen, *Diseases of Women*, p.851; *Canadian Medical Association Journal* (hereafter *CMAJ*), **22**, (4), April 1930, 467.

25 *CPMR*, **27**, (11), November, 1902, 662; *Dominion Medical Monthly* (hereafter *DMM*), **23**, (5), November 1904, 323; *CL*, **38**, (5), 1905, 432; Dudley, *The Principles and Practice of Gynecology*, p.27; *CL*, **43**, (5), January 1910, 400.

26 *DMM*, **23**, (5), November, 1904, 323; *Maclean's*, **33**, 1 September 1920, 73; *CL*, **38**, (5), 1905, 432; *The Canada Lancet and National Hygiene* (hereafter *CLNH*), **60**, (6), June 1923, 208; Gilliam, *A Text-book of Practical Gynecology*, p.4; *The Hospital World* (hereafter *HW*), **22**, (5), November 1922, 187; *CL*, **38**, (5), 1905, 432; *PHJ*, **4**, (12), December 1913, 649.

27 *PHJ*, **10**, (11), November 1919, 493.

28 Rinaldo William Armstrong, *Sex, Temperance and Right Thinking*, Ottawa: Graphic Publishers Ltd, 1931, p.53.

29 *Dalhousie Review*, **10**, July 1930, 150. Only rarely was a voice raised to suggest that education was not a problem. W. Blair Bell, in his article 'Disorders of Function', referred to a study by Catherine Chisholm which suggested that there did not seem to be any link between study and menstrual-ill health. However, Blair was not sure, not because he had evidence to the contrary, but because he felt that her assertions lacked support. See Eden and Lockyer (eds), *The New System of Gynaecology*, vol. I, p.297.

30 *CPMR* **26**, (5) (May, 1901): 251; Bland-Sutton and Giles, *The Diseases of Women*, p.397; Dudley, *The Principles and Practice of Gynecology*, p.748. In an article by Bell in Eden and Lockyer (eds), *The New System of Gynaecology*, vol. I, there was a recognition (pp.327–8) that marriage might also cause amenorrhoea.

31 Crossen and Crossen, *Diseases of Women*, pp.837, 859; *CMAJ*, **42**, (4), February, 1940, 149.

32 *CMAJ*, **56**, (3), March 1947, 345; *University of Toronto Medical Journal* (hereafter *UTMJ*), **23**, (3), December 1945, 110.

33 'How to Obtain True Womanhood', Vancouver: English Herbal Dispensary, 1932); *Canadian Journal of Medicine and Surgery* (hereafter *CJMS*), **35**, (4), April 1914, 214; *PHJ*, **15**, (5), May 1924, 209.

34 *DMM*, **23**, (5), November 1904, 327.

35 *Canadian Magazine* (hereafter *CM*), **30**, (6), April 1908, 76; *CM*, **16**, (3), July 1908, 91; Cecilia Benoit, 'Mothering in a Newfoundland Community: 1900–1940', in Arnup, Lévesque and Pierson (eds), *Delivering Motherhood*, p.178; *UTMJ*, **18**, (1), November 1940, 48; *Popular Sex Science*, **2**, 1 August 1940, 18; *University of Western Ontario Quarterly*, **16**, (2), 1946, 74.

36 *The Canadian Doctor*, **12**, (5), May 1946, 50; *The Canadian Doctor*, **15**, (7), July 1949, 35.
37 Alfred Henry Tyrer, *Sex, Marriage and Birth Control*, Toronto: Marriage Welfare Bureau, 1943, pp.14–15; Percy Ryberg, *Health, Sex and Birth Control*, Toronto: Anchor Press, 1942, p.24.
38 Charles Reed (ed.), *A Text-Book of Gynecology*, New York: D. Appleton, 1901, p.701; E.E. Montgomery, *Practical Gynecology*, Philadelphia: Blakiston, 1912, p.180; *How to Obtain True Womanhood*, p.91; Hirst, *A Text-Book of Obstetrics*, p.86; Crossen and Crossen, *Diseases of Women*, p.869; Tyrer, *Sex, Marriage and Birth Control*, p.231; Ryberg, *Health, Sex and Birth Controll*, p.122; Adair, (ed.), *Obstetrics and Gynecology*, vol. I, pp.524, 539; Benoit, 'Mothering in a Newfoundland Community', p.178; Novak, *Textbook of Gynecology*, p.508; *Saturday Night*, **62**, 8 March 1947, 16.
39 Reed, (ed.), *A Text-Book of Gynecology*, p.701; Hall, *Sexual Knowledge*, p.129; Bland-Sutton and Giles, *The Diseases of Women*, p.69; Eden and Lockyer (eds), *The New System of Gynaecology*, vol. I, p.402; *CLNH*, **60**, (1), January 1923, 24.
40 *CLNH*, **60**, (1), January 1923, 23; *PHJ*, **15**, (5), May 1924, 207–8; Tyrer, *Sex, Marriage and Birth Control*, p.138; Adair (ed.), *Obstetrics and Gynecology*, vol. I, p.539; Ryberg, *Health, Sex and Birth Control*, p.115.
41 Eden and Lockyer (eds), *The New System of Gynaecology*, p.402; *CPMR*, **42**, (10), October 1917, 419; *CPMR*, **41**, (2), February 1916, 90; Ryberg, *Health, Sex and Birth Control*, pp.61–2.
42 Ryberg, *Health, Sex and Birth Control*, p.130.
43 Angus McLaren, *A History of Contraception from Antiquity to the Present Day*, Oxford: Basil Blackwell, 1990, p.49.
44 Munro Kerr *et al.*, *Combined Textbook of Obstetrics and Gynaecology*, p.731.
45 Davis (ed.), *Gynecology and Obstetrics*, vol. III, ch. 8, p.17; Edgar, *The Practice of Obstetrics*, pp.26–7; Hirst, *A Text-Book of Obstetrics*, p.86; Adair (ed.), *Obstetrics and Gynecology*, vol. I, p.524; Novak, *Textbook of Gynecology*, p.595; Curtis and Huffman, *A Textbook of Gynecology*, p.563.
46 This seems to contradict the historiography which suggests a definite shift from the Victorian stress on difference to the twentieth-century notion of similarity. See Janice M. Irvine, *Disorders of Desire: Sex and Gender in Modern American Sexology*, Philadelphia: Temple University Press, 1990, p.87.
47 Adair (ed.), *Obstetrics and Gynecology*, vol. I, p.540; Ryberg, *Health, Sex and Birth Control*, pp.121, 127.
48 Ryberg, *Health, Sex and Birth Control*, pp.115, 126.
49 W.H.B. Stoddart, *Mind and Its Disorders: A Textbook for Students and Practitioners of Medicine*, Philadelphia: P. Blakiston's Sons & Co., 1919, p.190; Adair (ed.), *Obstetrics and Gynecology*, vol. I, p.545; *Maclean's*, **63**, 15 August 1950, 6; Tyrer, *Sex, Marriage and Birth Control*, pp.52, 136, 142; Crossen and Crossen, *Diseases of Women*, p.869; Ryberg, *Health, Sex and Birth Control*, p.25 (Ryberg told his readers that the left side of women's bodies was more susceptible to arousal than the right (p.135)).
50 Tyrer, *Sex, Marriage and Birth Control*, p.133; Ryberg, *Health, Sex and Birth Control*, pp.133–4.
51 Ryberg, *Health, Sex and Birth Control*, p.44.
52 Ellen Joyce Trott, 'Attitudes Towards Birth Control: Canada 1885–1935', MA thesis, Carleton University, 1984, 108; Edgar, *The Practice of Obstetrics*, pp.26–7; Hirst, *A Text-Book of Obstetrics*, p.86; Davis (ed.), *Gynecology and Obstetrics*, vol. III, ch. 8, p.17; Ryberg, *Health, Sex and Birth Control*, p.136; Tyrer, *Sex, Marriage and Birth Control*, p.41; Thurman B. Rice, *In Training: For Boys of High School Age*, Chicago: American Medical Association, 1951, p.28; in British Columbia Archives and Record Service, Marion Noel (Bostock) Sherman Papers, Add Mss, 409, Box 3, file on 'Mental Health'.

53 Tyrer, *Sex Marriage and Birth Control*, pp.8–9, 43, 153; A. Herbert Gray, *The Relations of Men and Women*, Toronto: Student Christian Movement, 1926, p.7; *UTMJ*, **17**, (3), January 1940, 130; *National Hygiene and Public Welfare* (hereafter *NHPW*), **28**, (5), May 1922, 249–50; *CMAJ*, **36**, (2), February 1937, 155; Adair, (ed), *Obstetrics and Gynecology*, vol. I, pp.543, 544, 546–7; *CL*, **43**, (12), August 1910, 909; Howard Atwood Kelly, *Gynecology*, New York: D. Appleton, 1928, p.1008; *CMAJ*, **25**, (2), August 1931, 142; *Maclean's*, **59**, 15 November 1946, 8; *Saturday Night*, **60**, 16 June 1945, 39; Graves, *Gynecology*, p.159; Eden and Lockyer (eds.), *The New System of Gynaecology*, vol. I, pp.299, 396–7; *UTMJ*, **21**, (1), October 1943, 24; Montgomery, *Practical Gynecology*, p.180; Novak, *Textbook of Gynecology*, p.509; *Modern Medicine of Canada* (hereafter *MMC*), **3**, (1), January 1948, 35; Curtis and Huffman, *A Textbook of Gynecology*, p.97; Queen's University Archives, Faculty of Medicine, Series VI, Notes and Lectures, Box 5, November 1945, *The Book of the Post Graduate Course*; Ryberg, *Health, Sex and Birth Control*, pp.137, 140; Reed (ed.), *A Text-Book of Gynecology*, p.9; *CMAJ*, **26**, (6), June 1932, 705; *How to Obtain True Womanhood*, p.9; *CL*, **44**, (2), October 1910, 128; Henry Holdich Morton, *Genito-Urinary Diseases and Syphilis*, Philadelphia: F.A. Davis, 1906, pp.90, 93, 467; Henry Jellett, *A Manual of Midwifery for Students and Practitioners*, London: Bailliere Tindall & Cox, 1910, p.587; *CMAJ*, **14**, (2), February 1924, 138; *CMAJ*, **48**, (3), March 1943, 231–2; *CMAJ*, **55**, (2), August 1946, 138; *CMAJ*, **60**, (1), January 1949, 32.

54 Stoddart, *Mind and Its Disorders*, p.190; Adair (ed.), *Obstetrics and Gynecology*, vol. I, p.545. These concerns only touch on marital sexuality. They do not address the concerns physicians addressed about non-marital sexuality.

55 *CMAJ*, **5**, (5), May 1915, 391; Bell, *The Principles of Gynaecology*, p.87; Dudley, *The Principles and Practice of Gynecology*, p.29; Alice Stockham, *Tokology: A Book for Every Woman*, Toronto: McClelland, Goodchild and Stewart, 1916, p.276; Eden and Lockyer (eds), *The New System of Gynaecology* vol. I, p.382; Stoddart, *Mind and Its Disorders*, p.196; *Ontario Journal of Neuro-Psychiatry*, **1**, (2), July 1922, 23; *CJMS*, **61**, (2), February 1927, 40; Davis (ed.), *Gynecology and Obstetrics*, vol. I, ch. 2, p.16; Hugh Dobson Papers B9 file L, Union College Lectures on the Family, Vancouver Theological College, synopsis of an address, 4 March 1938, p.3; *Manitoba Medical Review*, **24**, (4), April 1944, 104; William Albert Scott and H. Brookfield Van Wyck, *The Essentials of Obstetrics and Gynecology*, Philadelphia: Lea & Febiger, 1946, p.32; *UTMJ*, **24**, (3), December 1946, 71; *CMAJ*, **60**, (3), March 1949, 309.

56 J. Clarence Webster, *A Text-Book of Diseases of Women*, Philadelphia: W.B. Saunders, 1907, p.115; Dudley, *The Principles and Practice of Gynecology*, p.29; *CL*, **43**, (9) May 1910, 682; Stockham, *Tokology*, p.278; *CJMS*, **61**, (2), February 1927, 40; Ten Teachers, *Diseases of Women*, p.54; *Canadian Nurse*, **46**, November 1950, 880. Ryberg, in his manual, expressed uncertainty about the influence of climate: *Health, Sex and Birth Control*, p.184.

57 Webster, *A Text-Book of Diseases of Women*, p.115; Aleck William Bourne, *Synopsis of Midwifery and Gynaecology*, Toronto: The Macmillan Co. of Canada Ltd., 1925, p.272; Graves, *Gynecology*, p.37; Davis (ed.), *Gynecology and Obstetrics*, vol. I, ch. 2, p.16.

58 *CL*, **43**, (9), May, 1910, 682.

59 Montgomery, *Practical Gynecology*, p.179; Davis (ed.), *Gynecology and Obstetrics*, vol. I, ch. 2, p.16.

60 Webster, *A Text-Book of Diseases of Women*, p.115; Davis (ed.), *Gynecology and Obstetrics*, vol. I, ch. 2, p.16.

61 *Canadian Nurse*, **46**, November 1950, 880.

62 Webster, *A Text-Book of Diseases of Women*, p.115; *The Saskatchewan Medical Journal*, **2**, (4), April 1910, 99; Hall, *Sexual Knowledge*, p.204; Bourne, *Synopsis of*

Midwifery and Gynaecology, p.272; Graves, *Gynecology*, p.37; Munro Kerr *et al.*, *Combined Textbook of Obstetrics and Gynaecology*, p.52; *CMAJ*, **37**, (4), October 1937, 350–51; Adair (ed.), *Obstetrics and Gynecology*, vol. I, p.531; Novak, *Textbook of Gynecology*, p.114; Scott and Van Wyck, *The Essentials of Obstetrics and Gynecology*, p.32; Alfred C. Beck, *Obstetrical Practice*, Baltimore: The Williams & Wilkins Co, 1947, p.18; *Canadian Nurse*, **46**, November 1950, 880; Curtis and Huffman, *A Textbook of Gynecology*, p.102.

63 Webster, *A Text-Book of Diseases of Women*, p.115; *The Saskatchewan Medical Journal*, **2**, (4), April 1910, 99; Eden and Lockyer (eds), *The New System of Gynaecology*, vol. I, p.382.

64 *CL*, **48**, (2), October 1914, 79.

65 Bland-Sutton and Giles, *The Diseases of Women*, p.22; *CL*, **43**, (9), May 1910, 682; Stockham, *Tokology*, p.278; Eden and Lockyer (eds), *The New System of Gynaecology*, vol. I, p.385; Graves, *Gynecology*, p.36, *CMAJ*, **25**, (3), September 1931, 361; *CPHJ*, **23**, (3), March 1932, 124; *CMAJ*, **29**, (6), December 1933, 588; *CMAJ*, **37**, (4), October 1937, 354; *CMAJ*, **45**, (3), September 1941, 281; Ryberg, *Health, Sex and Birth Control*, p.182; *Canadian Home Journal*, **40**, August 1943, 11; *UTMJ*, **24**, (3), December 1946, 70; Helen Dunbar, *Emotions and Bodily Changes*, New York: Columbia University Press, 1947, p.149; *MMC*, **4**, (6), June 1949, 26–7; *Canadian Nurse*, **46**, November 1950, 880

66 Reed (ed.), *A Text-Book of Gynecology*, p.742; *CPMR*, **26**, (3), March 1901, 123; Edgar, *The Practice of Obstetrics*, p.26; Eden and Lockyer (eds), *The New System of Gynaecology*, vol. I, p.381; *Saturday Night*, **33**, 20 December 1919, 38; *American Journal of Psychiatry*, **10**, (6), May 1931, 1038; Ryberg, *Health, Sex and Birth Control*, p.182; *Canadian Home Journal*, **40**, August 1943, 10; *UTMJ*, **24**, (3), December 1946, 71.

67 *CL*, **48**, (2), October 1914, 79; Thomas Clifford Allbutt, W.S. Playfair and Thomas Watts Eden (eds), *A System of Gynaecology*, London: Macmillan and Co. Ltd., 1906, p.106; *CMAJ*, **27**, (1), July 1932, 100; *CMAJ*, **26**, (1), January, 1932, 59; Curtis and Huffman, *A Textbook of Gynecology*, p.103.

68 Reed (ed.), *A Text-book of Gynecology*, p.742; Dudley, *The Principles and Practice of Gynecology*, p.31; Hall, *Sexual Knowledge*, p.206; Eden and Lockyer (eds), *The New System of Gynaecology*, vol. I, p.385; Harry Oxorn, *Harold Benge Atlee M.D.: A Biography*, Hantsport, Nova Scotia: Lancelot Press, 1983, p.124; *CMAJ*, **26**, (1), January 1932, 59; *CPHJ*, **23**, (10), October 1932, 479; *Chatelaine*, **8**, (3), March 1935, 35; Davis (ed.), *Gynecology and Obstetrics*, vol. I, ch. 2, p.16; *CMAJ*, **37**, (4), October 1937, 352; *CMAJ*, **40**, (1), January 1939, 40; Adair (ed.), *Obstetrics and Gynecology*, vol. II, p.854; *Canadian Home Journal*, **40**, August 1943, 10; *UTMJ*, **24**, (3), December 1946, 70; *CMAJ*, **56**, (4), April 1947, 402; *Chatelaine*, **21**, (4), April 1948, 31; *UTMJ*, **27**, (2), November 1949, 45; *Alberta Medical Bulletin*, **15**, (1), January 1950, 13; *Manitoba Medical Review*, **30**, (5), May 1950, 291.

69 Bland-Sutton and Giles, *The Diseases of Women*, p.22; Edgar, *The Practice of Obstetrics*, p.26; Dudley, *The Principles and Practice of Gynecology*, p.29–30; Bell, *The Principles of Gynaecology*, p.91; Hall, *Sexual Knowledge*, p.206; *CMAJ*, **13**, (11), November 1923, 783; Bourne, *Synopsis of Midwifery and Gynaecology*, p.239; *International Journal of Psychoanalysis*, **65**, part 1, 1984, p.56, referring to the work of Helene Deutsch; Graves, *Gynecology*, p.36; *CMAJ*, **27**, (1), July 1932, 100; *CMAJ*, **45**, (3), September 1941, 280–82; Scott and Van Wyck, *The Essentials of Obstetrics and Gynecology*, p.33; *UTMJ*, **24**, (3), December 1946, 71; *Alberta Medical Bulletin*, **13**, (1), January 1948, 64; *Manitoba Medical Review*, **28**, (10), October 1948, 524; *Alberta Medical Bulletin*, **15**, (1), January, 1950, 13.

70 Dr Williams Medical Co., *Canadian Incidents from Real Life*, 1903, 8, personal collection; *PHJ*, **4**, (12), December 1913, 649; *PHJ*, **10**, (11), November 1919, 491; *CMAJ*, **37**, (4), October 1937, 350.

71 Eden and Lockyer (eds), *The New System of Gynaecology*, vol. I, p.385; Bland-Sutton and Giles, *The Diseases of Women*, p.22.
72. *Ontario Journal of Neuro-Psychiatry*, **1**, (2), July 1922, 23; *American Journal of Psychiatry*, **10**, (6), May 1931, 1036; *UTMJ*, **10**, (1), November 1932, 48; *CPHJ*, **23**, (10), October 1932, 479; *CPHJ*, **23**, (3), March 1932, 118; *CMAJ*, **37**, (4), October 1937, 352; *Canadian Home Journal*, **40**, August 1943, 10–11, 50; *Manitoba Medical Review*, **30**, (5), May 1950, 290.
73 Benjamin F. Miller and Clair Brackman Keane, *Encyclopedia and Dictionary of Medicine, Nursing and Allied Health*, Toronto: W.B. Saunders, 1978.
74 Gilliam, *A Text-book of Practical Gynecology*, p.66; Edgar, *The Practice of Obstetrics*, p.26; Bell, *The Principles of Gynaecology*, p.89; Hall, *Sexual Knowledge*, p.206; *International Journal of Psychoanalysis*, **65**, Part 1, 1984, p.56, with reference to Helene Deutsch in 1925; Graves, *Gynecology*, p.38; Ryberg, *Health, Sex and Birth Control*, p.77; Scott and Van Wyck, *The Essentials of Obstetrics and Gynecology*, p.33; *CMAJ*, **58**, (3), March 1948, 253; *Alberta Medical Bulletin*, **15**, (1), January 1950, 13.
75 Bland-Sutton and Giles, *The Diseases of Women*, p.22; Gilliam, *A Text-book of Practical Gynecology*, p.65; Bell, *The Principles of Gynaecology*, p.89; Hall, *Sexual Knowledge*, p.206; Stockham, *Tokology*, p.280; *CMAJ*, **19**, (6), December 1928, 680; Graves, *Gynecology*, p.69; *Chatelaine*, **3**, (10), October 1930, 40; *CMAJ*, **29**, (6), December 1933, 588; *CMAJ*, **34**, (4), April 1936, 406; *CMAJ*, **40**, (1), January 1939, 40; Ryberg, *Health, Sex and Birth Control*, 185–6; *Canadian Home Journal*, **40**, August 1943, 11; *Chatelaine*, **21**, (4), April 1948, 30; *CMAJ*, **58**, (3), March 1948, 253; Curtis and Huffman, *A Textbook of Gynecology*, p.104; *Canadian Nurse*, **46**, November, 1950, 880–81; *Alberta Medical Bulletin*, **15**, (1), January 1950, 13.
76 Alfred Lewis Galabin, *The Student's Guide to the Diseases of Women*, London: J & A. Churchill, 1884, p.406; Dr Williams Medical Co., *Canadian Incidents from Real Life*, 8; Bland-Sutton and Giles, *The Diseases of Women*, p.22; Gilliam, *A Text-book of Practical Gynecology*, p.65; Public Archives of Nova Scotia, Victoria General Hospital Papers, RG Series B III. 141 Clinical Records Patient no. 6, J.R. admitted Oct. 5, 1911; Stockham, *Tokology*, p.280; Hall, *Sexual Knowledge*, pp.205–6; *Ontario Journal of Neuro-Psychiatry*, **1**, (2), July 1922, 23; *CJMS*, **61**, (2), February 1927, 41; Thomas Watts Eden and Cuthbert Lockyer, *Gynecology for Students and Practitioners*, New York: J.&A. Churchill, 1928, p.91; *CMAJ*, **34**, (5), May 1936, 597; *CMAJ*, **34**, (4), April 1936, 406; Ryberg, *Health, Sex and Birth Control*, pp.185–6; *Manitoba Medical Review*, **24**, (4), April 1944, 104; *Chatelaine*, **21**, (4), April 1948, 30; *Alberta Medical Bulletin*, **13**, (1), January 1948, 64; Curtis and Huffman, *A Textbook of Gynecology*, p.103; *Alberta Medical Bulletin*, **15**, (1), January 1950, 13.
77 *CL*, **48**, (2), October 1914, 79; Public Archives of Nova Scotia, Victoria General Hospital Papers, box 89 patient M.P. admitted 1905; A.H.F. Barbour and B.P. Watson, *Gynecological Diagnosis and Pathology*, Edinburgh: William Green & Sons Publishers, 1913, p.4; Stockham, *Tokology*, pp.279–80; *CMAJ*, **27**, (1), July 1932, 100; Adair (ed.), *Obstetrics and Gynecology*, vol. I, p.537; *Alberta Medical Bulletin*, **15**, (1), January 1950, 14.
78 Jan Moran and Norah C. Keating, 'Making Sense Out of Feeling Different: The Experience of Menopause', *Canadian Woman Studies*, **12**, (2), Winter, 1992, 17.
79 Susan E. Bell, 'Changing Ideas: The Medicalization of Menopause', *Social Science and Medicine*, **24**, (6), 1987, 538.
80 Gilliam, *A Text-book of Practical Gynecology*, p.65; Hall, *Sexual Knowledge*, pp.204–5; Stockham, *Tokology*, p.284; *CMAJ*, **29**, (6), December 1933, 588; *CMAJ*, **34**, (5), May 1936, 597; *CMAJ*, **34**, (4), April 1936, 406; Ryberg, *Health, Sex and Birth Control*, pp.185–6; *Alberta Medical Bulletin*, **13**, (1), January 1948, 64; *Chatelaine*, **21**, (4), April 1948, 30.
81 Yet even hot flushes seemed to be culturally influenced, with Japanese women not experiencing them anywhere to the extent that western women do.

82 Bland-Sutton and Giles, *The Diseases of Women*, p.22.
83 See Margaret Lock, *Encounters with Aging: Mythologies of Menopause in Japan and North America*, Berkeley: University of California Press, 1993.
84 Physicians at the time discussed what they termed the 'male menopause', but the discussions were few and far between.

3 Female and Disabled: A Human Rights Perspective on Law and Medicine

MELINDA JONES AND LEE ANN MARKS

> Human dignity requires that the whole personality be respected: the right to physical integrity is a condition of human dignity but the gravity of any invasion of physical integrity depends on its effect not only on the body but also upon the mind and self-perception.[1]

The provision of medical treatment entails both positive and negative rights. Of most importance is the claim against the state to provide a minimum standard of health care: access to medical treatment and drugs, access to adequate food and shelter as preventative measures, and provision of a safe home and work environment. Our concern here, however, is with the negative aspects of the right to medical treatment. This involves a focus on what people and/or the state must refrain from doing, rather than considering what is required of the (ideal) state. A human rights perspective on this aspect of the provision of medical treatment is concerned with the administration of medical treatment: its mode and content, the equality of its provision; and the criterion of decision-making about whether to treat or not.

Because there is a positive right to medical treatment, there has been a tendency to consider that the provision of medical treatment is an inherent good. Doctors and other health care professionals have become used to the idea that they have unrestricted access to knowledge about what is best, and that medical intervention, over which they have power, is in almost all cases desirable. This ignores issues of human rights. The most significant of these are autonomy, consent, competence and incompetence, which focus on the individual and make assumptions about rationality as the basis of human identity. Beyond this is the issue of the rights of individuals within the family. The ideological smokescreen surrounding the liberal conception of family autonomy and family privacy has been defused, and we can no longer assume that relationships within the family are inherently good or that the family has not been used to shield abuses of human rights (McGillvray, 1992; Naffine, 1995; O'Donovan, 1993; Olsen, 1985; Thornton, 1995; Jones and Marks, 1994). Another difficulty in ensuring human rights in medical decision-making concerns the issue of the rights, duties and responsibilities of service providers, the criteria of decision-making powers with respect to non-therapeutic decisions or recommendations and factors relevant to risk–benefit analysis.

Overall, ensuring that human rights are protected in the context of medical decision making requires careful delineation of the layers of complexity involved. Human rights are not simply objects to be asserted, but values which mediate the boundaries between individuals and the complexities of relationships within which we all live. The hard case which provides the challenge to human rights discourse in this area is that of the incompetent individual. The person may be thought of as incompetent because of an intellectual disability, a physical disability, a psychiatric disability or because of her status as a child. Drawing boundaries in these cases involves balancing what are often conflicting demands of concerned and compassionate carers and professionals as well as the rights of the patient. Most of the stories we recount which mediate these problems involve young women, many of whom carry the triple disadvantage of gender, age and (dis)ability.

The Right to Bodily Integrity

There is a basic principle in common law, as well as in human rights, that the body is sacrosanct:[2] 'each person has a unique dignity which the law respects and will protect'.[3] The criminal and civil law relating to assault and battery derive from this basic human right. Battery is any intentional touching without consent (Brazier, 1992, p.73). The law makes no distinction between different degrees of violence; all touching is prohibited. Only in very limited circumstances, such as the jostling that arises from the exigencies of everyday life and where necessity dictates, does the law allow a violation of bodily integrity in the absence of consent (Mason and McCall Smith, 1994, pp.218–19). Underlying the common law recognition of the right to bodily integrity is a limited right to autonomy – that is, a person's right to choose what happens to her body. Questions of who has property in the body are particularly relevant in the brave new world of biotechnology.[4] Control is an important incident of ownership. Clearly, the right to bodily integrity confers a right to 'possess, use and manage' one's body and a person who is legally competent may waive his or her right to bodily integrity unless to do so would be against the public interest. One example of this is that no-one can consent to the infliction of bodily harm without good reason.[5]

The idea of individual autonomy has always been limited by ethical, theological and public policy considerations. Even within the confines of religion, however, there is a movement away from the idea that the body cannot be mistreated to the idea that the body must be treated. Within many ethical codes the greatest virtue is to save another's life. Such a position underpins the common law doctrine of necessity, empowering and requiring doctors to act to preserve life and health. Otherwise a medical practitioner who administers medical treatment without the consent of the patient could be civilly and criminally liable for trespass to the person, in particular the tort of battery. The common law doctrine of necessity provides an exception to the rule requiring consent to medical treatment (Mason and McCall Smith, 1994, pp.220–21). The doctrine of necessity renders lawful the actions of a medical practitioner administering treatment or surgery to save a person's life or to prevent serious, permanent disability. Accordingly, in such circumstances where a competent adult is unconscious or where the parents of a child cannot be contacted, medical treatment or surgery may be undertaken in the absence of consent. However, treatment is limited to that which is necessary in the circumstances, rather than that which is convenient (Law Reform Commission of Western Australia, 1988).

The Requirement of Consent to Medical Treatment

Where the patient is 'competent', the right to 'decide for herself whether to agree to ... treatment is endorsed as a basic human right' (Brazier, 1992, p.73). The ethical principle of autonomy, as encapsulated by the requirement of consent, pervades current medical practice.[6] Consent in the context of an action in trespass 'means consent to the general nature and quality of the proposed procedure' (Law Reform Commission of Victoria *et al.*, 1986, p.13). For a consent to be valid the person giving it must have a general understanding of the nature and purpose of the proposed treatment (Blackwood, 1991; 1992). The individual concerned must be legally competent to consent. An adult who has attained 18 years of age is presumed in law to be competent to make decisions. There is no requirement, in law, that the decision be rational or reasonable, provided the person concerned is cognitively competent at the time the decision is made. Legal notions of competence differ from medical definitions (Mendelson, 1993). Consent may be expressed or it may be implied from the circumstances of the case (Brazier, 1992, p.75).

There may be situations in which a patient's consent will not protect a medical practitioner from legal liability. This would be the case where failure to provide sufficient information about the particular medical treatment and associated risks might vitiate the consent and render the doctor liable in negligence where harm is suffered as a result of treatment.[7] The action will lie even if the doctor has not been negligent in carrying out the procedure but the harm is one of the risks associated with that procedure. The onus is on the applicant to prove that consent would have been withheld if the information had been given.

Another situation in which consent of an individual may not be binding, and therefore may not protect a doctor from legal liability, is where the individual concerned does not have the legal capacity to consent to medical treatment. The common law presumes an adult has the requisite capacity to make decisions concerning her bodily integrity, subject to public policy considerations which limit the right to consent to bodily harm.[8] However, the question arises – what is the 'requisite legal capacity'? When are the autonomy rights of people with disabilities accorded the same respect in law as the autonomy rights of the able-bodied? When is a child able to exercise such autonomy rights?[9] In each case, who is entitled to make the decision to treat or not to treat where the patient is deemed not legally competent?

To answer these questions, the starting point is the House of Lords decision in the *Gillick Case*.[10] The question in that case was whether a child under the age of 16 years could consent to contraceptive advice and treatment. Although all the Law Lords gave separate and somewhat distinct judgements, the case was a landmark in the development of children's rights. After *Gillick*, the capacity of the child (and by analogy that of the adult with disabilities) to consent to medical treatment is dependent on the child's own developmental maturity. The test of competence is whether the child has sufficient intelligence and maturity to understand the nature and consequences of the proposed medical treatment. If she has sufficient intelligence and maturity to satisfy the *Gillick* test, the child is competent to make her own decision.[11] The principle in *Gillick* not only challenges previously accepted notions of rationality and legal competence, but also provides for the right to bodily integrity to be claimed and controlled by the child.[12]

The *Gillick* test, in providing a new standard of legal competence and in acknowledging the emerging autonomy and self-control granted to children, provides a starting point from which to reassess the rights of people with disabilities. For a long time disability was constructed in a way which assumed that the individual labelled 'disabled' was incapable of ever exercising independent decision-making power. Some seven years after the House of Lords considered the position of the child, the High Court of Australia, in *Marion's Case*, considered the position of people with disabilities in the course of a judgement canvassing the extent of children's rights and the limits of parental authority. The medical treatment at issue in this case was sterilization: full hysterectomy and ovariectomy. At the commencement of the case, the child, Marion, was 13 years old. She was multiply disabled and on the evidence legally incompetent to consent to any medical treatment. The issue before the High Court was who, if anybody, could consent to such medical treatment. At the time the scope of parental authority was unclear. The same issue had been considered in a number of well publicized first instance hearings in the Family Court of Australia which were equally divided as to whether or not parents could consent to such treatment.[13] Marion's parents, who were clearly caring and compassionate, sought a declaration that they had power to act on behalf of their daughter.

In the event the High Court of Australia held that no parent could consent to serious, invasive, irreversible medical treatment such as that proposed. In considering the question of who can consent to medical treatment of a child, the High Court set down an approach which is respectful of all children, including children with disabilities. The High Court of Australia held that the *Gillick* test applied to all children regardless of (dis)ability. The question to be asked is, 'Is the child "*Gillick*-competent" – does she have sufficient intelligence and maturity to understand the nature and consequences of the proposed medical treatment?'[14] If the answer to this question is yes, then the person concerned (be she a child or an adult with disabilities) is competent to consent to treatment.[15] Like the House of Lords, the High Court saw competence as context-dependent. An individual might be competent to determine whether or not to have her broken arm set, but not competent to make decisions relating to sterilization procedures. Human rights issues arise even in the context of routine medical treatment, such as filling a tooth, setting a fracture, immunization or drug therapy for epilepsy. Even such apparently uncontroversial treatment may be highly invasive and, in the case of a person with a disability, the intrusion may be exacerbated and intensified by the individual's inability to cooperate in the usual way: for example, where a person with a disability is unable to provide a urine sample, a catheter may be used.

Where the individual is not in a position to make a determination about treatment, the next issue is who can make such a determination? Here a distinction has to be made between the child and the adult deemed legally incompetent. In the case of the child who is not *Gillick*-competent, it is controversial whether it is her parents, the courts or some other state agency who can make a determination on her behalf. This issue has arisen in a number of common law jurisdictions in a series of cases relating to the sterilization procedures. These cases tested the limits of parental power and the extent of the power of the state, particular through its courts. Prior to the case of *Re D*[16] in England in 1975, the limits of parental power in the area of medical treatment were unknown and largely untested. The English decision in *Gillick* in 1985 and the Australian decision in *Marion's Case* in 1992 clarified the position of parents and the role of the courts. In each of these cases it was held that parents have authority to consent to medical treatment on behalf of their children until the child is legally competent to make her own determination. However, parental authority is limited (*Marion's Case*) to therapeutic medical treatment and does not include procedures which are major medical interventions which have serious, irreversible consequences. Such treatment may only be authorized by courts exercising *parens patriae* powers (see below).

A Case in Point: Gender Reassignment

One of the early applications of these principles in Australia concerned gender reassignment of a child. The case of *In re A*[17] is worthy of consideration as it illustrates the difficulty of contextualizing human rights in medical treatment decision-making. As in all cases where courts are approached to authorize medical treatment, there were a number of potentially conflicting rights claims. The best interests of the child had to be determined taking account of the claims and interests of the parents and the stated desire of the child in the light of the assumption that the matter was urgent (Jones and Marks, 1996). *Marion's Case* had established that a *Gillick*-competent child could determine her own medical outcomes. In this case the surgeon was willing to carry out the necessary procedures if the court sanctioned the gender reassignment. On the evidence it was clear that the child was not *Gillick*-competent and the judge held that the procedures were beyond parental power.

At the time of the application for gender reassignment surgery, the child A, 13-years-old and genetically female, was born with an extreme degree of masculinization. Shortly after her birth, A was diagnosed as having a condition known as adrenal hyperplasia, which arises from the overproduction of male hormones by a dysfunctional adrenal gland. Despite her appearance as a baby boy, the doctors confirmed that she was sexually female and performed corrective surgery. Her parents were counselled about the importance of hormone therapy for A. The parents seem to have been confused about her identity. In their eyes, A was male and although subsequently A was known by a female name, she was given a male name at birth. It is interesting to note that the judge in the report refers to A as 'he' throughout the judgement. Millbank argues that the judge was relying 'upon the authoritative "legal" male birth certificate rather than the "social" history of a female life or "medical" fact of female diagnosis to refer to the child "by his male name throughout the judgement"' (Millbank, 1995, p.175). At the time of the hearing, A was fourteen and a half years old, she was confused about her gender and determined to be male. She dressed accordingly and used a male name. Hormone therapy had been erratic and her external genitalia had masculinized again. The evidence of the endocrinologist was as follows:

> By the age of 13 she looked and felt like a boy, and the clitoris had regrown to a considerable degree, such that she described painful erections in the presence of women. Her sexual orientation was towards females. Her request was 'Just make me back into a boy, just like I was when I was born'. (Per Mushin J, p.718)

The procedures sought were a complete hysterectomy, including removal of the ovaries and a bilateral mastectomy. It would then be necessary for A to undergo reconstructive surgery to create a penis. Mushin J heard the evidence of the mother and the experts called by her, including a psychologist who had been treating A, and authorized the procedure. The Public Advocate was represented and he supported the application. There was no separate legal representative for the child, as the guidelines developed in the later cases require. As no-one appeared to oppose the application, the evidence was accepted uncontested. It is of particular concern that there was no questioning of the evidence that it would be damaging to A to wait until she was 18 and was competent to consent on her own behalf. The result of the judgement was that A would undergo two or three major surgical procedures over the following 12 months which would render her infertile, remove healthy body parts and replace them with imperfect and artificial male body parts.

There are a number of problems with this decision. The most significant of these is the unquestioning acceptance of the evidence. In the course of making the decision, and without investigating other options, the judge accepted the necessity for these procedures. He assumed that gender reassignment would solve A's problems by 'correcting' the medical condition. By giving too much attention to the 'abnormal' aspects of A's physical characteristics, the judge was unduly swayed by the angst coming from the confusion which is a 'normal' part of adolescent grasping with issues of sexuality and sexual identity. The judge's and the doctor's conservative views about heterosexuality and homosexuality and the overriding value of masculinity thus become apparent.

The case is an example of the problem of basing the alternate decision-making process within the adversarial system.[18] Such decisions are not meant to be heard in an adversarial context. The alternate decision maker has to conduct an inquiry into what is best for the child or the person with disabilities. This means looking beyond evidence lead in court and refusing to simply accept that evidence where long-term considerations with respect to welfare and rights require this. While we do not doubt the difficulty of the judge's task, a human rights approach to the question of gender reassignment would inevitably result in a 'hands off' approach. The 'urgency' in this case was certainly not such that it would give rise to the doctrine of necessity. The proposed medical treatment was extremely invasive and clearly not the least restrictive alternative available. A's human rights would best be respected in all the circumstances of the case by refusing to authorize treatment and leaving matters in abeyance until A was legally competent.

An Interesting Contrast: Michael's Story

Michael's story provides an interesting contrast and perhaps is an example of a more measured approach. In this case, the state actively intervened in a private matter in the interests of the welfare of the child. Michael was born with a congenital heart abnormality: the tubes leading into his heart were reversed. This is a very serious and life-threatening condition. Shortly after birth, on the advice of doctors, Michael had a balloon septosomy. This procedure was performed to give him some 'breathing time' and the parents were advised that he needed a more radical procedure known as a Senning Procedure three to six months later, depending on his condition. Michael's parents were naturally very concerned about his well-being and they undertook extensive research into the Senning Procedure. As a result of that research they refused to consent to it. They were concerned that much could go wrong during the procedure, which could result in Michael's death, or that post-operative complications could lead to death. Their child had survived against the odds longer than any other child with his condition and they were not prepared to take the risk. Michael continued to have medical check-ups with his local doctor and a cardiac specialist and during that time the pressure increased to consent to the Senning Procedure. In 1990, when the parents again refused to consent to the Senning Procedure, the social welfare authorities became involved. Although they concluded that this was not a matter for care proceedings, the Public Advocate's Office was involved in the case.[19] The Acting Public Advocate brought proceedings in the Family Court in 1993 for authorization to consent to the Senning Procedure. In the event, the matter was settled with the parents undertaking that Michael would have regular medical checks and would himself be informed of his condition by the time he was 12, so that he could participate in the decision-making process. The case was adjourned *sine die* on the basis that, once the *parens patriae* jurisdiction of a court is invoked, it is necessary for the court to continue to supervise the welfare of the child, at least where the matter has not been finally resolved.

The issues in this case were difficult, involving a child with a life-threatening disability, courageous, caring and well-informed parents and a great deal of interference from the state, all in the cause of 'the best interests of the child'. Furthermore, the medical treatment was clearly therapeutic, although it did carry considerable risks. In this case the clash between the interests of the state, the child and the family are highlighted. In the event, the state fulfilled its responsibilities to supervise Michael's welfare in a way which respected the family's autonomy while protecting the individual's rights.

Parens Patriae and Non-therapeutic Medical Treatment

What of the adult who lacks legal competence? How is his or her welfare protected? While the legal authority of the parent ceases at the age of majority, the state retains a role in these cases. Superior Courts of Record, in common law countries, have an inherent jurisdiction, known as *parens patriae,* to supervise the welfare of 'infants, lunatics and idiots'.[20] Generally it is this jurisdiction which is invoked when courts supervise the welfare of children and adults with disabilities.[21] The principle of 'best interests' is the determining factor in the exercise of this jurisdiction.[22] It has been argued that, where intrusive medical treatment is at issue, courts are the proper place for a full consideration of the legal complexities.[23] Indeed, this was the position favoured by the English Law Commission when it considered the matter.[24] Despite these arguments the trend, particularly where adults are concerned, has been for guardianship boards to be preferred to courts (Tait *et al.*, 1994, p.142). The advantage of such tribunals is that they locate the individual in the community, are non-adversarial and informal and are best placed to promote individual autonomy and respect the human dignity of the person with a disability (Shaw, 1990, p.91; Carney and Tait, 1994).

Despite this trend, courts in a number of common law jurisdictions have, in recent years, invoked their *parens patriae* powers in the context of medical treatment decisions for adults with disabilities and 'special' medical procedures in children. In particular, the courts have become involved in decision-making where the proposed medical treatment could be viewed as 'non-therapeutic' (*Re A*) or at least as significantly intrusive/controversial decisions (*Re Michael; Re R*[25] and *Re W*[26]). Many of the cases have concerned sterilization procedures. It is interesting to note that in the United Kingdom and in Canada (in contrast to Australia and New Zealand) the procedure has been the less invasive tubal ligation.

The very concept that medical treatment can be conceived of as either therapeutic or non-therapeutic is highly problematic and is predetermined by concepts of wellness and illness, impairment and ability, the perfect or imperfect body. The first issue to be disentangled is the purpose of medical intervention. Where a person has a clearly defined medical illness, for example one caused by bacterial or viral infection, the purpose of medical intervention is to limit or reverse the effects of the infection and this would appear to be uncontroversial within the realm of the therapeutic. However, it is possible to define all treatment as therapeutic when medical people consider intervention desirable. Mason and McCall Smith are correct in their assertion that little divides the decision in *Eve*, which denies the right to undertake non-therapeutic treatment, and *B*, which permits sterilization for the purpose of menstrual management, which is viewed as a medical issue (Mason and McCall Smith, 1994, pp.86–7) This is because illness is a social construct and the ideology makers with regard to health matters tend to be medical. The 'medicalization' of menstruation is part of the wider movement to medicalize women's bodies and all aspects of human reproduction (Callaghan, 1995; Corea, 1984; Karpin, 1992). Once this occurs it becomes straightforward to assume that all decisions about menstrual management are 'therapeutic'.

The medical model of disability involves a similar mode of thinking.[27] While medicine clearly has a role to play in understanding and dealing with many aspects of disabling conditions, our concern is where medical practice overreaches itself and presumes to have solutions which, when applied, ignore the reality of the situation of the person with a disability. This is a result of the medical model elevating the disabling condition to the status of 'illness', and the primary and overriding focus on disability as a medical problem.[28]

This can be illustrated by the recent change in the understanding of the effect of Down's syndrome on an individual. While Down's syndrome was viewed through a medical lens, the life pattern of the affected person was circumscribed. A person with Down's syndrome was expected to follow a particular life course which was generally very limited in potential and relatively short in duration. Parents were routinely advised to institutionalize their newborn child. Little was offered to the child in terms of education, of fulfilling his or her potential or experiencing 'normal' family or interpersonal relationships. Not surprisingly, expectations about such a life were self-fulfilling prophesies. The position has changed significantly in the last decade and a half. The politicization of disability and the normalization movement, which adopt a social rather than medical model of disability, have led to a reassessment of the capabilities of all people (Brown and Smith, 1992; Oliver, 1990). Early intervention strategies and policies of deinstitutionalization have resulted in many individuals with Down's syndrome reaching a previously unimagined potential such that some are able to function with a degree of independence and to operate as contributing members of society. In the process, expectations to do with quality of life and life expectancy have improved dramatically. What this shows is the danger of decisions about treatment and outcomes which are based purely on medical constructions.

In determining appropriate medical treatment, the focus should be on the person *qua* person rather than on the impairment. Where the individual lacks the legal capacity to consent to medical treatment, the alternate decision maker, be it doctor, court or guardian, must be cognizant of all the ramifications of the proposed treatment as well as the medical and non-medical alternatives to the treatment. The alternate decision maker should not be satisfied with an assurance that the proposed treatment is therapeutic and therefore desirable. The responsibility of making life-affecting decisions on behalf of another should not be taken lightly and in some cases may raise the issue of conflict of interest between decision maker and the person with a disability.

A significant problem related to the reliance on the medical model of disability is a lowering of standard in the risk–benefit analysis which is an inherent part of informed medical decision-making. Questions of what amounts to treatment, known outcomes of procedures and even the degree of invasion involved in the treatment can be seen to collapse where there is seen to be an overriding feature which is the disability. As we have already seen, a patient's consent to medical treatment may be vitiated if that consent is based on insufficient information. Where an alternate decision maker is involved because of the patient's legal incapacity to consent to treatment, it is essential that the same range of factors should be taken into account in the risk–benefit analysis that is associated with making a determination about treatment. While the disability may be a factor to be taken into account in making such an assessment, the same standards should be applied regardless of ability. In evaluating whether or not this has in fact happened, it is recommended that a 'but for' test be applied to the decision. Would this treatment be authorized with respect to a person in similar circumstances who is not affected by the disability?[29] Then and only then would it be acceptable for the treatment to be administered to the person with a disability.[30]

A Case Study: Sterilizing Young Women

It is startling to learn that many young women around the world are being sterilized for no reason other than a perceived disability (Family Law Council of Australia, 1994); Freeman, 1988; Goldhar, 1991; Scott, 1986; Shaw, 1990). There are many forms of sterilization procedures. For women these are tubal ligation, laparoscopic sterilization, endometrial ablation with tubal ligation, endometrial ablation, hysterectomy and ovariectomy; and for men orchidectomy (removal of both testes) and vasectomy are available. Hysterectomy, which is major intrusive abdominal surgery, has been the most common procedure sought in a number of recent court cases concerning the sterilization of girls with intellectual disabilities. Hysterectomy involves the removal of the uterus and in some cases it is accompanied by the removal of the Fallopian tubes and possibly the ovaries. In prepubescent girls, the result is a failure to develop secondary sexual characteristics with all the concomitant psychological trauma. In all cases where the ovaries are removed, premature menopause with its accompanying problems will occur. Hysterectomy is appropriate when it is therapeutically indicated, for example where there is uterine or cervical cancer, or recurrent, severe dysfunctional uterine bleeding which does not respond to hormonal therapy (Thompson and Birch, 1981, p.1249).

> Hysterectomy for sterilization is not appropriate except in selected patients in whom there is a clear indication for hysterectomy over and beyond the desire for sterilization. ... The risk of complications following hysterectomy is greater than the risk of complications following tubal ligation; therefore hysterectomy should not be chosen as the most acceptable method of surgical sterilization unless significant gynaecological disease or symptoms are present. (Ibid., p.1254)

Historically, sterilization has been considered to be the solution to problems of personal hygiene, sexuality and fertility. In the common law world, sterilizations have been carried out without public scrutiny, sometimes at the behest of the family and sometimes at the behest of the institution caring for the girl (Freeman, 1988, pp.56–60; Goldhar, 1991, pp.61–75; Hayes and Hayes, 1982, pp.76–7; Scott, 1986, pp.806 fn 2, 809–16). The extent of such sterilizations is unknown. However, it is clear that such procedures have been performed on girls and women in the absence of medical necessity. Patient consent has rarely been sought and in many cases the patients have not been informed of the true nature of the operation, some being deliberately deceived (for example, they were told they were having an appendectomy). Even though sterilizations are generally performed in hospitals, until recently statistics were not usually kept (Carlson, 1996, p.9; Goldhar, 1991, p.157). Many of these cases have concerned pre-pubescent girls, the purpose being to prevent the onset of menstruation.

Although decisions about sterilization were until recently largely a matter for private concern, they have been the subject of public debate and often the debate favoured sterilization. In the last 20 years, and particularly in the last 10 years, the issue of sterilization of those with intellectual disabilities has moved into the public forum of the courts. It has also been the subject of investigation by law reform bodies in the UK, Australia and Canada. Despite the fact that, in the absence of statutory provision, court authorization of sterilizations is now required in a number of jurisdictions, in a majority of cases the courts have concluded that the sterilization should be performed on the woman concerned. Further, where non-consensual sterilization has been illegal, as in Germany, or where the court involvement is strictly speaking required, there is significant evidence that sterilizations are nonetheless performed in the absence of state sanction (Brady, 1996; Carlson, 1996; Shaw, 1990).

The court cases have involved the sterilization of women, including girls as young as 11, many pre-pubescent. The level of intellectual disabilities varied greatly from 'dull normal' through to mild, to moderate, to severe and profound. In some cases, the person with a disability was physically and intellectually disabled; in some cases they lived at home and in others they were institutionalized. While the cases appear to be based on the discourse of rights, the rights of the person with a disability are not taken seriously. The interests of parents, carers and other family members are considered and at times supersede the rights of the person with a disability. Indeed, at times the latter do not even seem to be in the equation. The New Zealand case, *Re X*,[31] is just one case in point. That case concerned a pre-pubescent girl with severe, multiple disabilities. Hillyer J, in authorizing the sterilization, was principally concerned with her carer's capacity to cope with her menstruation.

The sterilization of women with intellectual disabilities has been justified, in the absence of therapeutic need, on four grounds: eugenics, fertility control, protection from sexual abuse and menstrual management (including counteracting blood phobias). The most common rationale prior to the Second World War was the theory of eugenics. In the later nineteenth century and the earlier part of this century there was a widespread belief that a variety of personal traits, including intellectual disability (and pauperism) were inherited (Morris, 1991, p.45). In the western world, eugenics received support across the political spectrum and for a variety of reasons (Goldhar, 1991). Social Darwinists were concerned to improve the human species. Socialists were attracted to eugenics for the betterment of society: effective contraception would lead to smaller families and an improved standard of living for working-class people. Often sterilization was a precondition for both living in the community and being accepted into an institution.

The practice of eugenics was enthusiastically adopted in the 1930s in Hitler's Germany. Nazi policy and practice during the Second World War was a key factor in the decline of the eugenics movement. Eugenics is now largely discredited and there is an understanding that heredity is not as simple a process as its proponents believed. Nevertheless, arguments based on eugenics do surface from time to time in the modern cases. For example, in *Re D*, D's mother argued in favour of her daughter's sterilization on the grounds of eugenics.[32] Furthermore, while the theory is no longer creditable, its influence persists in popular attitudes and indeed in the guidelines for determining whether sterilization is medically indicated which are found in the medical and legal literature and in some of the cases.[33] One of the criteria in these guidelines is the patient's disability; disability itself is taken to be one indicator of the therapeutic value of the proposed sterilization (Kaunitz *et al.*, 1986, p.438; Sheth and Malpani, 1991, p.320).

With the demise of the eugenic justification for sterilization, the focus shifted to fertility control, protection from sexual abuse and menstrual management. Ironically, the move to normalization and deinstitutionalization empowered those arguing in favour of sterilization on these grounds. In this context, the rationale for sterilization has been that the person with a disability can more fully participate in the community if she is free of the risk of pregnancy, childbirth, parenting and sexual exploitation. This rationale was persuasive in the English decisions, *Re F*[34] and *Re B*, and in the recent unreported Scottish decision of *Lawrence*.[35] Arguments promoting sterilization for the purpose of eliminating fertility have found favour with some judges (*Re B*; *P and P* (1995)). However, in the context of social policy promoting the least restrictive alternatives in the care of people with intellectual disabilities, sterilization is rather an extreme form of fertility control, especially as a number of less intrusive methods of contraception are readily available.

Even where the fallacies of the fertility control argument have been recognized by the courts, the arguments relating to menstrual management and personal hygiene remain very influential (Kaunitz *et al.*, 1986; Sheth and Malpani, 1991). Indeed, menstruation is effectively classified as an illness, and menstrual management in some cases is regarded as providing a therapeutic indicator for hysterectomy.[36] Once again principles of least restrictive alternative (as required by the principles of normalization) are turned inside out to justify a major intervention in the woman's 'best interests'. In many of the court cases, the girl concerned had not yet begun to menstruate, and arguments about pain and discomfort associated with menstruation were purely speculative. In two cases there was anecdotal evidence that the girls concerned had blood phobias.[37] This of course is an issue which must be addressed, but frequently the solution sought in the cases was not the least restrictive alternative but that which categorically deals with the issue of menstruation by removing the uterus.

Much is made in the cases of the difficulties menstruation causes for the carers. Menstruation is one of the last taboos left in our society and it seems to touch a very sensitive core in our being. However, menstruation is a normal womanly function and not all women experience problems with it (Elkins *et al.*, 1986). Menstrual management is part of personal hygiene and as such may form part of a personal training programme. Generally, menstrual management is only an issue where a person is not toilet-trained. In such cases the carers have to attend to the woman's personal hygiene on a daily basis, several times a day, not just when the woman is menstruating. No-one argues that a catheter or a colostomy are appropriate measures for dealing with those who are incapable of being toilet-trained. Normalization is best achieved through counselling, information and practical training for carers and for the women. Where necessary this could be supplemented by medication. Sterilization is an extreme way to deal with menstruation and should be avoided in the absence of therapeutic necessity (Family Law Council of Australia, 1994, p.29; Carlson *et al.*, 1994, p.13).

Finally, hysterectomy has been said to protect a woman from sexual abuse and the consequences of abuse. This argument is patently absurd. It is ridiculous to argue that hysterectomy is a deterrent which will protect a girl from sexual exploitation. If the girl is known to be infertile and is intellectually disabled, especially if she is mute, she is more likely to be subject to abuse, as the perpetrator may well escape detection.

Traditional approaches to rights have been insufficient to protect the intrinsic right to bodily integrity in the case of girls with intellectual disabilities. It is interesting to note that at one time the importance of women's fertility was such that her autonomy, her power to control what happened to her body, was constrained by a public policy which limited her access to sterilization procedures. Ironically, at the same time, a condition of entry into normal society for women with disabilities was their compulsory sterilization.[38]

Certain of the landmark decisions of courts with respect to applications for sterilization gave heart to those in the human rights camp. It appeared that judges were able to move wisely from medical conceptualizations to a ready acceptance of the human dignity of the person with a disability, and embrace concepts of inclusion. This was apparent in the early decision of Heilbron J in *Re D* where her Honour refused to authorize the sterilization procedure sought by the mother. *Re Eve* provides another example. There the Supreme Court of Canada, in a seminal judgement, held that no-one could authorize a non-therapeutic sterilization on behalf of a person with a disability. The individual's human dignity and right to bodily integrity overrides mere convenience.

From a human rights perspective, the Australian case of *Marion's Case* could be considered a watershed. The judgements are informed by concepts of inclusion and 'least restrictive alternative'. While in the event the child Marion was sterilized, the language of the judgements gave grounds for the belief that it was a base from which people with disabilities would be treated with equal concern and respect. This belief was supported in some of the first instance cases that followed the High Court decision, such as *P and P*, before Moore J and the decision of Warnick J in *Sarah's case*.[39] In all these cases disability was but one factor in the equation.

The dominance of principles of inclusion in the judgements of courts exercising *parens patriae* jurisdiction has been short-lived. In England, the Court of Appeal beat a hasty retreat from *Gillick* in *Re R* and *Re W*, with the Master of the Rolls artificially distinguishing a right to make a determination from a right to consent. Surely, if a person is legally competent to consent, that person is legally competent to refuse treatment. If, indeed, parental authority decreases in direct proportion to the child's emerging competence, it is ridiculous to hold that the parent can override the child's refusal. There is however, a safeguard against folly: the court in its *parens patriae* jurisdiction still has supervisory power until the child is 18.

In Australia, the Full Court of the Family Court in overturning the decision of Moore J in *P and P* rejected the principles of inclusion and least restrictive alternative set out in *Marion's Case*. This case concerned a young woman, Lessli, who required constant supervision but who was quite competent at managing her own personal hygiene. While her case was complicated by her epilepsy, there was medical evidence that hysterectomy was not the least restrictive alternative. Other forms of contraception could safely be tried prior to surgery. Should surgery have proved necessary, this was surely a case where the less invasive tubal ligation was more appropriate. The court seems to have been very concerned with the mother's position as carer. The evidence was that Lessli would live with her mother once she finished school and that menstrual management, which was not an issue for the carers at school, was an issue in her relationship with her mother. The Full Court was very critical of the decision at first instance and yet a close examination of that judgement reveals that it followed in the spirit of the High Court in *Marion's Case*.

Conclusion

What these case studies demonstrate is that three human rights issues arise in relation to medical decision making. The most fundamental human right, a right embedded in the common law, is the right to bodily integrity. This right to autonomy, we have argued, is not dependent on rationality. Rather, it arises from human dignity and personhood. The problem for people with disabilities is not whether they have a right to bodily integrity, but how we ensure that their rights are respected where the person with a disability is not legally competent to make medical treatment decisions on her own behalf.

In challenging rationality as the basis of rights, we do not assume that individuals are atomistic and independent. We acknowledge the reality of interdependence and that rights exist in relationships. The most significant relationships for most people are to be found within the family structure. The second human rights issue is how to protect the rights of individuals in the context of the family at the same time as acknowledging and supporting the needs of carers. The veil of family privacy has been raised by feminist scholars and it has been demonstrated that there is inevitably state intervention in the family. Given the pervasive nature of state intervention in social life, it is appropriate that the state mediates 'private' medical treatment decisions. The question is how we ensure that, when there is intervention, a decision is made that reflects the rights of the individual concerned.

Finally, where there is an alternate decision maker, that decision maker has onerous responsibilities to ensure that the basis of the decision is the fundamental rights of the patient. In particular, it is essential that decision makers analyse their own value position and do not take into account irrelevant considerations such as those relating to (dis)ability, sexuality, sexual orientation or images of the body. Over and beyond this, the alternate decision maker has a responsibility to examine and question all the evidence concerning the treatment under consideration, not only the pros and cons of particular treatment but also alternate procedures and the long-term social and other consequences.

The issues with respect to medical decision-making, raised where the overlay of disability is present, provide the hard cases for establishing human rights in this area. However, these same issues arise whenever there is provision of medical treatment. A human rights perspective requires that a multifaceted analysis of the patient's needs be adopted, and that the bodily integrity and human dignity of the patient be respected. Such an approach is essential whether the patient be a person with a disability, a man, a woman or a child.

Notes

1 *Secretary, Department of Health and Community Services (NT)* v. *JWB & SMB* (1992) 106 ALR 385, 418 (hereinafter *Marion's Case*) per Brennan J in *Marion's Case*.

2 See *Collins* v. *Wilcock* [1984] 1 WLR 1172 per Robert Goff LJ. For a further discussion of the right to bodily integrity, see generally Brazier (1992, ch. 4); Jones and Marks (1994 pp.265, 289–90); Mason and McCall Smith (1994, ch. 10); Kennedy and Grubb (1994, ch. 3). See also *Marion's Case*.

3 Per Brennan J (as he then was) in *Marion's Case*, 417.

4 See, for example, *Moore* v. *Regents of University of California* 793 P 2d 479 (Ca 1990) where the question of whether an individual has full ownership and control of his body parts was considered. For a discussion of this case and of the issue generally, see Griggs (1994); Magnussen (1992).

5 See *Attorney-General's Reference (No. 6 of 1980)* [1981] 1 QB 719. For further discussion, see *Marion's Case* by Mason CJ, Dawson, Toohey and Gaudron JJ, pp.391–2, by Brennan J, pp.417–19 and by McHugh J, p.452.

6 For an overview of the emergence of bioethics in the field of medical ethics and the forces of change at work in this field, see Darvall (1993).

7 Disclosure requirements vary between common law jurisdictions. In the UK, medical negligence is judged according to whether or not a doctor 'acts in accordance with a practice accepted at the time as proper by a responsible body of medical opinion' (per McNair J in *Bolam* v. *Friern Hospital Management Committee* [1957] 2 All ER 118, 122). This professional standard of disclosure was upheld by the House of Lords in *Sidaway* v. *Board of Governors of the Bethlem Royal Hospital* [1985] AC 871. However, in the latter case, the House of Lords held that material risks of a procedure must be disclosed to a patient unless the doctor can justify withholding information on the grounds of therapeutic privilege. In such a case the onus is on the doctor to establish that disclosure might be psychologically damaging to the patient. By contrast, in Australia, the High Court in *Rogers* v. *Whittacker* (1992) 175 CLR 479 rejected the *Bolam* test. Professional practices were held to be relevant to the standard of reasonable skill and care required in diagnosis and treatment. However, where the provision of information and advice was concerned the High Court held that the standard of care is based on an objective standard judged from the

viewpoint of the patient (per the majority at p.490). For a more detailed explication, see Mason and McCall Smith (1994, pp.237–47). See also McSherry (1993).

8 *R* v. *Donovan* [1934] 2 KB 498, endorsed in *R* v. *Brown* [1993] 2 All ER 75. For a more detailed discussion, see Mason and McCall Smith (1994, pp.218–19).

9 For a more detailed discussion of children's rights, see Jones and Marks (1994; 1996, p.313); Freeman (1983); Alston *et al.* (1992); Alston (1994).

10 *Gillick* v. *West Norfolk and Wisbech Area Health Authority* [1986] AC 112.

11 For a more detailed discussion of the *Gillick* case, see Bainham (1992); Brazier (1992, pp.331–9); Devereux (1991); Mason and McCall Smith (1994, pp.218–31); Morgan (1986); Wilson (1986).

12 Until very recent times, children have been treated as the property of their parents or, more particularly, their fathers. See further: Freeman (1983); Marks (1993); Montgomery (1988).

13 *In re a Teenager* (1988) 94 FLR 181; *Re Jane* (1988) 94 FLR 26; *Re Elizabeth* [1989] FLC 92-023; *Attorney-General (Old)* v. *Parents (Re S)* (1989) 98 FLR 41.

14 *Marion's Case* per Mason CJ, Dawson, Toohey and Gaudron JJ at 395.

15 Ibid., 395–6.

16 [1976] Fam 185.

17 (1993) 16 Fam L R 715.

18 *Marion's Case* established the *parens patriae* jurisdiction of the Family Court of Australia. This ancient jurisdiction is essentially inquisitorial in nature, rather than adversarial.

19 This is a statutory office set up under the Guardianship and Administration Board Act 1986 (Vic).

20 For a more detailed discussion of the *parens patriae* jurisdiction, see *Re Eve* (1986) 31 DLR (4th) 1, 13–16; discussed in, Dickens (1987); Lowe and White (1979); Hoggett (1988).

21 In the UK, these powers have been revoked in relation to adults. As a consequence, there is said to be a 'therapeutic lacuna' with respect to legally providing medical treatment for adults with disabilities (Mason and McCall Smith, 1994, p.225).

22 For a critique of the best interests test, see Jones and Marks (1994, p.275 fn 28); Parker (1994).

23 In Australia this position is strongly supported by the Chief Justice of the Family Court of Australia (Nicholson, 1993). See also Nicholson, Harrison and Sandor (1996). For a critical analysis of this position, see Tait *et al.* (1994).

24 The Law Commission (1993).

25 [1992] Fam 11.

26 [1992] 4 All ER 627.

27 For a detailed analysis of the various models of disability, see Bickenbach (1993).

28 According to the World Health Organisation's *International Classification of Impairments, Disabilities and Handicaps*, an 'impairment' is any abnormality of physiological or anatomical structure of function, a 'disability' is the limitation which results from the impairment and 'handicap' is the resulting disadvantage to the individual that limits the fulfilment of a normal role or occupation. This definition has been subject to much criticism; see, for example Barnes (1991, pp.1–3); Bickenbach, *Physical Disability*; Oliver (1990, ch. 1).

29 For a thoughtful expliction of this, see the judgement of Moore J in *P and P*, No SY4034 of 1989, 23 September 1994 (Fam Ct of Australia).

30 For a different view, see *P and P* (1995) 19 Fam LR 1.

31 (1991) 2 NZLR 365.

32 It is interesting to note that D's disability was regarded as severe by her mother, where the court found it was very mild.

33 For example, in two Australian cases, *Re Jane* (1988) 12 Fam LR 662, and *Re Marion (No 2)* (1993) 17 Fam LR 336, 351–352, the factors to be taken into account included the likelihood of the young woman engaging in sexual intercourse, the possibility of pregnancy, her parenting capacity and the views of her carers, as well as alternate courses of treatment. See also *P & P* (1995) 19 Fam LR 1, analysed in Rhoades (1995).
34 [1989] 2 WLR 1025.
35 Unreported judgement of Lord MacLean, 22 February 1996.
36 See particularly *Re X*, 369, 371, where Hillyer J was at pains to emphasize that the purpose of the medical procedure was to prevent menstruation and to distance himself from a rationale of fertility control.
37 *Re K and the Public Trustee* (1985) 19 DRL (4th) 255; *Re X*.
38 This practice was institutionalized in many states of the USA in the compulsory sterilization statutes. This practice also highlights the shifting category, 'disabled': many young women and young men were sterilized in the USA who were indigent but not impaired. One famous example is *Buck* v. *Bell* 274 US 200 (1927). For a more detailed discussion, see Freeman (1988, pp.56–60); Goldhar, 1991, pp.163–4; Scott, 1986, pp.809–10.
39 *Re L and M, Director-General of Family Services and Aboriginal and Islander Affairs* (1993) 17 Fam LR 357.

References

Alston, P. (ed.) (1994), *The Best Interests of the Child*, Oxford: Clarendon.

Alston, P., S Parker and J. Seymour (eds) (1992), *Children, Rights and the Law*, Oxford: Clarendon.

Bainham, A. (1992), 'The Judge and the Competent Minor', *Law Quarterly Review*, 108.

Barnes, C. (1991), *Disabled People in Britain and Discrimination*, London: Hurst & Co.

Bickenbach, J. (1993), *Physical Disability and Social Policy*, Toronto: Toronto Press.

Blackwood, J. (1991), 'Sterilising the Intellectually Disabled: The Need for Legislative Reform', *Australian Journal of Family Law*, **5**, 138.

Blackwood, J. (1992), 'Sexuality and the Disabled: Legal Issues', *University of Tasmania Law Review*, **11**, 187.

Brady, Susan (1996), 'What Price a Womb?', paper presented at the Rights, Ethics and Justice for People with Disabilities Conference, Brisbane, 11–12 April.

Brazier, Margaret (1992), *Medicine, Patients and the Law*, 2nd edn, London: Penguin.

Brown, H. and Smith, S. (1992), 'Normalisation: A Reader for the Nineties', London: Routledge.

Callaghan, J.C. (ed.) (1995), *Reproduction, Ethics and the Law: Feminist Perspectives*, Bloomington, Indiana University Press.

Carlson, Glenys (1996), 'Sterilising People who have Intellectual Disability: the questions that are not being asked', paper presented at the Rights, Ethics and Justice for People with Disabilities Conference, Brisbane, 11–12 April.

Carlson, G., M. Taylor, J. Wilson and J. Griffin (1992), *Menstrual Management and Fertility Management for Women who have an Intellectual Disability: An Analysis of Australian Policy*, research project, Canberra: Commonwealth Department of Health, Housing and Community Services.

Carney, T. and D. Tait (1994), 'Guardianship Boards in Australia: Accessible and Accountable Justice?', in S Verdun-Jones and M. Clayton (eds), *Mental Health Law and Practice through the Lifecycle*, Burnaby: Simon Fraser University.

Corea, G. (1985), *The Mother Machine*, London: The Women's Press.

Darvell, Leanna (1993), *Medicine, Law and Social Change*, Aldershot: Dartmouth.

Devereaux, J. (1991), 'The Capacity of the Child in Australia to Consent to Medical Treatment – Gillick Revisited', *Oxford Journal of Legal Studies*, **11**.

Dickens, B. (1987), 'No Parental or Parens Patriae Power to Authorise Non-therapeutic Sterilisation of Mentally Incompetent Persons', *Canadian Family Law Quarterly*, **2**, 103.

Elkins, T., L. Gafferd, C. Wilks, D. Muram and G. Golden (1986), 'A Model Clinical Approach to the Reproductive Health Concerns of the Mentally Handicapped', *Obstetrics & Gynaecology*, **68**, 185.

Family Law Council of Australia (1994), *Sterilisation and Other Medical Procedures on Children: A Report to the Attorney General*, Canberra: AGPS.

Freeman, M.D.A. (1983), *The Rights and Wrongs of Children*, London: Frances Pinter.

Freeman, M.D.A. (1988), 'Sterlising the Mentally Handicapped', in M.D.A. Freeman (ed.), *Medicine, Ethics and Law: Current Legal Problems*, London: Stevens and Sons.

Goldhar, J. (1991), 'The Sterilization of Women with an Intellectual Disability', University of Tasmania Law Review, **10**, 157.

Griggs, L. (1994), 'The Ownership of Excised Body Parts: Does an Individual Have a Right to Sell?', *Journal of Law and Medicine*, **1**, 223.

Hayes, Susan and Robert Hayes (1982), 'Mental Retardation: Law, Policy and Administration', Sydney: Law Book Company.

Hoggett, B. (1988), 'The Royal Prerogative in Relation to the Mentally Disordered: Resurrection, Resuscitation or Rejection', in M.D.A. Freeman (ed.), *Medicine, Ethics and Law; Current Legal Problems*, London: Stevens and Sons.

Jones, M. and L.A.B. Marks (1994), 'The Dynamic Developmental Model of the Rights of the Child: A Feminist Approach to Rights and Sterilisation', *International Journal of Children's Rights*, **2**, 265.

Jones, M. and L.A.B. Marks (1996), 'Mediating Rights: Children, Parents and the State', *Australian Journal of Human Rights*, **2**, 313.

Karpin, I. (1992), 'Legislating the Female Body: Reproductive Technology and the Reconstruction of Woman', *Columbia Journal of Gender and the Law*, **3**, 325.

Kaunitz, A., J. Thompson and K. Kaunitz (1986), 'Mental Retardation: A Controversial Indication For Hysterectomy', *Obstetrics & Gynaecology*, **68**, 436.

Kennedy, I. and A. Grubb (1994), *Medical Law: Text with materials*, 2nd edn, London: Butterworths.

Law Reform Commission of Victoria (Report 24), Australian Law Reform Commission (Report 50) and Law Reform Commission of Western Australia (June 1988), *Medical Treatment for Minors*, Discussion Paper No. 77.

Lowe, N.V. and R.A.H. White (1979), *Wards of Court*, ch. 1, London: Butterworths.

McGillvray, A. (1992), 'Reconstructing Child Abuse: Western Definitions and Non-Western Experience', in M.D.A. Freeman and P. Veerman (eds), *The Ideologies of Children's Rights*, Dordrecht: Kluwer.

McSherry, B. (1993), 'Failing to Advise and Warn of Inherent Risks in Medical Treatment: When Does Negligence Occur?', *Journal of Law and Medicine*, **1**, 5.

Magnussen, R. (1992), 'Recognition of Proprietary Rights in Human Tissue in Common Law Jurisdictions', *Melbourne University Law Review*, **18**, 601.

Marks, L.A.B. (1993), 'Family Privacy Versus Individual Autonomy: The Role of the State in Children's Medical Treatment Decisions', paper presented at the 4th Australian Family Research Conference, Sydney, February.

Mason, J.K. and R.A. McCall Smith (1994), *Law and Medical Ethics*, 4th edn, Edinburgh: Butterworths.

Mendelson, D. (1993), 'Medico-Legal Aspects of the "Right to Die" Legislation in Australia', *Melbourne University Law Review*, **19**, 112.

Millbank, Jenny (1995), 'When is a Girl a Boy? *Re A (a child)*', *Australian Journal of Family Law*, 173.

Montgomery, J. (1988), 'Children as Property', *Modern Law Review*, **51**, 323.
Morgan, J.M. (1986), 'Controlling Minors' Fertility', *Monash University Law Review*, **12**, 161.
Morris, Jenny (1991), *Pride Against Prejudice*, London: The Women's Press.
Naffine, N. (1995), 'Sexing the Subject of Law', in M. Thornton (ed.), *Public and Private: Feminist Legal Debates*, Melbourne: Oxford University Press.
Law Reform Commission of Victoria (Report 24), Australian Law Reform Commission (Report 50) and New South Wales Law Reform Commission (Report 62), *Informed Decisions about Medical Procedures*, (1989), Victoria.
Nicholson, A. (1993), 'The Medical Treatment of Minors and Intellectually Disabled Persons – United Nations Convention on the Rights of the Child, Article 3', paper presented at the First World Congress on Family Law and Children's Rights, Sydney, 4–9 July.
Nicholson, A., M. Harrison and D. Sandor (1996), 'The Role of the Family Court in Medical Procedure Cases', *Australian Journal of Human Rights*, **2**, 242.
O'Donovan, Katherine (1993), *Family Law Matters*, London: Pluto Press.
Oliver, M. (1990), *The Politics of Disablement*, Basingstoke: Macmillan.
Olsen, F. (1985), 'The Myth of State Intervention in the Family', *University of Michigan Journal of Law Reform*, **19**, 836.
Parker, S. (1994), 'The Best Interests of the Child – Principles and Problems', in P. Alston (ed.), *The Best Interests of the Child: Reconciling Culture and Human Rights*, Oxford: Clarendon Press.
Rhoades, H. (1995), 'Intellectual Disability and Sterilisation – An Inevitable Connection?', *Australian Journal of Family Law*, **9**, 234.
Scott, Elizabeth S. (1986), 'Sterilisation of Mentally Retarded Persons: Reproductive Rights and Family Privacy', *Duke Law Journal*, 806.
Shaw, Josephine (1990), 'Sterilisation of Mentally Handicapped People: Judges Rule OK?', *Modern Law Review*, **53**, 91.
Sheth, S. and A. Malpani (1991), 'Vaginal Hysterectomy for the Management of Menstruation in Mentally Retarded Women', *International Journal of Gynaecology & Obstetrics*, **35**, 319.
Tait, D., T. Carney and K. Deane (1994), 'Legal Regulation of Sterilisation: The Role of Guardianship Tribunals in NSW and Victoria', *Australian Journal of Family Law*, **8**, 141.
The Law Commission (1993), *Mentally Incompetent Adults and Decision Making*, Consultation Paper No. 128, London: HMSO.
Thompson, J. and H. Birch (1981), 'Indications for Hysterectomy', *Clinical Obstetrics and Gynaecology*, **24**, 1245.
Thornton, M. (1995), 'The Cartography of Public and Private', in M. Thornton (ed.), *Public and Private: Feminist Legal Debates*, Melbourne: Oxford University Press.
Wilson, R. (1986), 'The Gillick Crusade', *Australian Journal of Forensic Science*, 8.

Cases

Attourney-General (Qld) v. Parents (Res) (1989) 98 FLR 41.
Attourney-General's Reference (No. 6 of 1980) [1981] 1 QB 719.
Bolam v. *Friern Hospital Management Committee* [1957] 2 All ER 118.
Buck v. *Bell* 274 US 200 (1927).
Collins v. *Wilcock* [1984] 1 WLR 1172; [1984] 3 All ER 374.
Gillick v. West Norfolk and Wisbech Area Health Authority [1986] AC 112.
Lawrence, Unreported Judgement of Lord MacLean, 22 February 1996.
Moore v. *Regents of University of California* 793 P 2d 479 (Ca 1990).

P and P, No SY4034 of 1989, 23 September 1994 (Fam Ct of Australia).
P and P and Legal Aid Commission of NSW; Human Rights and Equal Opportunity Commission (Intervener) (1995) 19 Fam LR 1.
R v. *Donovan* [1934] 2 KB 498.
R v. *Brown* [1993] 2 All ER 75.

In re A (1993) 16 Fam LR 715.
Re a Teenager (1988) 94 FLR.
Re B [1987] 1 All ER 206.

Re D [1976] Fam 185.
Re Elizabeth [1989] FLC 92-023.
Re Eve (1986) 31 DLR (4th) 1.

Re F [1989] 2 WLR 1025.

Re Jane (1988) 12 Fam LR 662; (1988) 94 FLR 26.

Re K and the Public Trustee (1985) 19 DLR (4th) 255.
Re L & M, Director-General of Family Services and Aboriginal and Islander Affairs (1993) 17 Fam LR 357.

Re Marion (No 2) (1993) 17 Fam LR 336.
Re Michael (1994) 18 Fam LR 27.
Re R [1992] Fam 11.
Re W [1992] 4 All ER 627.
Re X [1991] 2 NZLR 365.
Rogers v. *Whittacker* (1992) 175 CLR 479.
Secretary, Department of Health and Community Services (NT) v. *JWB & SMB [Marion]* (1992) 106 ALR 385.
Secretary, Department of Health and Community Services (NT) v. *JWB & SMB* (1992) 175 CLR 218 (Marion's Case).
Sidaway v. *Board of Governors of the Bethlem Royal Hospital* [1985] AC 871.

4 The Interaction Between Family Planning Policies and the Introduction of New Reproductive Technologies

R. ALTA CHARO

> Once during the trip I was trying to push [Presidential candidate George] Bush to be more personal and reflective on the subject of the family – its role in society, what it means to him ... Finally, exasperated, I said, 'Well what made you have a family anyhow? Why did you start having kids?' Mrs. Bush's eyes went wide. 'Why Peggy!' 'Oh my!' I said embarrassed, 'That *was* personal and I do apologize.' The vice president began to laugh ... [and said:] 'Don't apologize. That's a perfectly appropriate question for your generation, because, of course, for all of you the decision to have a baby is truly a decision. But in our time it was different, you married and had children, it was what you did. And we did it too.' (Noonan, 1990, p.314)

Introduction

Family planning is not a new idea. Women in ancient times are known to have tried a variety of methods to control their fertility, ranging from potions to intravaginal and intrauterine plugs (Gordon, 1990, p.28; Petchesky, 1990, pp.27–8). The Bible speaks of Onan 'spilling his seed' rather than risking impregnation (Genesis 38:7–10). The impulse to defy nature goes very deep.

It is this very defiance of nature that links contraceptive policy, abortion politics and infertility relief technology. The Vatican opposes all separation of sexual intercourse from procreation and marriage (its so-called 'procreative and unitive' functions) whether its goal is to prevent the birth of a child, as in contraception, or the creation of a child, as in artificial insemination or in *in vitro* fertilization (IVF) (Congregation for the Doctrine of the Faith, 1987). Its reasons rest not only upon a rejection of sexual pleasure as a good in and of itself, or on its conception of the family and the sanctity of monogamous marriage, but also on the notion that man and woman should not be completely free of the vicissitudes of life or the dictates of God and nature. To separate the primal act of intercourse from its natural outcomes is an act of tremendous hubris, a failure to recognize the appropriate place of humankind in the creation (McCormick, 1985). More specifically, it bespeaks a rejection of women's roles as wives and mothers, which in turn can be viewed either as a rejection of biological determinism, social determinism, or both. As Kristin Luker's research on abortion politics in the USA reveals, this attitude is not restricted to ancient times or to Vatican celibates. It is very much alive today (Luker, 1984, pp.58–62).

This chapter explores some aspects of the significance of human control over fertility. Specifically, it notes the commonality of questions raised once technical control over fertility is achieved, and the similarity of some of the public policy responses. For example, if there is fertility control, then what is its purpose? Is it to be used to achieve general goals of the community, public health goals or the fulfilment of personal aspirations? In the light of its stated goals, who has the control over the control? In other words, who decides which forms of control can be used and by whom? Finally, if there are to be limits to the use of fertility control techniques, what are those limits and, again, who is going to set them?

Fertility Control in Context

Family planning is now an accepted part of American life. Planned Parenthood, for example, is supported by 250 000 donors and has 24 000 volunteers and staff (Steinbrook, 1988, p.3). Yet only recently in the USA, contraceptives were considered obscene. They were also considered illegal, and there were several vigorous campaigns in the 1950s and 1960s to keep them that way. The battle in the USA was lost, however, when the Supreme Court ruled, first in *Griswold* v. *Connecticut* in 1965 and then in *Eisenstadt* v. *Baird* in 1972, that there is a constitutionally protected zone of privacy.[1] It would be a mistake, however, to view that battle as centred simply on contraception or even sexual morality. Rather, it was part of a larger debate about the power of women to control their reproductive capabilities and their lives. It began with nineteenth-century 'voluntary motherhood' organizations fighting for contraception. This movement did not reject the idealization of motherhood; it fought merely to make the timing a matter of discretion rather than chance. Many of its motivations were based on concerns for women's health: maternal and infant mortality rates were very high, and birth spacing and birth limitation were considered crucial to improving survival (Gordon, 1990, pp.93–113).

Nineteenth-century Birth Control Movements

In nineteenth-century America, abortion services were widely advertised, but their quality varied widely (Mohr, 1978, pp.91–2, 126–7). The morbidity and mortality associated with abortion was not tremendously high, but as health services began to improve it appeared unreasonably high. Thus feminists did not resist efforts to criminalize abortion. Legal abortion would only enhance a problem of disproportionate responsibility for the consequences of sexual activity, in which men would be free to engage in sexual activity without significant physical consequence, while women would be faced with either the physical and social burdens of unwanted pregnancy or the prospect of possibly dangerous and certainly painful abortion procedures. The possibility of safe, painless abortions seemed too remote (Petchesky, 1990, p.76).

The movement to criminalize abortion began, not within the women's movement, however, but within the medical community and the American Medical Association. Its goals were threefold: to obtain a monopoly on health and childbirth (Petchesky, 1990, p.81); to promote the birth of more white Protestant babies (whose mothers used abortion and contraception much more frequently than immigrant and Catholic women) for the purpose of maintaining a particular demographic make-up of the USA (Mohr, 1978, pp.187–8; Haller, 1984, p.160); and to reduce the dangers associated with abortion (Mohr, 1978, p.160). By the end of the Civil War, most American states had abortion statutes in their criminal codes.

Feminist thinking on contraceptives was different. Prohibitions against contraception, such as the American Comstock laws, appeared to be premissed upon an expectation that sexual activity without procreation was dangerous to a social order that tried to ensure that women fulfilled specified functions. For example, they were not to stray from their marital partner; they were to provide the labour to create and nurture heirs; and they were not to compete equally in the growing cash economy of industrial America. Thus contraception, for the women's movement, spelled relief from socially imposed gender roles. Although cloaking their demands under the banner of 'safe motherhood', these feminists saw contraception as a blow to the 'scientific' biological determinism that was rampant in nineteenth-century America (Hubbard, 1990).

It was not until the twentieth century that the feminist movement fully addressed biological determinism of women's roles. Even then, however, many of the women's movement accepted eugenic doctrines and often advocated eugenic contraception and immigration laws (Gordon, 1990, pp.299–309). This argument gained the birth control proponents wider support than they could gain by appealing only to arguments based on women's rights to control their lives or to protect their health. Indeed, health arguments were subsumed under eugenic arguments by the assertion that birth spacing and limitation led to 'better' babies (Goldman, 1976).

Twentieth-century Birth Control Movements

Of course, the eugenics argument had several pitfalls beyond the obvious problems of exacerbating racism and pseudo-scientific public policy planning. First, it invited analysis of the effect of birth control on overall population size, and not merely population make-up. This, in turn, led to President Theodore Roosevelt's 1905 accusation that the birth control proponents were traitors to their country and their gender by advocating a technique that could lead to 'race suicide' (Gordon, 1990, pp.133–4). This debate, about the obligation of women to submerge individual aspirations concerning childbearing to the community's demographic needs, raged from 1905 to 1910, and is still the basis of discussion in regimes as diverse as pro-natalist cold war Romania[2] and anti-natalist modern China (*Proceedings of the International Conference in Beijing on Improving Birth Quality and Child Upbringing*, 1992).

A second damaging aspect of the eugenic justification for birth control is that it led to differential contraceptive access for desired and undesired portions of the community. African-Americans were identified by the white government as a growing, undesirable portion of the population, and several southern states led the way in providing birth control 'education' specifically for the black population (Gordon, 1990, p.349). This set the stage for what became a permanent distrust of contraceptive technologies within this ethnic group; the same pattern of abuse and resulting distrust began to operate on a global scale when the USA entered the international family planning field later in the century (Charo, 1991).

Another significant development in the first half of the twentieth century was the growing 'professionalization' of birth control. Previously a technique developed and disseminated by women and 'irregular' (this is, non-medical) doctors, it became increasingly subject to the control of doctors (Gordon, 1990, pp.245–96). Medical doctors, who for years had opposed birth control, often inaccurately criticizing it as dangerous or ineffective, became increasingly involved in its development and distribution as it became clear that even the Comstock laws would be unable to prevent its use. Margaret Sanger herself was instrumental in medicalizing birth control when she specifically invited physicians to become the new proponents of contraceptives. In part, her strategy reflected her experiences in court, where a judge speculated that her conviction for distribution of contraceptives would not have been upheld had they been distributed by a doctor for 'health' reasons (Sanger, 1931, p.145). Seizing upon this new angle – that anti-contraceptive laws interfere with the physician's ability to deliver appropriate health care – she placed physicians in prominent positions in her organization and began advocating the liberalization of these laws (Chelser, 1992).

By the 1940s, birth control as an aspect of women's rights and women's health began to be eclipsed by the population control movement (Gordon, 1990, pp.386–8). The Planned Parenthood Federation of America ardently supported using birth control for the twin goals of enhancing personal control and achieving population goals. Indeed, once again, it was the threat of 'others' (such as Africans and Asians) reproducing more than 'us' (that is, Caucasian Americans) that drew support for the liberalization of contraceptive access and the spread of contraceptive education and supplies abroad. Thus, in many ways, American women only achieved full domestic access to contraceptives when it became a matter of foreign policy.

The Medical Community's Dominance in Birth Control

It took nearly 70 years for the birth control movement to become completely successful, culminating in the 1960s with the declaration that the Comstock laws were unconstitutional. In that time the medical community had thoroughly displaced much of the midwifery and non-medical assistance associated with pregnancy and childbirth. Delivery moved into the hospital, and was accomplished under anaesthesia. Episiotomy became routine and Caesarean section rates began their long, upward climb. The professionalization of both contraception and pregnancy was nearly complete (Borst, 1990, pp.197–216; Davis-Floyd, 1992).

It seemed natural, then, that the great new advance in contraception would come from the medical community. Gregory Pincus and others were responsible in the 1950s and 1960s for the development of the birth control pill, a breakthrough in fertility control because it promised reliability, secrecy and convenience. It was lauded as a revolution in fertility control and was opposed by the Vatican and others as an invitation to promiscuity without consequence (Charo, 1991). It appeared at the same time as the increase in sexual activity among unmarried women. The 1960s ethos of 'free love' appeared to spell gender equality, until later years revealed that sexual freedom for women also spelled a reduction in sexual responsibility by men. Some feminists assert it became practically a demand on the part of men for free access to the sexual favours of women, who could no longer hide behind the fear of pregnancy. This was, of course, exactly what was feared by nineteenth-century feminists who, with some exceptions, refused to adopt the 'free love' movement. (Klein *et al.*, 1991).

Another feminist backlash against the pill was triggered by concerns about its effect on women's health. Stories about the development of the pill and its clinical trials in Puerto Rico revealed a lack of informed consent coupled with a rather high rate of significant side-effects. Feminists identified and advertised these side-effects, and complained that the medical researchers and pharmaceutical companies were routinely discounting reports of discomfort and disease from its use (Petchesky, 1990, pp.171–8). They also charged medical personnel with having little regard for non-medical, female-controlled forms of birth control, such as the diaphragm and sponge, asserting that this was part of a general tendency to assert control over all aspects of female physiology, and to turn ordinary health 'events' into health 'problems'. The incidence of hysterectomies was also evidence that the medical community fundamentally viewed women's bodies as inherently disordered, and that the general cure was to reshape those bodies – by surgery if necessary – to resemble male bodies in which hormonal fluctuations were fewer and simpler to comprehend (Bale, 1990, pp.430–39; Poirier, 1990, pp.230–32; Petchesky, 1990, pp.110–80).

The division between some wings of the women's movement and the medical community was exacerbated by medical developments in the 1970s, such as the inattention to the infection rates associated with the Dalkon Shield intra-uterine device (IUD), and the advent of routine amniocentesis and fetal monitoring (Davis-Floyd, 1992). Ironically, however, the women's movement had a great need for cooperation from the medical community on issues surrounding abortion politics. The pre-1973 anti-abortion statutes routinely had exceptions for 'therapeutic' abortions done to preserve the life or health of the pregnant women, and it was doctors who were entitled to decide whether this exception applied. Physicians helped in leading the public health-based arguments for liberalization or decriminalization of abortion laws prior to *Roe* v. *Wade* (Mohr, 1978, pp.253–8). In its analyses, the *Roe* court explicitly relied upon the existence of a doctor–patient relationship to bolster its finding that abortion is a fundamental right deserving the highest level of constitutional protection.

In some ways, however, the 1973 *Roe* decision freed the women's movement from its most pressing needs for political cooperation with the medical community. Indeed, as abortion became more and more controversial, physicians dropped abortion as a routine aspect of medical practice. By the late 1980s, only 15 per cent of those completing obstetric/gynaecological residencies were trained in even simple first trimester suction abortion, a technique that had been taught to lay persons prior to the advent of legal medicalized abortion in the early 1970s (Institute of Medicine, 1989).

Instead, medicine began to focus on prenatal care and the development of the fetus as a separate patient, leading to the well-documented rise of so-called 'maternal–fetal conflict' and all its attendant efforts to control women's behaviour during pregnancy (Rothman, 1986). These control efforts began with a rapid rise in court-ordered Caesarean sections. Later efforts were made to incarcerate or prosecute women who engaged in behaviour such as drinking, smoking or use of illicit drugs that were deemed unhealthy for the fetus (Charo, 1992). The arguments for such drastic actions were not couched in terms of what was needed to preserve the woman's health, but rather what was needed to preserve the health of the fetus. Using the newly acquired bioethics language of autonomy and patients' rights, many physicians abandoned paternalistic efforts to help women change their behaviour.

The Medical Community's Dominance in Infertility Treatment

It is against this backdrop that infertility services began to proliferate in the late 1970s and the 1980s. The advent of the birth control pill spelled a decline in barrier methods that had provided some relief from transmission of venereal diseases, leading to an increase in sterility due to infection. The unsafe IUDs of the late 1960s and early 1970s added to that toll. The change in sexual and cultural mores, in part due to the advent of more effective contraception, was leading to later childbearing, by which time more years had elapsed during which infections could take their toll in terms of impaired fertility (US Congress Office of Technology Assessment, 1988). Among the insured population, worry about inability to conceive increased, even though actual infertility rates remained stable. Physicians responded with a growing range of medical and surgical treatments. It was IVF, however, that appeared to be the most dramatic development in the treatment of infertility (ibid.).

IVF was first developed to overcome one specific cause of infertility: blocked Fallopian tubes. By obtaining the ova surgically, technicians could manage to achieve fertilization in a laboratory dish, and then attempt to reintroduce the fertilized ovum into a woman's body. IVF required a variety of complex steps, including the use of stimulation drugs, surgical egg retrieval, fertilization, initial development in vitro, and timed transfer to the uterus for implementation. Each step entailed significant emotional and physical side-effects. But those side-effects seemed minimal compared to the hope the procedure offered to those who had tried every other method for infertility relief (ibid.). Unfortunately, IVF moved too rapidly from experimental to clinical use. Moreover, researchers and physicians appeared to deliberately mislead patients about its prospects for success. Long before its techniques had been thoroughly studied and standardized, the procedure was being offered to paying patients at a growing number of clinics. Clinics often quoted 'success' rates that reflected a researcher's rather than a patient's version of success, for example citing pregnancies per transfer rather than live births per IVF attempt. Given that many patients' ova failed to fertilize and that over a third who did experience implantation would subsequently miscarry, the gap between illusion and reality was enormous (Medical Research International and American Fertility Society Special Interest Group, 1988, pp.212–15).

Ironically, one of the reasons for the low success rate and the overly rapid expansion of 'therapeutic' IVF services was the debate over abortion and family planning. Because of the furore over these developments, a number of efforts had been made by Democratic and Republican administrations alike to make symbolic statements about the sanctity of embryonic and fetal life. One result was that researchers were unofficially banned from using Federal monies to do any research using fertilized eggs (Charo, 1995). While basic research continued in Europe and Australia, the USA was left to do unfunded research in the course of performing therapeutic fertilization procedures on private patients. The same ban slowed development of a contraceptive vaccine that was being studied in Australia (US Congress Office of Technology Assessment, 1988). As a result, the health of IVF patients was jeopardized. Prior to the advent of embryo freezing, the most prominent IVF clinics would force women to undergo repeated surgery for frequent retrievals of small numbers of ova, or to undergo attempted implantation of too many ova (thereby risking dangerous multiple births), to avoid 'surplus' embryos in the laboratory.[3] This was probably the most dramatic example of the debate over abortion and contraception directly compromising the quality of infertility care for women in the USA.

Feminist critics of reproductive technologies were quick to point out that IVF was a technique born of physical control over procreation. They attacked physicians for being more concerned with public relations and leftover embryonic tissue than with women's physical health. They noted that, as with the birth control pill, physicians routinely discounted women's complaints about side-effects from the stimulation drugs. They also referred to a multitude of problems associated with these developments (Arditti *et al.*, 1984; Corea, 1985; Wikler, 1986).

More importantly, feminist critics complained, IVF was once again an example of manipulation of the female body and female desires for the purpose of serving male needs. Whether it was encouraging a healthy women to undergo surgical removal of ova to help out a male partner with a low sperm count, or encouraging an infertile woman to go to these extraordinary lengths to satisfy a partner's desire for a child, IVF was viewed as another example of putting all risk and responsibility for reproductive failure on women. Further, IVF, which often entails costs amounting to $15 000 and months of discomfort and emotional stress, all for a success rate of less than 10 per cent, would not be considered a reasonable choice in a world in which childbearing was seen as only one optional part of complex lifestyles. Thus the very excitement over IVF and the existence of a demand for the service was evidence of society's profound attachment to perceiving women as unfulfilled unless they produce children (Arditti *et al.*, 1984).

Finally, some feminist critics argued that IVF, and surrogacy, bespoke a profound attachment to genetic lineage that was not equally shared by the sexes. Men, they contended, could feel related to their children only when they saw their own physical characteristics reflected in them, as men often spent less time with their children, and of course could not have the sensation of gestation and delivery. This genetic fascination tended to distort women's stated desires concerning infertility relief.

While other wings of the women's movement did not speak so stridently of their concern about the rapidity with which IVF was sold to the public – especially to women – as the ultimate cure for infertility, most agreed that an unsavoury aspect of the technique was its transfer of power to physicians and the social screening of patients (Andrews, 1987). As with surrogacy and artificial insemination, physicians and legislators routinely attempted to limit use of the techniques to heterosexual, financially stable, married women. Resistance by married women with infertile husbands to having sex with a man whom they do not love (that is, extramarital intercourse) in order to conceive was labelled a 'health' problem (deserving a medical/surgical remedy), thus laying the groundwork for demanding public financing of these services as a part of an overall health care package (US Congress Office of Technology Assessment, 1988). Single or gay women would not be covered, however, as their resistance to sex with a man whom they do not love as a means to conceive was a 'social' rather than a 'health' problem.

Abortifacients and the Distrustful Women's Movement

In the 1980s, eugenic politics and generic distrust of reproductive technologies fostered by the history of birth control and reproductive health services were taking their toll in another arena: a new reproductive technology designed to provide a medical form of abortion. RU-486, the French abortion pill (known generically as 'misopristol') offers the prospect of abortion in the fourth to seventh week: that is, earlier than is possible using suction techniques. It has been extensively tested and found to be safe for most prospective users, and has been approved in France and the UK, where it is chosen by almost a third of the women undergoing first trimester abortion (Charo, 1991). The French company, Roussel-Uclaf, decided to promote this new antiprogestin abortifacient (Greenhouse, 1989, p.23) and, on 23 September 1988, the French Minister of Health approved the pill for marketing (Foreman, 1988, p.1). Instead of the protests dying down, as Roussel-Uclaf had hoped, they escalated. The influential Archbishop of Paris condemned the pill (Greenhouse 1989 p.23). Even Judy Norsigian of the National Women's Health Network in the USA was less than completely supportive of the decision: 'Women think this is a great idea and it does offer an option to women ambivalent about abortion, but it's too early to say if it is a good thing until it has been around longer' (Foreman, 1988, p.1).

Norsigian's ambivalence was noted and her remarks were repeated in the *National Right to Life News*, in which the education director of the National Right to Life Committee (NRLC) expressed concerns about fetal life, the safety of women and human experimentation (Glasow, 1988). These were the same kinds of charges made earlier by women's groups who had opposed the proposed injectable Searle contraceptive 'Depo-Provera', and they reflect the NRLC's clever decision to coopt the rhetoric and the fears of the women's movement in its opposition to the drug.

The autonomy offered by RU-486, however, overcame feminist scepticism towards contraceptive innovations.[4] The drug may enable abortion to be performed in a physician's office and even at home. The prospect of eliminating abortion clinics, which are easy targets for picketing and bombing by the radical anti-abortion movement, has made some feminists enthusiastic supporters of the drug. This has alarmed abortion opponents, who characterized RU-486 as ushering in an era of hedonistic and guilt-free chemical abortions (Andrusko, 1989). In fact, in an editorial of 6 October 1988 entitled 'Pills and Parallels', the *Boston Globe* noted the connections between the fears of rampant and rapacious sexuality following introduction of the birth control pill and those preceding the introduction of RU-486:

> Historic parallels between the two pills are remarkable in the extent to which American pharmaceutical companies fear political and religious backlash against the new abortifacient, just as they did 30 years ago against the contraceptive. Such fears about the 'pill' turned out to be groundless, as they should about the abortifacient.
>
> In the 1950s, America's mightiest drug companies did not dare to market the contraceptive pill, fearing they would become the target of boycotts over the 'immorality' of birth control. The identical fear now – of a vast boycott threatened by the NRLC over the 'immorality' of abortion – intimidated the pharmaceutical industry (Rivera, 1996). For-profit firms steered away from the drug, though one group of investors started a small company – Delta Science Research Foundation – dedicated to investigating RU 486 (and therefore immune to secondary boycotts of collateral product lines). In the end, however, it was a dedicated not-for-profit institute – The Population Council – that beat all the commercial concerns to the punch, and was the first to seek licensing and approval for RU 486. (F-D-C Reports, 1995)

It was this obstacle to marketing RU-486 for abortion that led to great interest in another drug, already on the US market for non-abortion indications, called methotrexate. As reports surfaced of physician use of this drug to induce medical (as opposed to surgical) abortion, interest grew in documenting its safety and efficacy. It was the introduction of an already approved drug into the equation that began to quell fears of boycotts and political backlash and, by the mid-1990s, Delta Pharmaceuticals had begun testing a methotrexate/misopristol combination that was 96 per cent effective at inducing abortion without report of serious side-effects (ibid.), though some investigators still advocated surgical abortion as the superior choice because of the reduced risk of incomplete abortions lost to follow-up (Ferris and Basinski, 1996).

Population Control Versus Family Planning

As mentioned earlier, birth control was introduced into American public opinion by linking it to neo-Malthusian arguments about population limitation. The early 1960s environmental movement embraced this point of view, and explicitly called for zero population growth (ZPG) as an essential aspect of environmental planning. The USA became a leader in the financing of third world population control projects, and vast sums were spent to convince third world governments that population limitation was the key to economic growth and environmental protection. This was a difficult argument to make in many parts of the world.

First, population appeared to spell power. In the artificial nation-states of Africa, for example, where colonialist powers drew unnatural boundaries that followed neither geographic nor tribal lines, diverse ethnic groups found themselves locked in power struggles exacerbated by a traditional policy structure based on family, village and ethnic group. The key to survival appeared to be greater numbers for one's own group. Population limitation seemed a self-destructive strategy. It also appeared to be the tool of political repression in the countries, such as Burundi, where the ruling group, an ethnic minority, was seen to be attempting to foist birth control upon the majority ethnic group (Barclay *et al.*, 1970; Mass, 1976; Greer, 1984, p.33).

Second, population control entailed a long term investment by countries suffering from seemingly more immediate problems. Family planning requires trained personnel, contraceptive supplies, warehouse and accounting facilities, and massive public education. This investment does not fully pay off for generations. Under these circumstances, it was unlikely to be a high priority for these governments.

Third, population control involves birth limitation that goes against the cultural and religious traditions of many of these countries. Even granting that these traditions are exceedingly repressive for women, they are nonetheless embraced by most of the population, including women (Gordon, 1990, pp.393–6).

Finally, population control was seen as an outgrowth of the old eugenic movements of the first half of the century. At a time when developed countries were concerned about fertility and its high-technology treatments, enormous sums were being spent to prevent the non-white populations of the world from reproducing. This disparity in focus was unmistakeable. Further, arguments were made that birth rates would fall when the social and economic conditions improved, as had happened in developed countries (ibid., pp.388–9).

It took nearly 20 years for western demographers and policy analysts to persuade developing country governments that population control was indeed necessary to give those countries a fighting chance to develop educational, physical plant and transport systems to meet existing and projected demand. During that time, a rising chorus of protest was heard from portions of the women's movement and the political parties of the left, who asserted that population control was being achieved through coercive measures that took no account of the reality of women's lives. For example, it ignored the need to produce children as a condition of marriage, and therefore of economic survival. The programmes failed to correct the underlying economic drives towards large families, such as the need for agricultural labour, household help and support in old age (Littlewood, 1977). Population control also failed to provide women with alternatives to bearing large families, as these alternatives depended upon making education and cash employment accessible to women – a task seen as largely out of the jurisdiction of population planners.[5] While so-called 'women in development' modules were attached to the US Agency for International Development (USAID) projects, they appeared to be an afterthought in project design.

Despite these criticisms and the concerns of the developing countries' governments, by the early 1980s it was a truism that population control was the cornerstone of economic and environmental policy. It was, therefore, a shocking blow to the international population planning movement when the Reagan administration announced at a world population congress in 1984 in Mexico City that it no longer believed that population control was a primary goal of US foreign assistance in contraception. The effect of this change was felt most of all within the American government itself, as USAID scrambled to recreate a justification for its population planning programmes. This justification was found in a far more women-oriented, progressive line of analysis.

Family planning, it was asserted, is something to be done for the benefit of the individual and the individual's family, not for the benefit of overall economic or environmental needs of the nation. Birth spacing enhances maternal health and child survival. Thus family planning became a pro-family measure (USAID, 1986). Interestingly enough, this is true. Studies in Turkey and North Africa reveal that birth spacing by 18–24 months is more effective at lowering infant mortality than any other intervention, including oral rehydration therapy, vaccination, or maternal nutrition programmes (Maine and McNamara, 1985). Ironically, this switch to a health-based justification for family planning programmes also provides a justification for abortion law reform in the developing world, much of which has inherited repressive laws from their former colonial governments. This was certainly not the intention of the Reagan administration, which in fact made receipt of US assistance for family planning conditional upon a complete separation of abortion services and the imposition of a gag rule concerning abortion referrals for all clinics receiving American monies (Cook, 1987, pp.93–140). Other unanticipated effects included extending the definition of family planning to include both contraception and infertility relief,[6] and making health programmes – which now included contraception – controversial.[7]

The Purposes of Fertility Control

The Reagan administration's announcement in Mexico City invited a fresh inquiry into the true purpose of fertility control. There are three options: community goals, such as population increase or decrease; public health goals, such as reduction in maternal and infant mortality; and fulfilment of individual aspiration, as an aspect of human rights. All three elements exist in most national population policies (Posner, 1992, 187–96).

Fertility Control for Demographic Planning

Public interest in the size and make-up of a relevant population is of course significant. Most professionals in demography and population studies agree that a population may become too large for a country's economic base to support. The problem can be exacerbated by population compositions. For example, in many countries with a high birth rate, the percentage of the population below the economically productive age of 15 years may cause impossible burdens of support to rest on the shoulders of adults (Ehrlich, 1987, p.9). Conversely, in the USA and many other industrialized nations, increased lifespan coupled with low birth rates may lead to an unusually high percentage of the population in the post-productive years (roughly over 70 years of age). This places a significant burden on working adults to create goods and services to meet their own needs and those of aging parents (Teitelbaum and Winter, 1985, pp.105–10).

On a purely economic basis, then, a strong argument can be made to regulate the number and timing of new entrants into the population via birth regulation. Without a doubt, this was the justification used by both China and Romania for their unusually interventionist population policies of the 1970s and 1980s. China's family planning policy has been marked by controversy over its 'one-child' programme, a policy adopted as the result of a perception that the inertia of demographics was rapidly dooming China to long-term poverty and illiteracy. The policy had several components, including delayed childbirth (via restrictions on early marriage and sanctions against births outside marriage), universal access to contraception, community pressure for compliance and abortion as a back-up to failed contraception. Overall, the China programme has all the hallmarks of a social policy enforced on the backs of women. It is women who are the subject of lengthy village inquiries and education sessions designed to bring recalcitrant women in line with government policy. Also it is women who risk benefits and promotions through work-unit enforcement of the policy.

These extreme costs are borne by women despite the fact that less burdensome means exist to meet the public goal of reducing the rate of population growth. Education is the strongest single correlate with reduced family size and yet the Chinese government did not choose to emphasize the education of women for its population programme, even after the 1991 passage of major legislation purporting to guarantee equal education and economic opportunities to women. When questioned whether enforcement of this law might not provide the socioeconomic circumstances associated with declining birth rates at a lower cost to women, family planning officials in at least one province replied that the urgency of the population problem in China required drastic measures with short-term returns. The readiness with which the Chinese government adopted the one-child policy also indicates a ready acceptance of the notion that, in the end, woman's bodies as reproductive propensities are legitimate tools of state interests.

Consistent with this emphasis on birth reduction, the Chinese government has not emphasized infertility services. Even basic education to combat sexually transmitted diseases (STDs) that cause infertility is hampered by a sexual prudery that prevents open acknowledgement of premarital and extramarital sex. As infertility is not a government priority, infertility prevention is not the subject of government action, even though childlessness for women often results in divorce and economic isolation. Overall, the demographic justification for fertility control in China has failed to address the full spectrum of women's needs and focuses instead on short-term relief for the nation's overcrowding.

Romanian pro-natalist policies were equally interventionist. To ensure an adequate supply of labour for the postwar economy, women were forbidden access to contraceptives. Many were subjected to repeated pregnancy tests at their places of work. Pregnant women were required to submit to follow-up examinations. A miscarriage would result in an investigation to determine whether it had been induced. Induced miscarriage, of course, was a crime – not against the fetus, as is argued in the USA, but against the state and the community.

Once again, despite non-interventionist options for meeting state policy goals (such as increasing immigration from the impoverished countries which have too many people to support), the community and government reaction was to look for the most immediate solution. By definition, that entailed using women as a means to state ends.

In his concurring opinion in *Planned Parenthood of Southeastern Pennsylvania* v. *Casey*, Supreme Court Justice Blackmun recognized the dangers of coercing reproductive choices to meet state goals, and explicitly related it to questions of gender equality:

> By restricting the right to terminate pregnancies, the State conscripts women's bodies into its service, forcing women to continue their pregnancies, suffer the pains of childbirth, and in most instances, provide years of maternal care. The State does not compensate women for their services, instead, it assumes that they owe this duty as a matter of course. This assumption – that women can simply be forced to accept the 'natural' status and incidents of motherhood – appears to rest upon a conception of women's role that has triggered the protection of the Equal Protection Clause. (At 2846–7)

If one accepts this analysis, unprecedented in Supreme Court opinions, fertility control based upon demographic needs must be viewed first as a question of gender equality. Unless men's reproductive options are similarly circumscribed, coercive programmes for community good must be judged by whether they serve legitimate goals in an acceptable fashion. The failure to try non-coercive solutions to demographic problems first would appear to condemn these programmes. Only in the presence of demographic disaster and an absence of reasonable alternatives can coercive programmes be fashioned and justified.

It is worth noting that the effort to connect gender equality to reproductive freedom is the hallmark of the United Nations Convention on the Elimination of All Forms of Discrimination Against Women. Seemingly neutral or sound policies may offend if they hinder women from attaining full potential. Laws which permit women to enjoy a status equal to that of men are still considered discriminatory if they prevent such women from pursuing further goals. Thus laws that would equally prohibit men and women having children violate women's rights to use their bodies for experiencing pregnancy if they so wish. Conversely, laws which equally prohibit men and women from using contraception are unacceptable because they interfere with unhindered use of a woman's body, as pregnancy can be highly limiting.

Fertility Control for Public Health

The Reagan administration's reconceptualization of American population assistance as a public health measure was taken seriously by grantees. In 1988, in Chad, government officials embarked together upon an exploration of their version of family planning, renamed 'bien-être familiale', or 'family well-being' rather than birth control.[8] The name change was significant. The focus became birth spacing, rather than birth limitation, which made the programme acceptable to Muslim leaders. It is true that the 1988 statement by the influential Fatwa Committee of the Al-Azhar Islamic Research Academy in Cairo appears to accept demographic justifications for family planning when it states that some countries, needing more population for workers, should embrace high birth rates, while others who are poor in resources should content themselves with fewer people, but it continues later in its statement to say that birth limitation, as opposed to spacing, is contrary to Islamic law. Spacing is allowed if necessary to ensure adequate education, religious training, food or other resources for one's children, or when needed to enhance maternal and child health. Furthermore, it states that no country may pass a law mandating birth limitation or augmentation, as this ought to be the personal choice of a husband and wife (Sachedina, 1990, pp.107–14).

It was against this backdrop that the Chadians explicitly included a right to infertility prevention and treatment services, as well as a host of maternal and child health services, in their package entitled 'bien-être familiale'. The conference featured speakers from Niger and Senegal who reported on the estimated 10 per cent infertility rate in Central Africa. Traditional remedies for infertility, ranging from potions to magic tokens, and the problem of STDs were discussed. No reference was made to reproductive technologies which are too expensive and labour-intensive for the still preliminary family planning programme in N'Djamena and surrounding areas. While USAID may be more interested in overall population reduction, it supported this portion of the conference in an effort to make family planning acceptable to the Chadian Ministry of Health.

The health justification of family planning is also of importance under international law, where one line of analysis in support of access to contraception and abortion rests on assertions that there is a basic human right to access to health care, including all forms of reproductive health care. Following constitutional changes in 1988, the Colombian government proceeded to authorize Ministry of Health regulations that, when issued in 1991, explicitly approved of a wide range of infertility treatments and contraceptives. The regulations thus authorize the use of donor gametes and possibly surrogacy as solutions to infertility, as well as IVF where it does not involve discard of fertilized ova.[9]

Use of a 'right to health' as the basis for access to both contraception and infertility services has limitations. It invites restrictive abortion laws that make exceptions to a general prohibition only when physical health is threatened, or perhaps grave psychological harm is imminent. It is not an adequate basis for a generalized and unobstructed right to abortion. Further, it supports birth spacing but not necessarily unconditional birth limitation. The Fatwa Committee, for example, singled out sterilization, except for serious health reasons, as unacceptable. Even where accepted, it is subjected to significant restrictions. Moreover, at the Chadian conference a sterilization law akin to that in Niger – where it is available only to older women with at least five children and older men with at least seven children – was discussed in approving terms. Health justifications do not assist single or homosexual men and women seeking to use medical infertility services to bypass the social dilemma posed by their status. Thus public health justifications only permit a narrow range of reproductive rights.

Furthermore, public health justifications can lead to implementation of eugenic measures. In China, for example, birth limitation has led to a culture of female infanticide and infanticide of disabled newborns (*Proceedings on the International Conference in Beijing on Improving Birth Quality and Child Upbringing*, 1992) and several provincial governments have adopted a eugenic model forcing the sterilization of people with intellectual disabilities where there are doubts about parenting capacities and concerns about passing the disability on to children. Interest in genetic screening services appears to be running very high in China and, despite an incipient cult of 'individual rights' analysis, public health arguments for eugenics appear to be widely accepted (ibid.).

Another issue raised by public health justifications for fertility control concerns professionalization of services and invites the conclusion that doctors, pharmacists and nurses should control distribution of commodities and access to services. This can be counterproductive. In Ghana, for example, the Ministry of Health has inherited outdated British poison legislation which requires prescriptions for most contraceptives. However, Ghana is a country with only 700 pharmacists and a doctor–patient ratio over 30 times smaller than that in the UK (Charo, 1990). Efforts to change the prescription regulations have met with a variety of responses, most of them reminiscent of the birth control battles fought in the USA. First, reform would be an embarrassment to the country, as it would admit the dearth of trained professionals; second, it would suggest that Ghanaian women are not entitled to the same degree of safety as British or American women, who rely upon professionals to screen out inappropriate candidates for specific contraceptives; and third, family planning is more acceptable to the government and the populace when it is seen as actively endorsed and promoted by health professionals as a health service. A recent meeting held by the Alan Guttmacher Institute concerning prospects for eliminating the prescription requirement for the birth control pill in the USA met with similar concerns, despite evidence that the modern low dose version would be safer than most drugs already sold over the counter.[10]

Discussions concerning the appropriateness of medical control over simple technologies like artificial insemination by donor (AID) and medical vacuum aspirations (MVA) also run into resistance. AID for example, can easily be performed by women themselves. While screening of semen donors is best done by a professional with laboratory facilities, the actual insemination takes little technique. Many state laws, however, grant women the benefit of having the donor declared a 'non-father' only if the insemination is done by a physician (US Congress Office of Technology Assessment, 1988). There appears to be a magic created by the physician's presence. The depersonalization and medicalization of the procedure is sanitizing and makes it more acceptable to the public. It is not a circumvention of the need to commit adultery to provide one's husband with a child if it is a 'treatment' for a disorder.

From a child's point of view, the physician's presence means nothing. If conceived by intercourse rather than artificial insemination, a child's wish to be recognized as the legal offspring of the genetic father would be recognized at law. The physician's presence changes all those rules, just as the physician's prescription transforms birth control from an act of self-assertion into an act of health preservation.

Manual vacuum aspiration picks up another thread in this tapestry. The technique is highly appropriate for many parts of the world, including the USA, but it is being developed specifically for third world markets, where few physicians are available as abortion providers. The nineteenth-century campaign to remove abortion from the hands of 'irregular' practitioners is still having its effects. There is an underlying presumption that abortion cannot be done safely by non-physicians and that anything less than perfect safety is intolerable – despite the large number of deaths due to pregnancy, untrained and (unsafe) abortion or delivery (WHO, 1990). This presumption promotes the continued interest in RU-486 as a medical abortifacient for the third world. Women and governments from developing countries are suspicious of any technique that is not planned to be offered to American women. In turn, American women are suspicious of any technique developed for third world women, who presumably are not getting techniques as safe as those in the USA.

Fertility Control for the Attainment of Individual Aspirations

Arguments for access to fertility control based on a right to autonomy raise issues about the significance of fertility control. Justices O'Connor, Kennedy and Souter address these issues in *Planned Parenthood of Southeastern Pennsylvania* v. *Casey* by stating that the rights to marry, to form a family, to practise contraception, to procreate and to rear children are at the heart of 'liberty', which they describe as the 'right to define one's own concept of existence, of meaning, of the universe'. Dissenting Justice Scalia noted that throughout the majority opinion there is resort to a series of terms, including 'personal autonomy', 'intimate views', 'basic decisions' and 'bodily integrity'. The need to use so many terms, he asserts, demonstrates that those writing the majority opinion do not know exactly what they mean by liberty and certainly do not know how liberty encompasses the right to terminate a pregnancy.

Justice Blackmun takes the view that decisions which 'profoundly affect bodily integrity, identity ... should be largely beyond the reach of government' (at 2846). The language used by Justice Blackmun and the majority is important because it focuses on the rights of the individual, as opposed to the marital unit. The *Casey* decision explicitly reaffirms the right to practise contraception established in *Griswold* and *Eisenstadt* and upholds (with some limitations) *Roe*'s right to terminate pregnancy. Further, it would appear to fully embrace the notion of an affirmative right to procreate, which until now has not been articulated, though presumed to be buried within decisions prohibiting coercive sterilization.

Even given that there are rights to procreate, to practise contraception and to obtain an abortion, the *Casey* decision leaves open the question of how these rights will be treated in law. Until 1992, these rights were viewed as 'fundamental', that is, essential to our notions of ordered liberty, and therefore state interference was subject to strict judicial scrutiny. By lowering the standard of review in the context of abortion, the *Casey* court leaves open the possibility of a lower level of review for procreation and contraception cases. An assertion of 'legitimate' state interest could be made in relation to the right to procreate. Specifically, the state interest in ensuring that children, as far as possible, are born into two-parent, heterosexual homes is probably 'legitimate' under current constitutional jurisprudence. After all, a court that can uphold state prohibitions on sodomy and, to date, leave untouched a nineteenth-century decision upholding prohibitions on polygamy, surely can find a legitimate interest in maximizing a child's chance of having a 'traditional' home. Thus the court's attempt to find a middle ground in abortion jurisprudence has directly threatened the integrity of jurisprudence concerning both infertility relief technologies – which are often sought by unmarried people – and contraception. It is ironic that the very jurisprudence of abortion that was once used by commentators to bolster arguments in favour of unfettered access to AID, IVF and surrogacy may now become the downfall of these family creation techniques.

Outside the USA, arguments based on individual rights analysis may not have equally strong emotional appeal. In Western Europe there is a stronger tradition of trading off individual responsibilities against rights (Glendon, 1991). If one looks further, towards China, one finds a country in which there is a flirtation with individual rights analysis but still an exceedingly strong communitarian tendency. This somewhat different balance between rights and responsibilities is struck in the very language used in international conventions that attempt to guarantee both access to contraception and protection from forced sterilization or other attempts to limit an affirmative right to procreate. Article 23 of the International Covenant on Civil and Political Rights ('the Political Covenant') and Article 10 of the Economic Covenant recognize the family as the fundamental unit of society and the 'right to marry and to found a family'. The Woman's Convention, building on earlier General Assembly resolutions approving of family planning and recognizing the interrelatedness of the right to found or not to found a family, refers to the right to decide on the number and spacing of children, responsibly and freely. This provision links family planning with a right to procreate and with a responsibility to exercise that right with discretion.

What is left unanswered, however, is the meaning of 'responsible'. It appears to be an invitation to constrain individual rights to procreate or practise contraception when needed for the good of someone. As the *Casey* decision demonstrates, the question of what constitutes a 'legitimate' third party interest is highly political and subjective. It leaves the door wide open to control over fertility technologies as the subject of a continuing struggle among women, physicians and the state.

Conclusion

Both contraceptive technology and reproductive technologies for infertility relief separate sexual intercourse from procreation. Many commentators have noted this similarity and concluded that the jurisprudence surrounding the use of both technologies should be linked. However, the two are linked perhaps even more tightly by a shared political history. The history has certain recurring themes: woman's equality premised on personal control over the capability and timing of childbearing; struggles for control over technology between women (the users) and professionals (the providers) and the state (the affected community); and a series of almost irresistible tendencies towards eugenic manipulation of the population. Depending upon whether the purpose of fertility control is the satisfaction of broad community needs, public health or individual preference, different players are granted control over the technology, and different limitations on its use apply. It is probably unrealistic to expect any government to be able to state clearly which of the above is its primary purpose in making fertility control available. It is not too much to demand, however, that its underlying purposes be revealed and discussed before limitations are set in law and practice.

Women benefit most from a regime in which fertility control is viewed as a technique that sometimes is best practised with medical assistance but should always be done to fulfil individual aspirations. Where the technique is available primarily for community benefit, as with for example demographic control, individual women's preferences are secondary to national interests. This transforms birthing or birth control into a form of uncompensated and involuntary public service. Where the technique is available primarily as a public health measure, it may serve the physical needs of individual women, such as those who would sicken or die from repeated pregnancies, but ignores the physical, emotional and economic toll pregnancy can take on healthy women. In sum, it treats women as physiological human beings, but as not as fully entitled citizens with rights.

Unfortunately, premising access to contraception and infertility relief on women's rights to political self-determination eliminates some of the economically powerful arguments behind the population control and public health justifications. Indeed, it requires that the general population accept women's equality as a paramount policy goal even though it has not yet accepted it as a paramount cultural goal. Even among ardent feminist supporters of fertility control, there will be the temptation to use economic and public health arguments to legitimize their claims for access to and financing of fertility control services. The possible loss of control over these services either to government officials or to the medical community is seen as an unfortunate but necessary correlate.

This was the dynamic in play in the 1890s and 1940s, when birth control clinics were being founded in North America. In the 1990s, this is still the driving dynamic in the USA, where the debate rages within the feminist and reproductive health communities over strategies to ensure coverage for abortion care in any reformed national health care system.

Notes

1 For more recent developments, see the 1992 *Planned Parenthood of Southeastern Pennsylvania* v. *Casey* decision.
2 Personal communication from Kathleen Hunt, National Public Radio reporter, Bucharest, June 1992.
3 Personal communication, Dr Howard Jones, Director, Jones IVF Institute, Norfolk VA, October 1987.
4 RU-486 is now being attacked by the anti-reproductive technology wing of the feminist movement. In *RU 486: Misconceptions, Myths and Morals*, Klein *et al.* focus almost exclusively on parallels between the development of RU-486 and

the development of other reproductive technologies such as IVF and various failed forms of birth control. They claim that abortions using RU-486 and a follow-up dose of prostaglandin ('RU/PG abortion'), went from animal testing to human trials in record time, that reports of side-effects were routinely discounted, and that long-term follow-up was insufficient. Further, they argue that both the press and physicians misled women by billing the drug as an advance towards making abortion a more private procedure that offered greater personal control to women.

5 Personal communication, Dr Judith Seltzer, Director, Policy Planning Division, Office of Population, Bureau of Science and Technology, US Agency for International Development, May 1988.

6 For example, see the OPTIONS project of the Office of Population, US Agency for International Development (contracted to The Futures Group, Washington, DC), especially its 1988 conference, 'Bien-être familiale', in N'Djamena, Chad, October 1988.

7 Personal observations of the author during her 1988–9 employment as a policy analyst at the Office of Population, US Agency for International Developments and during her field trips to Chad, Mali, Côte d'Ivoire (1988) and Indonesia (1989).

8 The following discussion of the Chadian conference is based upon the author's own notes of her attendance. Further details are available from the official conference report available from the Office of Population, US Agency for International Development, or from the Futures Group, Washington, DC, which acted as USAID's contractor for the OPTIONS project, which supported the conference.

9 Remarks of Dr Isabel Plata at the meeting of Latin American participants to the Third International Conference on Law, Medicine and Ethics, Toronto, July 1991.

10 Meeting at offices of the Alan Guttmacher Institute, February 1992. The report on the meeting is based on the author's notes of her attendance.

References

Andrews, L.B. (1987), 'Feminist Perspectives on Reproductive Technologies', presented at A Forum on Reproductive Law for the 1990s, New York, 18 May.

Andrusko, D. (1989), 'Feminist Leaders Mount Campaign for Abortion Pill', *United Press International*, 1.

Arditti, R., R. Duelli-Klein and S. Minden (eds), (1984), *Test Tube Women*, Boston: Pandora Press.

Bale, A. (1990), 'Women's Toxic Experience', in R. Apple (ed.), *Women, Health and Medicine in America*, New Brunswick: Rutgers University Press.

Barclay, W., J. Enright and R.T. Reynolds (1970), 'The Social Context of US Population Control Programs in the Third World', paper presented to the Population Association of America, 17 April.

Borst, C.G. (1990), 'The Professionalization of Obstetrics: Childbirth Becomes a Medical Specialty', in R. Apple (ed.), *Women, Health and Medicine in America*, New Brunswick: Rutgers University Press.

Charo, R.A. (1990), *Legal and Regulatory Obstacles to Expanding Family Planning Services in Ghana*, Report to the US Agency for International Development.

Charo, R.A. (1991), 'A Political History of RU-486', in K. Hanna (ed.), *Biomedical Politics*, Washington, DC: National Academy Press.

Charo, R.A. (1992), 'Mandatory Contraception in the US', *The Lancet*, **339**, 1104.

Charo, R.A. (1995), 'The Hunting of the Snark: The Moral Status of Embryos, Right-to-Lifers, and Third World Women', *Stanford Law and Policy Review* **6**, (2), 1–38.
Chesler, E. (1992), *Woman of Valor: Margaret Sanger and the Birth Control Movement in America*, New York: Simon & Schuster.
Congregation for the Doctrine of the Faith (1987), *Instruction on Respect for Human Life in its Origin and on the Dignity of Procreation*, Rome: Vatican City.
Cook, R. (1987), 'Population Policy, Sex Discrimination and Principles of Equality Under International Law', *New York University Journal of International Law and Policy*, **20**, 93.
Corea, G. (1985), *The Mother Machine*, New York: Harper & Row.
Davis-Floyd, R.E. (1992), *Birth as an American Rite of Passage*, Berkeley: University of California Press.
Ehrlich, P. (1987), *The Population Bomb*, London: Ballantine Friends of the Earth.
F-D-C Reports Inc. (1995), **57**, (36), The Pink Sheet T&G-9, 10 (4 September).
Ferris L.E. and A.S. Basinski (1996), 'Medical abortion: what does the research tell us?', *Canadian Medical Association Journal*, **154**, (2), 15 January, 185–7.
Foreman, J. (1988), 'France OK's Use of New Abortion Pill', *The Boston Globe*, 24 September.
Glasow, R. (1988), 'Abortion Pill RU 486 Approved for Use in France, China; Pro-Life Spokesmen Condemn Death Drug', *National Right to Life News*, 6 October.
Glendon, M. (1991), *Rights Talk*, New York: The Free Press.
Goldman, E. (1976), 'Love and Marriage', in A. Baskin (ed.), *Woman Rebel*, New York: Archives of Social History.
Gordon, L. (1990), *Woman's Body, Woman's Right*, New York: Penguin Books.
Greenhouse, S. (1989), 'A New Pill, A New Battle', *New York Times Magazine*, 12 February.
Greer, G. (1984), *Sex and Destiny*, New York: Harper & Row.
Haller, M.H. (1984), *Eugenics: Hereditarian Attitudes in American Thought*, New Jersey: Rutgers University Press.
Hubbard, R. (1990), *The Politics of Women's Biology*, New Brunswick: Rutgers University Press.
Institute of Medicine (1989), *Medical Professional Liability and the Delivery of Obstetrical Care*, ed. B. Potter, Washington, DC: National Academy Press.
Klein, R., J. Raymond and L. Dumble (1991), *RU 486: Misconceptions, Myths and Morals*, North Melbourne: Spinifex Press.
Littlewood, T.B. (1977), *The Politics of Population Control*, Notre Dame: University of Notre Dame Press.
Luker, K. (1984), *Abortion and the Politics of Motherhood*, Berkeley: University of California Press.
McCormick, R. (1985), *Notes on Moral Theology 1981–1984*, Washington, DC: University Press of America.
Maine, D. and R. McNamara (1985), *Birth Spacing and Child Survival*, New York: Center for Population and Family Health.
Mass, B. (1976), *Population Target*, Toronto: Woman's Education Press.
Medical Research International and American Fertility Society Special Interest Group (1988), 'In Vitro Fertilization and Embryo Transfer in the United States: 1985 and 1986. Results from the National IVF/ET Registry', *Fertility and Sterility*, **49**, 212.
Mohr, J.C. (1978), *Abortion in America*, Oxford: Oxford University Press.
Noonan, P. (1990), *What I Saw at the Revolution*, US: Ballantine Books.
Petchesky, R.P. (1990), *Abortion and Woman's Choice*, Boston: Northeastern University Press.
Poirier, S. (1990), 'Women's Reproductive Health', in R. Apple (ed), *Women, Health and Medicine in America*, New Brunswick: Rutgers University Press.

Posner, R. (1992), *Sex and Reason*, Cambridge Mass.: Harvard University Press.
Proceedings of the International Conference in Beijing on Improving Birth Quality and Child Upbringing, 24–27 May 1992, Beijing: International Academic Publishers.
Rivera, R. (1996), 'Mad at the Mouse. Christian boycotts are becoming a popular way of protesting', *Christianity Today*, **2**, (12), 12.
Rothman, B.K. (1986), *The Tentative Pregnancy*, New York: Viking.
Sachedina, A. (1990), 'Islam, Procreation and the Law', *International Family Planning Perspectives*, **16**, 107.
Sanger, M. (1931), *My Fight For Birth Control*, New York: Farrar and Rinehart
Steinbrook, R. (1988), 'Wide Use of Nonsurgical Abortions is called likely', *Los Angles Times*, 4 February.
Teitelbaum, M.S. and J.M. Winter (1985), *The Fear of Population Decline*, Florida: Academia Press.
US Agency for International Development (1986), *Birth Spacing and Maternal Child Health Programs*, USAID.
US Congress Office of Technology Assessment (1988), *Infertility: Medical and Social Choices*. Washington, DC: US Government Printing Office.
Wikler, N.J. (1986), 'Society's Response to the New Reproductive Technologies: The Feminist Responses', *Southern California Law Review*, **59**, 1043.
World Health Organisation (1990), *1988–89 Report of the Special Programme of Research, Development and Research Training in Human Reproduction*, Geneva: World Health Organisation.

Cases

Eisenstadt v. *Baird* 405 US 438 (1972).
Griswold v. *Connecticut* 381 US 479 (1965).
Planned Parenthood of Southeastern Pennsylvania v. *Casey* 112 S CRT 1271 (1992).
Roe v. *Wade* 410 US 113 (1973).

5 Reproductive Autonomy and Reproductive Technology: Gender, Deviance and Infertility

SHARYN L. ROACH ANLEU[1]

Introduction

Reproductive autonomy refers to women's right to make choices about their reproductive lives, including decisions about whether and when to become pregnant. This liberal conception of choice implies that actors freely make decisions to maximize their self-interest. Reproductive choices, however, are constrained, but not completely determined, by various intersecting inequalities which structure opportunities, the medico-legal environment and the prevailing normative system.

One set of constraints stems from the dominant expectation that 'normal' women will become wives, then mothers. Cultural constructs of domesticity, sexuality and pathology distinguish between 'normal' and 'abnormal' women and structure the experiences of 'being female' (Carlen and Worrall, 1987, pp.2–8). Medical and legal discourses constitute women's bodies as problematic, diseased, pathological and as requiring medical management or legal regulation (Smart, 1991, pp.165–7). Thus (married, heterosexual) women who experience infertility deviate, albeit unintentionally, from motherhood and family norms, indeed from the norms of femininity *per se*; such a condition has come to entail medical intervention to facilitate conformity.

This chapter looks beyond the physiological causes of infertility and views involuntary childlessness as a social status resulting in deviation from parenthood norms. These norms differ for men and women and vary according to marital status, sexuality, age, class and race. The discussion below explores how gender informs views about infertility and how gender differentially shapes the experiences of infertility for men and women. Finally, the chapter examines the meaning of reproductive autonomy or choice in the context of conceptive technologies, especially *in vitro* fertilization (IVF).

Infertility, Deviance and Medicalization

Infertility has become defined as a medical condition, often leading to 'high-tech' treatments involving hormonal stimulation, sophisticated and expensive technology and medically managed fertilization of gametes in the laboratory. Biomedical interventions aimed at alleviating (rather than treating) infertility by producing a pregnancy have expanded rapidly since the birth of the first baby conceived through IVF in 1978 (Blank, 1990, pp.11–16; Scritchfield, 1989, p.99). Despite no increase in the overall incidence of infertility, visits to physicians for infertility services grew from about 600 000 in 1968 to around 1.6 million in 1984 and the number of infertility specialists steadily increased in the USA (Office of Technology Assessment, 1988, p.5). Infertility treatment and research have become distinct fields of medical specialization (Bonnicksen, 1989, pp.19–24).

Infertility has also emerged as a highly contentious public issue, with much of the controversy focusing on the development and application of IVF and its related procedures, including experimentation. At the centre of these debates is the status of the human embryo. Indeed, the embryo has become a site of struggle over the nature of human personhood, the status of women and the role of scientific experimentation. Religious leaders, infertility groups, right-to-life organizations, medical scientists, feminists, lawyers, academics and other interested individuals often make incompatible claims about the social, ethical, moral, therapeutic and legal dimensions of the so-called 'new reproductive' or 'procreative technologies'.[2] They seek to have their own specific world views and values incorporated into public policy.

Infertility specialists argue that embryo experimentation is essential to develop new treatments for infertility and to alleviate the plight of childless couples. Public policies and laws which prohibit or restrict experimentation and the clinical application of conceptive technologies, they argue, conflict with patient demands (Cant, 1992, p.43). In contrast, some opponents seek greater regulation over medical science and condemn the experimentation as unethical or immoral tampering with human life. Others criticize medical scientists' primary concern with producing babies and their consequent treatment of women as a means to that end.

Not all viewpoints are represented equally in policies or legislation dealing with conceptive technologies. Where such policies and laws exist, they focus overwhelmingly on the status of the human embryo (Gallagher, 1987, pp.140–41). This can be linked with the emerging discourses around fetal rights which assume certain ideologies of motherhood (DeGama, 1993, pp.116–19; Diduck, 1993, pp.472–9). Notably absent are concerns about the rights and status of women as patients in IVF programmes (Gaze, 1992, p.29). The new procreative technologies pose a number of dilemmas for women as individuals and for feminist theory – especially regarding the scope for individual choice, autonomy and agency.

Medical intervention in the area of conception suggests that infertility is a disease or illness. Infertility also entails deviation from pervasive parenthood and family norms. Broadly, deviance can be defined as behaviour which breaks social norms, with the consequences involving some kind of sanction. Thus to talk about deviance presupposes prescriptive notions of normality, which may or may not be widely shared. Attempts to eradicate or manage deviance are also attempts to 'normalize' the behaviour or activities of individuals in order to establish conformity and reaffirm particular social values or world views. Two general theoretical traditions exist in the sociology of deviance. The first focuses on the existence of social norms and seeks to explain why some people break them while others conform, by examining the underlying social, economic, opportunity structures and learning processes. This perspective is concerned with social control, that is the responses to deviance, which range from glances, gossip and embarrassment in everyday social interaction to fines and imprisonment for violation of the criminal law (so long as the violator is caught!).

Carol Smart (1976, pp.146–50) points out that men's deviance is more likely to be criminalized, whereas women's non-conformity is more likely to be interpreted from a medical model. Usually, men's deviance is explained as resulting from rational choices within particular opportunity structures. In contrast, women's deviance is often analysed as emanating from female biology – especially reproductive organs and hormones – which is presumed to be prone to pathology, or from their 'naturally' unstable emotions and problematic mental health. Even where women's deviation involves breaking the criminal law, their bodies and supposed 'nature' become the site of investigation and diagnosis (Carlen and Worrall, 1987, pp.6–7; Smart, 1991, p.166). This means that the sort of social control deviant women experience is often located within the medical profession rather than the criminal justice system.

The second main stream of deviance theory emphasizes the processes of definition. How and by whom are social rules, including laws, defined and constructed? How are ideas of normality constructed and which values and interests do such notions reflect or reaffirm? Alternatively, who is motivated and has power to define some activities or behaviour as acceptable or normal and others as unacceptable, given the often widespread disagreement about what constitutes deviance? Here the focus is on social reactions, that is the labelling process and its effect upon an individual's identity formation and self-conception. No activity or individual is inherently deviant: it just depends on the responses of others who identify and interpret activities or individuals as such. The definition of behaviour as deviant depends on the social audience, not just on the norm-breaking activity. According to Howard Becker,

> Deviance is *not* a quality of the act the person commits, but rather a consequence of the application by others of rules and sanctions to an 'offender'. The deviant is one to whom the label has successfully been applied; deviant behaviour is behaviour that people so label. (Becker, 1963, p.9; emphasis in original)

The central concern of labelling theorists, then, is to distinguish rule-breaking behaviour from deviance by separating the actual acts from the identification of an individual or group as deviant and ultimately their subjective view of themselves as such (Roach Anleu, 1995, pp.30–32). From within the labelling perspective, Schur catalogues a range of norms around self-presentation, marriage/maternity, sexuality and occupational choice which are applied to women but not to men (Schur, 1984, p.53). Indeed, the status of female is deviant without anything further; as male is the norm in many spheres of social life, even where the expectations appear gender-neutral, being female is *ipso facto* deviant (MacKinnon, 1987; 1989).

How, then, do conceptions of deviance and normative frameworks fit the medical model of infertility as a disease? Parsons (1951a; 1951b) first pointed out that illness is not just a physiological condition but a special type of deviant behaviour. The sick role is one alternative available to an individual facing strain; it is one way of avoiding social responsibilities (Parsons, 1951b, p.431). While not denying the organic causes of illness, he rejects the notion of illness as a purely physiological phenomenon. The test for whether being sick constitutes a social role is the existence of a set of institutionalized expectations and the corresponding sentiments and sanctions. By definition, the sick person is helpless and in need of help, has an obvious interest in getting well and should accept any necessary measure to achieve health. The therapeutic process therefore involves social control as the physician and the person in the sick role are concerned with achieving conformity to social roles.

Parsons (1951b, pp.455–6) identified four dimensions of the sick role. First, the sick person is exempt from the performance of certain normal social obligations. Second, a person defined as ill is not held responsible for her/his condition. Third, the legitimacy of the sick role rests upon the individual's seeking specialized, usually medical, assistance: the sick person is under an obligation to get well and stigmatizing illness as undesirable reaffirms the value of health. Finally, by entering a relationship with institutionalized medicine the sick person acquires the additional role of patient, thereby incurring specific obligations, especially cooperating with the physician in the process of trying to get well.

At first glance infertility, or involuntary childlessness, does not fit neatly into Parsons' conception of the sick role. Even so, dominant ideas of femininity conform to the characterization of the patient as helpless, frail and inevitably dependent on an authoritative (often male) expert (Smart, 1976, pp.148–9). Infertility may be curable, for example, blocked Fallopian tubes preventing conception may be unblocked via surgical procedure. For women participating in an IVF programme, however, their condition is similar to chronic illness, as the role of medical personnel is more akin to management of the symptoms than to treatment (Gallagher, 1976, pp.209–10). The aim of IVF is to enable a successful pregnancy and a live birth, it does not cure or alleviate infertility. Chronic illness can be distinguished from other illness on the basis of its long-term nature, the extent to which the illness and its treatment become focal concerns, and the uncertainty of the treatment trajectory. With the exception of a few couples whose physical impairments make conception impossible, infertile couples find it difficult to give up hope, thus suggesting that the possibility of treatment is a focal concern (Greil, 1992, p.23). Ironically, the same technological changes that make it possible for infertile couples to have realistic hope for a child make it difficult for the members of an infertile couple to accept their infertility or to ignore new treatment procedures (Greil, 1992, p.24). Management of the symptoms of infertility involves hormonal stimulation to initiate or increase ovulation and the *in vitro* procedures, neither of which cure ovulatory problems or enhance subsequent fertility. The successful outcome of IVF is the birth of a baby; the infertility remains (Mullens, 1990, pp.244–80).

Others suggest that involuntary childlessness can be conceptualized as a form of physical disability. For example: 'Involuntary childlessness is similar to other disabilities which are viewed as *accidental* or *involuntary deviance*. It is usually not motivated, and is typically associated with contingencies of inheritance, accidents of infection and trauma' (Freidson, 1966, p.81, as quoted in Miall, 1986, p.269; emphasis in original).

Unlike other examples of disability, infertility is invisible; infertile people possess a secret stigma in that they display no obvious stigmatizing features (Goffman, 1963; Greil, 1992, p.22). Indeed, infertility has been termed an 'un-disease' because it usually remains undiagnosed or unrecognized until a conception is sought. It is inferred from the absence of a pregnancy and birth rather than demonstrated by the presence of a disease (Sandelowski *et al.*, 1990, p.198). Infertility only restricts a person's performance of parental roles; they are not precluded, at least not physically, from fulfilling most other social roles.

Infertility has not always been a medical category. The activities of the medical profession, particularly the segments of obstetrics and gynaecology, have been instrumental in its designation as a medical condition requiring medical treatment and intervention (Becker and Nachtigall, 1992, p.457; Strickler, 1992, pp.113–15). Medicine is oriented to locating and identifying illness by creating social meanings of illness where such interpretations were previously absent (Freidson, 1988, p.252). The history of the medicalization of pregnancy and childbirth shows that 'natural' or 'normal' events and conditions have been redefined as medical problems requiring medical involvement and control (Ehrenreich and English, 1978). Research documents increasing medical intervention and diagnostic testing during pregnancy, the movement from home to hospital births and male physicians' progressive exclusion of female midwives from the birthing process (Rothman, 1983; 1986, pp.86–115; Sullivan and Weitz, 1988).

Medicalization may have more to do with professional claims making and achieving medical dominance than with underlying physiological conditions or causes (Conrad and Schneider, 1980, pp.261–76). As Freidson observes, 'just like law and religion the profession of medicine uses *normative* criteria to pick out what it is interested in' (1988, p.206; emphasis added). Medical scientists do not exist outside social life passively responding to natural conditions, but, subjected to the existing cultural values and norms regarding parenthood and childlessness, they actively define and redefine the conditions that constitute infertility. The mere fact that infertility programmes receive large-scale financial and medical resources affirms the conclusion that infertility should be remedied and couples' desires for children fulfilled. Moreover, infertility research is a pioneer area in which scientists have achieved a number of 'firsts', for example the first babies born after IVF (Rutnam, 1991, p.144). This results in widespread public attention and high status for the scientists, with consequent benefits to their careers (Reif and Strauss, 1965).

The medicalization of infertility, however, is incomplete: the 'success rate' is notoriously low; only between 10 and 20 per cent of all couples participating in programmes have a baby; private insurance companies, especially in the USA, have been reluctant to include fertility treatments; and unexplained infertility persists (National Perinatal Statistics Unit, 1992, pp.2–6; Office of Technology Assessment, 1988). The jurisdiction that medicine has established vis-à-vis infertility extends further than its demonstrable capacity to 'cure' (Freidson, 1988, p.251). Rather than accepting their current ineffectiveness in curing infertility medical scientists use the limitations of the techniques as a basis on which to make claims for more resources and the lifting of prohibitions on embryo research as necessary to improve 'success' rates (Cant, 1992, p.43; Roach Anleu, 1996).

Gender and Infertility

Most discussion of reproductive technology focuses on the couple and access to the programmes is usually restricted to married, heterosexual couples. However, references to and concerns with the 'infertile couple' gloss over the possibility that one partner is fertile and are insensitive to the different experiences of men and women resulting from infertility, regardless of the location of the physiological cause. In IVF programmes women are the patients who receive 'treatment' and undergo the procedures. This is true even if the woman is fertile and the male factor – for example, low sperm count or poor sperm motility – is the cause of the couple's inability to conceive (Lorber and Bandlamudi, 1993, p.33).

Referring to the infertile couple also diverts attention from pervasive norms regarding motherhood and fatherhood. It is important to consider how gender informs views about infertility and how gender differentially shapes the experiences of infertility for men and women. Considerable discussion exists in the literature regarding the gender norms relating to motherhood (Ferree, 1990, pp.868–71; Thorne with Yalom, 1982). While not all women become mothers, the ideology and imagery of specific forms of motherhood is pervasive at a cultural level (Fineman, 1991, p.276).

A range of norms surround women's reproductive capacities, resulting in certain social roles being widely viewed as normal and any variation deviant and stigmatized. Mothering is an area where women's activities are subject to widespread normative regulation and often medical intervention (Schur, 1984, pp.81–92). Central to this normative structure is that procreation occurs within marriage, or at least long-term heterosexual partnership, and all women should marry and have children (Veevers, 1980). Positively sanctioned motherhood involves economic and emotional dependence on the father, and the presence of the father and the mother in the home is deemed essential to the welfare of the child (Carlen and Worrall, 1987, p.3). Perceived violations include intentional non-motherhood, single motherhood and 'unfit' motherhood. Single motherhood is far less stigmatized than previously, yet there are still class and race distinctions. For example, over 90 per cent of the recipients of the Australian Commonwealth government's Sole Parent Benefit are women, which means that a large proportion of single mothers are subject to government control and surveillance (Roach Anleu, 1995, p.236). Here approved motherhood is responsible and cooperative within the welfare state (Carlen and Worrall, 1987, p.3). In poverty discourses and recent welfare reforms in the USA the social and economic deprivations poor children and their mothers suffer are attributed to their deviant family form; that is, the absence of the father/husband (Fineman, 1991, p.275). The idea of 'unfit motherhood' has arisen recently in custody cases, in the controversies surrounding surrogacy arrangements and regarding women's drug use during pregnancy.

Some evidence suggests that the standards for parental fitness are higher for women than for men in child custody cases. In the USA since the late 1970s, fathers suing for custody win in about half the cases because judges devalue the mother's caretaking functions in favour of the father's higher earning capacity and greater likelihood of remarrying, thereby re-establishing a 'normal' family (Polikoff, 1982). Mothers are not allowed to fail any of their obligations, whereas fathers who do anything for children are often perceived as better parents than mothers (Chesler, 1986, p.49).

In the infamous 'Baby M' case Mary Beth Whitehead – the birth (and genetic) mother – reneged on a surrogate mother contract and refused to relinquish her daughter to the genetic father and his wife, the commissioning parents. During the trial the testimony of mental health experts reflected middle-class biases about good mothers and good parenting and presented Mary Beth as narcissistic and as having an 'emotional over investment' with her children (Harrison, 1987, pp.307–9). In the wider debates around the case critics condemned the participation in a contract agreeing to relinquish a child as devaluing motherhood (Roach Anleu, 1992, p.40).

Finally, criminal prosecutions have been brought against women in the USA for drug abuse, especially for crack cocaine and alcohol use, during pregnancy, which allegedly harms the fetus. The emergence of a 'fetal rights' discourse establishes an adversarial relationship between a woman and her fetus and provides the state with power for defining women's behaviour during pregnancy as deviant, possibly involving court-ordered obstetrical interventions or incurring criminal sanctions (Bennett, 1991, pp.72–6; Johnsen, 1986, p.600; 1987, p.35; Note, 1988, p.1010). Viewing the fetus as a baby and endowing it with personhood rights renders the pregnant woman a mother with associated expectations and obligations (Petchesky, 1986, pp.338–41).

In sum, women can be deemed deviant if they are married and remain without children by choice, if they have children outside marriage or if they have children for the wrong reasons, or if the wrong kinds of women – poor, ethnic minorities, those already with large families – have children.

Experiences of Infertility

Being without children results from a decision not to procreate or from infertility. Both situations result in non-conformity to motherhood norms but entail very different consequences. Voluntarily childless women are often viewed as emotionally immature, abnormal, selfish, immoral, irresponsible, lonely, unhappy and sexually inadequate (Veevers, 1979, p.5). Even the term 'childless' connotes deviance, suggesting that a child is lacking and thereby a person must be less than complete or unfulfilled. In contrast, involuntarily childless women usually define their own infertility as negative or discreditable, representing an inability to function normally (Callan and Hennessey, 1988; Miall, 1985; 1986). Many display a personal sense of failure and find it difficult to disclose infertility to family and friends because of feelings of inadequacy and shame and the belief that others will view them in a new and damaging way (Miall, 1985, p.396; 1986, p.271). This points to the process of self-labelling, not labelling by a social audience, and indicates the importance of discerning the different experiences of infertility. The notion of self-labelling indicates that women who experience infertility may define themselves as impaired or deficient; as others do not know about their infertility, they cannot engage in the labelling process. Of course, ideas about the 'deviant' status of involuntary childlessness derive from dominant motherhood and domestic norms and from anticipating how others might react if they knew.

Regardless of the cause of infertility, men and women interpret, explain and react to infertility in radically different ways. Self-definitions as fertile or infertile seem to depend as much on a deep-seated fear of being unable to conceive as on medical probability. This perceived vulnerability to infertility relates to the greater relevance of fertility for female as compared with male identity and role enactment (Sandelowski *et al.*, 1990, p.200). Women are more likely to 'recognize' a problem and initiate medical attention than are their male partners (Becker and Nachtigall, 1992, p.462). They are also more likely to interpret the absence of a pregnancy as evidence of their own failure and to perceive themselves as abnormal, defective and incapable. In contrast, men give more scope to bad luck, rely on the female partner to initiate diagnosis and wait for a medical diagnosis which identifies the cause of the inability to conceive (Sandelowski *et al.*, 1990, p.201).

A study of 22 married infertile couples[3] contacted though a local chapter of Resolve – an infertility support group – in New York state indicates that consideration of the influence of gender on infertility is crucial to understanding how couples experience infertility (Greil *et al.*, 1988, p.173). Specifically:

> The existence of a physiological impairment in one or both partners does not in and of itself determine the course of the couples' experiences of infertility. Rather, the process of 'becoming infertile' is a dialectical one in which husbands and wives interpret, respond to, and give meaning to physical symptoms and physiological conditions. (Greil *et al.*, 1988, p.174)

The in-depth interviews revealed that the women tended to take the lead in pursuing medical treatment. In 21 out of the 22 cases, it was the wife who first presented herself to a physician for diagnosis, while the men tended to be supportive, which meant that they did not interfere with the treatment process. The women were more likely to see infertility as a devastating experience and suggested they experienced infertility as a cataclysmic role failure that spoiled their ability to live normal lives (ibid., p.181). They tended to retreat from interaction with fertile people and to become very focused on the problem of infertility; they thought about infertility often, constantly read about it and were often willing to do whatever was required to shed the infertility 'master' status.[4] Rather than being a person with problems conceiving, an individual becomes an infertile person, which in turn forms a part of their own self-identity.

The infertile women found it psychologically difficult to continue in previously satisfying activities. It is not so much that they are unable to continue their normal life as it is that they no longer find it meaningful to do so (Greil, 1992, p.33). The women sought to conform to the ideal of 'normal' womanhood. One woman commented on a general feeling of personal failure:

> It [the experience of infertility] affects your ego. It has an immense effect on self-concept, in all sorts of crazy ways. You ask, 'How can I be a normal woman?' By affecting the self concept, it affects sexuality, and it affected work for me for a while. 'How can I be good at this?; I'm not a normal person.' (Greil, 1992, p.25)

The men viewed infertility as disappointing but not devastating. They felt it was something they could accept and put into perspective and were chagrined that their wives were not also able to do likewise (Greil *et al.*, 1988, p.192). The authors suggest that, possibly because the expectation to be a father is not as important a part of male identity as the expectation to be a mother is of female identity, few husbands spoke in terms indicating that they experienced infertility as a role failure. Even where there was clearly a male reproductive impairment, wives still tended to view the situation as their problem. Regardless of who is biologically 'at fault', it is the woman who is unable to display the visible signs of an expected and desired change in status (Greil, 1992, p.32).

Following the analysis that infertility is a type of deviance, women will be perceived as deviating from norms which are specifically applied to them and not to their male partners. This suggests that women are more concerned with infertility because the social consequences of childlessness, that is the absence of children (unless of course they are adopted), are greater for them than for men because of the pervasive norms surrounding motherhood as central to an adult, heterosexual, married woman's identity. This links to Carlen and Worrall's suggestion that typifications of femininity distinguish between 'normal' and 'abnormal' women in terms of domesticity, sexuality and assumed pathological biology (1987, pp.2–3). Motherhood is promoted as a vocation, as a worthwhile career in itself, and the 'normal' woman is a mother who requires the adjacent female attributes of coping, caring, nurturing and altruism. Inability to conform with this ideal type denotes abnormality, which can be remedied by seeking medical assistance.

A Canadian study shows how 71 involuntarily childless women[5] perceived their own and their partners' 'problem' and how they managed its potentially stigmatizing implications in social interaction. Interestingly, the study initially sought to compare the reactions of men and women to their involuntary childlessness, but was unable to recruit a sufficient sample of men (Miall, 1986, p.271). The research identified strong themes of privacy and secrecy, feelings of a loss of control and autonomy, and reticence among the women to inform other people. There was an overwhelming sense of stigma and perception that involuntary childlessness entailed very negative consequences. Nearly all the women who themselves were infertile experienced feelings of anxiety, isolation and conflict as they explored the possibility of personal infertility. Most were concerned that an awareness of their infertility problems would cause others to view them differently and negatively. One respondent commented: 'I do believe it lessens you in some people's eyes, makes you different and possibly even morally suspect, like God is punishing you or something' (Miall, 1986, p.272).

Fertile women with infertile male partners were less likely to feel as personally stigmatized than did the infertile respondents, but they found it more difficult to disclose this information (Miall, 1986, p.273). These women shared a courtesy stigma; that is, they shared the stigma of infertility; their stigma is based on their association with someone who has a stigmatizing attribute – here infertility – and not on their own personal attributes. In other words, they allowed others to think that the origin of the problem was their own biology and not that of their male partner, thus permitting the social audience to view them negatively. Greil's research also found that wives willingly took responsibility for their husbands' reproductive impairments, but suggested that the term 'courtesy stigma' fails to capture the reality that these women experienced. They did not describe themselves as accepting responsibility for their husband's infertility, but actually thought of themselves as being infertile, which in a sense they were because of their inability to conceive in that particular relationship (Greil *et al.*, 1988, p.184). This suggests an inversion of Sykes and Matza's (1957) conception of 'techniques of neutralization' which are used by people deviating from social norms who disavow the deviance because, here, the women neutralized the deviance of their partner and deviantized themselves.

Perhaps women with a courtesy stigma have more difficulty telling others because of the greater perceived stigma associated with male infertility. There seems to be a conundrum here. On the one hand, it appears that the spectre of childlessness is not as traumatic for men as for women; they find it easier to return to normal life. On the other, the revelation of infertility appears more stigmatizing for men than for women. The explanation that, so long as the source of infertility is unknown, it will be assumed immediately that the problem lies with the woman resolves this apparent contradiction. Frequently, the general public, as well as infertile couples themselves and physicians, tend to view infertility as the woman's problem, regardless of its location or cause.

In managing the stigma of infertility, involuntarily childless women tend to engage in some form of information control. Specific strategies include selective concealment, therapeutic disclosure and preventive disclosure.

Selective Concealment

Apart from disclosures to professionals, nearly all the respondents decided whether to conceal or disclose their infertility on the basis of their perception of others as genuine or trustworthy. They learned to judge or recognize who might make them feel uncomfortable about their childlessness and to avoid them, or to use strategies of concealment in conversation. For example:

> On occasions at parties, I've tried to avoid the topic. Even though no one has done anything that might upset me, I believe in being prepared for the possibility of it happening. My whole approach is to be as low key as possible, not to get excited, *to show we are normal*. (Miall, 1986, p.275; emphasis added)

Therapeutic Disclosure

The selective disclosure of infertility to others may enhance self-esteem or serve to renegotiate personal perceptions of stigma. Therapeutic disclosure was a kind of catharsis providing an acceptable physiological rather than an unacceptable social explanation for being without children.

Preventive Disclosure

This entails the selective disclosure to others of the discreditable attribute, with a view to influencing others' actions or ideas about oneself, or about infertility in general. Several infertile women revealed their infertility by using the medical diagnosis of their condition to avoid greater perceived negative consequences. Or they revealed the infertility as an uncontrollable consequence of another medical condition such as diabetes. This indicates a shifting of responsibility from the individual to demonstrate that there is nothing that can be done, and therefore the individual is not blameworthy; she is not childless by choice. The deviation from motherhood norms is not intentional; it is not a matter of choice; 'normal' women do not choose to be without children. The apparent norm violation is neutralized (Sykes and Matza, 1957). This illustrates Parsons' point that an ill person is not responsible for his or her condition. In this case, illness constitutes one way of managing strain, and many infertile women seem to prefer the sick role than that of the voluntarily childfree. Moreover, entry into the sick role is more compatible with cultural ideas of femininity because it attests to the lack of intention or volition vis-à-vis being without children.

While both voluntary and involuntary childlessness deviate from motherhood and marital norms, the former is more like criminal deviance in that the woman will be regarded as responsible for choosing not to have children; an intention is presumed present. The latter is closer to the sick role, signifying disability or incapacity to fulfil social obligations, and intentional deviation is lacking (Aubert and Messinger, 1958). A consequence of adopting the sick role is the associated expectation or obligation to seek medical assistance; that is, to become a patient. Even so, the boundaries between voluntary and involuntary childlessness are unclear. Women may be blamed or held responsible for their present infertility viewed as resulting from past intentional actions or choices, including undergoing an induced termination for non-medical reasons. Medical literature often explains or theorizes women's biologic failure to reproduce as stemming from a lack of desire, albeit subconscious, or from such 'deviant' behaviour as delaying childbirth and concentrating on career development (Sandelowski, 1990a, p.478).

Reproductive Autonomy

On one level, the new procreative technologies offer women who are part of an 'infertile couple' an opportunity to conform to motherhood norms; they expand reproductive choices. Participation in an assisted conception programme makes available a route out of the deviant status, or at least attempting all available options, even without taking home a baby, attests to the involuntariness of being without children – it was never a choice.

On another level, given the kinds of normative constraints which may operate on women, the concept of reproductive choice, freedom or autonomy in the context of the medical and often technologically sophisticated solutions to infertility becomes problematic. Does the availability of conceptive technologies enhance or reduce reproductive autonomy? Their existence and development creates possibilities and hope, yet the low success rate means that many women are doubly disappointed (Klein, 1989). Medical dominance of infertility treatments which can be invasive and disruptive suggests a lack of control and freedom, as the recent history of abortion illustrates. Reproductive autonomy remains an abstract ideal unless choices are realizable.

The discussion of reproductive autonomy is most developed in the debates on abortion, with such slogans as 'Freedom to Choose', 'Reproductive Rights', 'Control Over Our Bodies' being catch phrases of women's movements since the 1960s. The US Supreme Court viewed reproductive choice as an issue of personal privacy in *Roe* v. *Wade* which resulted in the legalization of abortion in 1973. The court stated:

> This right of privacy ... is broad enough to encompass a woman's decision whether or not to terminate her pregnancy. The detriment that the State would impose upon the pregnant woman by denying this choice altogether is apparent. [The Court then listed a variety of

harms] ... All these are factors the woman and her responsible physician necessarily will consider in consultation. (*Roe* v. *Wade*, 1973, p.153)

Recent developments regarding abortion demonstrate that the notion of reproductive autonomy depends on social and historical contexts and its scope may ultimately depend on judicial decisions. Rather than deciding conclusively about women's right to abortion, *Roe* v. *Wade* galvanized opposition to the availability of abortion which has eroded the realization of reproductive rights for many women. Various Supreme Court judgements and governmental policies subsequently have minimized the possibilities for the exercise of the choice to have an abortion (Petersen, 1993, pp.157–66). The ideas of choice and autonomy are abstract and questions of access and the ability to exercise such 'choices' are constrained by social norms, economic circumstances, political agendas and narrowing legal interpretations.

While the privacy doctrine successfully established the foundation for the legal right to abortion, it has become a tenuous foundation with the growing opposition to legal abortion and the increasing formalism of the Supreme Court (Eisenstein, 1988, pp.187–9). Accordingly, pro-abortion or pro-choice arguments have shifted from privacy and choice to focus on equality and the social and economic conditions which enable the 'right to choose' to be exercised rather than just possessed. In an amicus brief for the 1989 case, *Webster* v. *Reproductive Health Services*, the National Abortion Rights Action League (NARAL) argued that restrictive abortion laws deprive women of their freedom to control the course of their lives and restrict their ability to participate in society equally with men. Equal participation rapidly erodes because of the financial constraints childbearing and rearing place on women. Consequently, it is argued, the reproductive rights must recast the language of 'pro-choice' in terms of race, economic class, geographical location, age and other factors which determine access (Eisenstein, 1991). However, such concerns were not incorporated by the majority of the US Supreme Court which emphasized the existence of choice as distinct from the opportunities to exercise such 'choice'. So long as women do not rely on public health facilities, their 'choices' are unimpeded. Others can still choose to have a termination but will have to fund it themselves if public facilities do not offer termination services. Chief Justice Rehnquist, delivering the judgement of the court in *Webster* declared:

Missouri's refusal to allow public employees to perform abortions in public hospitals leaves a pregnant woman with the same choices as if the State had chosen not to operate any public hospitals at all. The challenged provisions only restrict a woman's ability to obtain an

> abortion to the extent that she chooses to use a physician affiliated with a public hospital. (*Webster* v. *Reproductive Health Services*, 1989, p.3052)

In the abstract, *Webster* does not take away the right to abortion or limit the sphere of privacy but, by upholding states' right to restrict abortion services, it reduces access for women with few economic resources and without private health insurance who rely on public hospitals. This is a narrow, individualistic view of choice which does not take into account the social conditions under which choices can be implemented. The court is also becoming more concerned with the rights of the fetus which overshadow those of women.

More recently, in *Planned Parenthood of Southeastern Pennsylvania* v. *Casey* (1992), the Supreme Court, without overturning *Roe* v. *Wade*, reduced the fundamental right to abortion to a 'liberty interest', which no longer attracts maximum constitutional protection against governmental intrusion. The court upheld a state abortion statute requiring the provision of literature on the risks and alternatives to abortion; a 24-hour waiting period before the procedure; informed consent from a woman seeking an abortion and parental consent from a minor seeking an abortion. However, it rejected the provision that a married woman seeking an abortion notify her husband. The majority held as follows:

> Though the woman has a right to choose to terminate or continue her pregnancy before viability, it does not at all follow that the State is prohibited from taking steps to ensure that this choice is thoughtful and informed. Even in the earliest stages of pregnancy, the State may enact rules and regulations designed to encourage her to know that there are philosophic and social arguments of great weight that can be brought to bear in favor of continuing the pregnancy to full term and there are procedures and institutions to allow adoption of unwanted children as well as a certain degree of state assistance if the mother chooses to raise the child herself. ... It follows that States are free to enact laws to provide a reasonable framework for a woman to make a decision that has such profound and lasting meaning. (*Planned Parenthood* v. *Casey*, 1992, pp.711–12)

The decision establishes that the requirement of informed consent is satisfied even if only 'right-to-life' information is provided and public policies to persuade women to choose continuation of a pregnancy may not unduly burden her decision regarding termination. The court has shifted from a liberal view of women making the decision in private within the confidential doctor–patient relationship to a conception of women balancing various competing interests. The majority observed:

> Abortion is a unique act. It is an act fraught with consequences for others: for the woman who must live with the implications of her decision; for the persons who perform and assist in the procedure; for the spouse, family and society which must confront the knowledge that these procedures exist, procedures some deem nothing short of an act of violence against innocent human life; and, depending on one's beliefs, for the life or the potential life that is aborted. (*Planned Parenthood* v. *Casey*, 1992, p.698)

This statement accords with gender norms specifying that women ought to consider others' desires, needs and interests as well as their own. While not directly accepting the 'right-to-life' arguments, the court accords them more legitimacy than previously and agrees that more regulation be placed on the decision to terminate a pregnancy.

Reproductive Autonomy and Infertility

Many people, including medical scientists and potential consumers/ patients, argue that infertile couples should have the same choices as do fertile couples. The choice to have a child necessitates the availability of assisted reproductive technologies. The emphasis is on helping couples to conceive; on assisting their goal to have a child. This is enshrined in legislation which provides for counselling and information dissemination which reflects the concern that participants must make informed decisions and consent freely to the procedures.

Access to assisted reproduction programmes is restricted to certain kinds of infertile people. The possibility of artificial insemination and IVF where the male gametes are donated enables the formation of families without any kind of relationship with a man; indeed, the new medicotechnologies potentially pose a greater threat to fatherhood than to motherhood (DeGama, 1993, p.123). To counter this possibility, legislation (where it exists) clearly envisages only 'married' heterosexual couples as having access to reproductive technologies and where male gametes are donated the husband is presumed to be the father, with the donor having no rights or obligations vis-à-vis any offspring (Bennett, 1993, pp.42–4). In Victoria (Australia), the Infertility Treatment Act 1995 (which replaces the Infertility (Medical Procedures) Act 1984 as amended) requires that 'a woman who undergoes a treatment procedure [including IVF] must be married' (s.8(1)). In South Australia, the Reproductive Technology Act 1988 defines 'married' as including couples who have lived together for five years. Similarly, in Western Australia, the Human Reproductive Technology Act 1991 specifies that an IVF procedure may be carried out where

> the persons seeking to be treated as members of a couple are –
> (i) married to each other; or
> (ii) are co-habiting in a heterosexual relationship as husband and wife and have done so for periods aggregating at least 5 years, during the immediately preceding 6 years. (Section 23 (c))

The issue of marriage was a focus of considerable disagreement during the parliamentary debates on all the statutes passed in Australia. The salient theme among those who sought to restrict the availability of the programmes was that married couples are more stable, there is greater commitment between the partners and thus they are more deserving. During the debates on the Reproductive Technology Bill in 1987 one member of the South Australian Legislative Council asserted:

> It is not unreasonable, where people are asking the State and the taxpayer to assist them to achieve a pregnancy, that the safeguards of marriage should be a condition of that assistance. ... But, as a matter of principle, in fertilising unmarried people [that is, women] it would primarily be putting them in a position of being potential pensioners as it were, or potentially drawing supporting parent benefits, and it does seem to be a strange thing for a society to do. (Legislative Council [South Australia], 24 November 1987, p.1967)

The claim here is that, as female-headed or single parent families deviate from 'normal' family forms, they will necessarily be dependent on the state; the absence of a male breadwinner means that the family will be economically deprived and inadequate. Similarly, some members of the Victorian parliament during the debates before the passage of the 1984 legislation referred to the commitment and self-sacrifice that marriage entails and concluded that married couples are more deserving of access to IVF programmes. One member stated: 'If people are willing to commit themselves to the conventions of marriage, they are on the whole more likely to provide the environment we would want for the children produced through the *in vitro* fertilization programmes' (Legislative Council [Victoria], 11 October 1984, p.767).

Similarly, during the parliamentary discussion preceding passage of the 1995 legislation, a government member of the Victorian Legislative Council reinforced the argument: 'If you are not prepared to make whatever sacrifices are involved in getting married, then we question whether you are serious about putting the welfare of children first' (Legislative Council [Victoria], 7 June 1995, p.1301). A primary criterion for access to reproductive technology procedures is conformity with the nuclear family based on heterosexual coupling and marriage and the ideal of domesticity. Only certain people –

excluding single, lesbian, divorced women – have access to the technologies and are able to exercise the choice of whether or not to participate.

While feminists and 'right to life' activists hold diametrically opposed viewpoints in the abortion debates, this is not the case in the debates on IVF, surrogacy and embryo experimentation. Their arguments and value orientations differ, but their conclusions converge, namely that medical scientists are self-interested and should not be trusted; and that IVF programmes are harmful and should be discontinued. For conservative critics, the overwhelming harm is to the embryo – the so-called 'unborn child' – while feminist critics emphasize the harm suffered both by women as patients and women as a whole.

The meaning of reproductive autonomy in this context is a point of disagreement among many feminists. Some identify the dangers of participating in IVF programmes, especially stemming from the drugs used for superovulation, the mounting pressure on women to become mothers, the pain and anguish that can result from participating in a commercial surrogacy arrangement and the continuing 'medicalization' of women's bodies (Rothman, 1989, pp.62–3; Rowland, 1985, pp.540–41; 1987a; 1987b, pp.524–8). They stress the experimental nature of the procedures and the fact that few women actually leave an IVF programme with a baby and possibly that baby has received considerable neonatal attention. One critic, for example, writes: 'In presenting new reproductive technology as an exciting 'scientific breakthrough' and 'technological progress', and IVF as a 'standard procedure', scientists, doctors and the media alike misled the general public into believing that IVF is a successful technology. In reality it is a *failed* technology' (Klein, 1989, p.1; emphasis in original).

A central argument is that, rather than extending women's choices and reproductive autonomy, the new procreative technologies actually narrow them, subject women to greater social control and further pathologize their bodies. First, the availability of such programmes reinforces pro-natalist ideals and places additional pressures on women unable to conceive to participate; motherhood is reinforced as a necessary status for 'normal' women. Second, participants in IVF programmes may have little scope for making choices to refuse or vary treatments. The medical specialists may present the refusal to undergo a particular procedure as lowering the chances of conception.

Third, autonomy is reduced further, as the only sphere where women have some distinctive power and control – motherhood – is being steadily eroded by increasing medical intervention (Rothman, 1984; 1986; 1989, pp.152–8). Indeed, the whole notion of motherhood is being fragmented, especially in surrogacy arrangements where the genetic, gestational, social and legal mothers can all be different women. This has led to arguments about who is the real mother (given that we assume that there can only be one); in other words, who has the most authentic claim to motherhood (Taub, 1989, p.218)? Is this determination to be based on genetic links, pregnancy, conformity to certain cultural norms about mothering and family structure, or on the strongest demonstrated desire and commitment to be the mother? Finally, in the area of assisted reproduction, medicine and law intersect, with the latter regulating more and more aspects of women's reproductive lives as a consequence of rapid developments in the former (Smart, 1991, pp.168, 172–5).

Another concern is that, where the male partner is infertile, IVF and related technologies are now being extended to fertile women (Lorber, 1988, p.121; 1989, pp.24–6). In other words, fertile women are the patients undergoing the clinical procedures. Rather than there being a free choice or a freely given gift to an infertile partner, some women undergo the extensive treatment as a patriarchal bargain: They try to maintain a relationship and have a child within the bounds of monogamy, thereby conforming to family and parenthood norms (Lorber, 1989, pp.32–3).

Legislation in three Australian states – Victoria, South Australia and Western Australia – specifies the conditions under which IVF procedures may be carried out (Infertility Treatment Act 1995 (Vic): ss.8–11; Reproductive Technology Act 1988 (SA): s.13A(3)(d)(ii); Reproductive Technology Act 1991 (WA): s.23). A central criterion is that, except where any 'undesirable' hereditary disorder or 'genetic abnormality' (and in Victoria 'or a disease' (s.8(3)(b)) may be transmitted to the child of a pregnancy, only infertile couples can participate in an IVF programme. Even so, arguments are made to extend IVF to fertile people to facilitate some surrogacy arrangements, to enable couples to store embryos and to allow the testing of embryos for possible chromosomal disorders (Dawson and Singer, 1990, p.167). Medical scientists developed a technique to microinject sperm surgically into an oocyte (egg) which provides information about male infertility and assists conception. Researchers in Victoria obtained permission to engage in this research in 1987, and babies have been conceived through the procedure (Boreham, 1992, p.3; Waller, 1992, pp.27–9). This technique enables men to be the genetic fathers of children, yet the woman who is not infertile may be able to achieve a pregnancy through the much simpler procedure of artificial insemination. By allowing the microinjection technique, fertile women are being treated for male infertility. The new Victorian legislation provides that, before a woman undergoes a treatment procedure, a doctor must establish that 'she is unlikely to become pregnant from an oocyte produced by her and sperm produced by her husband other than by a treatment procedure' (s.8(3)(a)), or a genetic abnormality or a disease might be transmitted. This allows married fertile women to participate in a reproductive technology programme where their husbands are infertile, thus enabling genetic parentage within marital relations.

Disagreement and controversy exist regarding the nature of the relationship between womanhood and motherhood. Suggestions that motherhood is being fragmented, that this sphere of women's activity and special contribution may lead many to suspect essentialist assumptions about women's alleged distinctive and innate role as mothers (Stanworth, 1987, pp.16–18). Such an argument can be turned against women in the abortion debates and in their attempts to gain greater access to the labour market.

Other feminists reject images of women as victims incapable of resisting male domination who passively comply with the desires of a husband to 'father' children and the demands of the mostly male medical profession and are unable to transcend cultural prescriptions of pro-natalism (Paltrow, 1985; Stanworth, 1987; 1990, pp.296–300; Wikler, 1986, p.1053). They argue that such imagery dismisses women who have thought long and hard and decided to participate in an IVF programme and denies that the desires of women unable to conceive to have a child are real and concrete, not merely ephemeral or socially constructed.

Critics of assisted reproductive technologies place infertile women in an ambiguous position; they are portrayed (at least by implication) as far more convinced by pro-natalism and motherhood ideals and as far more susceptible to medical dominance than are fertile women. It is almost as though such women are more at the mercy of their irrational desires and emotions than are fertile women. Sandelowski writes: 'infertile women are viewed as neither authentically wanting nor freely choosing medical/technological assistance to reproduce' (1990b, p.40). This critical scenario offers little scope for agency or volition on the part of women who decide to participate in IVF programmes. Their decision to participate is less real than the decision of those not to participate. Sandelowski further suggests: 'When some feminist critics suggest that women's motivations for bearing children or their inclinations toward medically prescribed diagnostic and treatment regimens are spurious, or largely products of the social or gendered construction of choices, they are, in effect, dismissing or trivialising women's desires' (ibid., p.41).

Women who are physically infertile and those who are fertile but involuntarily childless experience considerable stigma and deviantization during everyday life which have profound effects on their social identity and behaviour (Miall, 1986). Research suggests that women experience infertility as a cataclysmic role failure that spoiled their ability to lead 'normal' lives and couples tend to see infertility as a problem for the female partner (Greil *et al.*, 1988, p.191).

To view infertile women who participate in IVF programmes as more persuaded by the promises of medical science further deviantizes their status. Indeed, they become doubly deviant: deviant from broad cultural norms about parenthood and family formation and deviant from feminist norms regarding the inappropriateness of assisted conception techniques. Sociological reductionism or determinism is as problematic as the argument that women become mothers and behave in distinct ways simply because of sex-specific biological imperatives (Carlen and Worrall, 1987, p.7).

A central issue, then, is the contest over the ever-changing and ill-defined boundaries between 'normal' and 'abnormal' women and the meaning of femininity (Carlen and Worrall, 1987, p.7; Erikson, 1966, pp.10–14). Debates surrounding the clinical and experimental application of assisted conception procedures illustrate that 'women's bodies are a site of contested meanings' (Smart, 1991, p.157). The debates raise questions about the prospects for reproductive autonomy versus continuing medical and legal control over women's reproductive lives, the constitution of the family and the relationship between motherhood and fatherhood.

Conclusion

In thinking about reproductive autonomy we need to link broad structural aspects of society to the opportunities for individuals to make choices and to exercise autonomy. As the recent history of abortion policies demonstrates, the abstract right to abortion is not the same as the ability to exercise that right, which is mediated by social and material conditions and resources. Women's choices are mediated by the following:

- the pervasiveness of gender inequality;
- dilemmas arising from the competing demands of motherhood and employment which may result in delayed childbirth decisions and a potentially greater demand for conceptive technologies;
- the gender norms which still render childlessness more deviant for women than for men;
- medical dominance, especially regarding pregnancy and childbirth, and the treatment of infertility as an 'illness';

- lack of widely available information on the success rates and side-effects of participating in assisted conception programmes.

The theoretical and policy choices are not between a liberal view of women as free agents actively pursing their own goals and a conception of women as subjugated by male domination and exploited by medical science. The challenge is to incorporate an understanding of individual women's concrete situations and experiences within broader structural conditions, including the organization and power of the medical profession. As Rosalind Petchesky suggests:

> The critical issue for feminists is not so much the content of women's choices, or even the 'right to choose', as it is the social and material conditions under which choices are made. ... The fact that individuals themselves do not determine the social framework in which they act does not nullify their choices nor their moral capacity to make them. (Petchesky, 1980, pp.674, 675)

Arguments that motherhood norms are social and that we live in a pro-natalist culture are not synonymous with suggestions that the experiences and perceptions of infertile individuals are not real. To view infertility as a medical construction and the desire to have a biologically related child as a social product is not to deny to the consequences of such definitions. While it is essential to critique the process of 'medicalization' and to be continually wary of the development of technologies and interventions that aim to alleviate infertility, these 'treatments' do not determine totally the capacity of individuals to make choices. That the available options are limited, restrictive and may involve medical intervention does not deny some scope for negotiation, bargaining and resistance. The portrayal of women who participate in conceptive technology programmes as acting contrary to their own interests suggests they experience false consciousness – a problematic argument which further deviantizes their status.

The development of assisted reproduction programmes and the 'medicalization' of infertility raise some of the most difficult questions for feminist theory and practice. Arguments about reproductive autonomy that have worked, at least in the short term, in the abortion controversies have become highly problematic and tenuous in the context of IVF programmes. The debates around the so-called 'new reproductive technologies' also highlight the difficulties, indeed impossibility, of speaking of women as an undifferentiated group with shared interests.

Notes

1 This chapter is part of a larger project, on the legal regulation of reproductive technology, funded by an Australian Research Council grant.
2 The terms 'reproduction', 'procreation' and 'conception' are used interchangeably and synonymously. Some of the procedures usually included in the term 'new reproductive technologies' are not new and others, for example artificial insemination, involve little technology.
3 In this study, infertility was due to a female reproductive impairment in nine cases, to a male reproductive impairment in four and to a combination of male and female in six. In the remaining three cases, the source of the infertility had not been identified (Greil *et al.* 1988, p.176).
4 A master status is an all-encompassing but single attribute which largely defines a person's whole identity (Hughes, 1945, p.353).
5 This research involved a pretested, standardized, open-ended interview with 30 involuntarily childless women; a further 41 involuntarily childless women completed a questionnaire identical to the interview schedule. A total of 12 respondents were fertile themselves but married to infertile men (Miall, 1986, p.271).

References

Aubert, V. and S.L. Messinger (1958), 'The Criminal and the Sick', *Inquiry*, **1**, 137.

Becker, G. and R.D. Nachtigall (1992), 'Eager for Medicalization: The Social Production of Infertility as a Disease', *Sociology of Health and Illness*, **14**, 456.

Becker, H. (1963), *Outsiders*, New York: The Free Press.

Bennett, B. (1991), 'Pregnant Women and the Duty to Rescue: A Feminist Response to the Fetal Rights Debate', *Law in Context*, **9**, 70.

Bennett, B. (1993), 'Gamete Donation, Reproductive Technology and the Law', *Law in Context*, **11**, 41.

Blank, R.H. (1990), *Regulating Reproduction*, New York: Columbia University Press.

Bonnicksen, A.L. (1989), *In Vitro Fertilization: Building Policy from Laboratories to Legislatures*, New York: Columbia University Press.

Boreham, G. (1992), 'IVF Method May Screen Embryos', *The Age*, 18 January, 3.

Callan, V. and J.F. Hennessey (1988), 'Emotional Aspects and Support in *in vitro* Fertilization and Embryo Transfer Programs', *Journal of In Vitro Fertilization and Embryo Transfer*, **5**, 290.

Cant, S. (1992), 'Governments Brought to Book by Frustrated IVF Innovator: Technology Leaving Legislators Behind', *The Weekend Australian*, 16–17 May, 43.

Carlen, P. and A. Worrall (1987), 'Introduction', in P. Carlen and A. Worrall (eds), *Gender, Crime and Justice*, Milton Keynes: Open University.

Chesler, P. (1986), *Mothers on Trial: The Battle for Children and Custody*, Seattle: Seal Press.

Conrad, P. and P. Schneider (1980), *Deviance and Medicalization: From Badness to Sickness*, St Louis: C.V. Mosby.

Dawson, K. and P. Singer (1990), 'Should Fertile People Have Access to In Vitro Fertilisation?', *British Medical Journal*, **300**, 167.

DeGama, K. (1993), 'A Brave New World? Rights Discourse and a Politics of Reproductive Autonomy', *Journal of Law and Society*, **20**, 114.

Diduck, A. (1993), 'Legislating Ideologies of Motherhood', *Social & Legal Studies*, **2**, 461.

Ehrenreich, B. and D. English (1978), *For Her Own Good: 150 Years of the Experts' Advice to Women*, London: Pluto Press.
Eisenstein, Z. (1988), *The Female Body and the Law*, Berkeley: University of California Press.
Eisenstein, Z. (1991), 'Privatizing the State: Reproductive Rights, Affirmative Action and the Problem of Democracy', *Frontiers*, **12**, 98.
Erikson, K.T. (1966), *Wayward Puritans: A Study in the Sociology of Deviance*, New York: Macmillan.
Ferree, M.M. (1990), 'Beyond Separate Spheres: Feminism and Family Research', *Journal of Marriage and the Family*, **52**, 866.
Fineman, M.L. (1991), 'Images of Mothers in Poverty Discourses', *Duke Law Journal*, 274.
Freidson, E. (1966), 'Disability as Social Deviance', in M. Sussman (ed.), *Sociology and Rehabilitation*, Washington, D.C.: American Sociological Association.
Freidson, E. (1988), *Profession of Medicine: A Study of the Sociology of Applied Knowledge*, Chicago: University of Chicago Press.
Gallagher, E.B. (1976), 'Lines of Reconstruction and Extension in the Parsonian Sociology of Illness', *Social Science and Medicine*, **10**, 207.
Gallagher, J. (1987), 'Eggs, Embryos and Foetuses: Anxiety and the Law,' in M. Stanworth (ed.), *Reproductive Technologies: Gender, Motherhood and Medicine*, Oxford: Polity.
Gaze, B. (1992), 'Controlling Medical Science: Reproductive Technology, Infertility and the Position of Women', *Law in Context*, **10**, 29.
Goffman, E. (1963), *Stigma: Notes on the Management of Spoiled Identity*, Harmondsworth: Penguin.
Greil, A. (1992), 'A Secret Stigma: The Analogy Between Infertility and Chronic Illness and Disability', *Advances in Medical Sociology*, **2**, 17.
Greil, A., T.A. Leitko and K.L. Porter (1988), 'Infertility: His and Hers', *Gender & Society*, **2**, 172.
Harrison, M. (1987), 'Social Construction of Mary Beth Whitehead', *Gender & Society*, **1**, 300.
Hughes, E.C. (1945), 'Dilemmas and Contradictions of Status', *American Journal of Sociology*, **50**, 353.
Johnsen, D. (1986), 'The Creation of Fetal Rights: Conflicts with Women's Constitutional Rights to Liberty, Privacy and Equal Protection', *Yale Law Journal*, **95**, 599.
Johnsen, D. (1987), 'A Threat to Pregnant Women's Autonomy', *Hastings Center Report*, 33.
Klein, R.D. (ed.) (1989), *Infertility: Women Speak Out About Their Experiences of Reproductive Medicine*, London: Pandora.
Legislative Council of South Australia (1987), *Parliamentary Debates*, 24 November, Adelaide: Government Printer.
Legislative Council of Victoria (1984), *Parliamentary Debates*, 11 October, Melbourne: Government Printer.
Legislative Council of Victoria (1995), *Parliamentary Debates*, 7 June, Melbourne: Government Printer.
Lorber, J. (1988), '*In Vitro* Fertilization and Gender Politics', *Women & Health*, **13**, 117.
Lorber, J. (1989), 'Choice, Gift, or Patriarchal Bargain? Women's Consent to *In Vitro* Fertilization in Male Infertility', *Hypatia*, **4**, 23.
Lorber, J. and L. Bandlamudi (1993), 'The Dynamics of Marital Bargaining in Male Infertility', *Gender & Society*, **7**, 32.
MacKinnon, C.A. (1987), *Feminism Unmodified*, Cambridge, Mass.: Harvard University Press.

MacKinnon, C.A. (1989), *Toward a Feminist Theory of the State*, Cambridge, Mass.: Harvard University Press.
Miall, C. (1985), 'Perceptions of Informal Sanctioning and the Stigma of Involuntary Childlessness', *Deviant Behavior*, **6**, 383.
Miall, C. (1986), 'The Stigma of Involuntary Childlessness', *Social Problems*, **33**, 268.
Mullens, A. (1990), *Missed Conceptions: Overcoming Infertility*, Toronto: McGraw-Hill Ryerson.
National Abortion Rights Action League (NARAL) (1989), 'Amicus Brief for *Webster v. Reproductive Health Services*', *Yale Journal of Law and Liberation*, **1**, 101.
National Perinatal Statistics Unit (1992), *Assisted Conception: Australia and New Zealand 1990*, Sydney: Fertility Society of Australia.
Note (1988), 'Maternal Rights and Fetal Wrongs: The Case Against the Criminalization of "Fetal Abuse"', *Harvard Law Review*, **101**, 994.
Office of Technology Assessment (1988), *Infertility: Medical and Social Choices*, Washington, DC: US Government Printing Office.
Paltrow, L.M. (1985), 'Book Review: *Test-Tube Women: What Future for Motherhood?*', *Women's Rights Law Reporter*, **8**, 303.
Parsons, T. (1951a), 'Illness and the Role of the Physician: A Sociological Perspective', *American Journal of Orthopsychiatry*, **21**, 452.
Parsons, T. (1951b), *The Social System*, Glencoe: The Free Press.
Petchesky, R.P. (1980), 'Reproductive Freedom: Beyond "A Women's Right to Choose"', *Signs: Journal of Women in Culture and Society*, **5**, 661.
Petchesky, R.P. (1986), *Abortion and Woman's Choice: The State, Sexuality and Reproductive Freedom*, London: Verso.
Petersen, K.A. (1993), *Abortion Regimes*, Aldershot: Dartmouth.
Polikoff, N. (1982), 'Why Are Mothers Losing? A Brief Analysis of Criteria Used in Child Custody Determinations', *Women's Rights Law Reporter*, **7**, 235.
Reif, F. and A. Strauss (1965), 'The Impact of Rapid Discovery Upon the Scientist's Career', *Social Problems*, **12**, 297.
Roach Anleu, S.L. (1992), 'Surrogacy: For Love But Not For Money?', *Gender & Society*, **6**, 30.
Roach Anleu, S.L. (1995), *Deviance, Conformity and Control*, 2nd edn, Melbourne: Longman Cheshire.
Roach Anleu, S.L. (1996), 'The Legal Regulation of Medical Science', unpublished ms, The Flinders University of South Australia.
Rothman, B.K. (1983), 'Midwives in Transition: The Structure of a Clinical Revolution', *Social Problems*, **30**, 262.
Rothman, B.K. (1984), 'The Meanings of Choice in Reproductive Technology', in R. Arditti, R. Duelli Klein and S. Minden (eds), *Test-Tube Women: What Future for Motherhood?*, London: Routledge.
Rothman, B.K. (1986), *The Tentative Pregnancy: Prenatal Diagnosis and the Future of Motherhood*, New York: Viking.
Rothman, B.K. (1989), *Recreating Motherhood*, New York: Norton.
Rowland, R. (1985), 'A Child At Any Price? An Overview of Issues in the Use of the New Reproductive Technologies and the Threat to Women', *Women's Studies International Forum*, **8**, 539.
Rowland, R. (1987a), 'Making Women Visible in the Embryo Experimentation Debate', *Bioethics*, **1**, 179.
Rowland, R. (1987b), 'Technology and Motherhood: Reproductive Choice Reconsidered', *Signs: Journal of Women in Culture and Society*, **12**, 512.
Rutnam, R. (1991), 'IVF in Australia: Towards a Feminist Technology Assessment', *Issues in Reproductive and Genetic Engineering*, **4**, 143.
Sandelowski, M. (1990a), 'Failures of Volition: Female Agency and Infertility in Historical Perspective', *Signs: Journal of Women in Culture and Society*, **15**, 475.

Sandelowski, M. (1990b), 'Fault Lines: Infertility and Imperiled Sisterhood,' *Feminist Studies*, **16**, 33.
Sandelowski, M., D. Holditch-Davis and B.G. Harris (1990), 'Living the Life: Explanations of Infertility', *Sociology of Health and Illness*, **12**, 195.
Schur, E.M. (1984), *Labeling Women Deviant: Gender, Stigma and Social Control*, New York: Random House.
Scritchfield, S.A. (1989), 'The Social Construction of Infertility; From Private Matter to Social Concern', in J. Best (ed.), *Images of Issues: Typifying Contemporary Social Problems*, New York: Aldine de Gruyter.
Smart, C. (1976), *Women, Crime and Criminology: A Feminist Critique*, London: Routledge & Kegan Paul.
Smart, C. (1991), 'Penetrating Women's Bodies: The Problem of Law and Medical Technology', in P. Abbott and C. Wallace (eds), *Gender, Power and Sexuality*, London: Macmillan.
Stanworth, M. (1987), 'Reproductive Technologies and the Deconstruction of Motherhood', in M. Stanworth (ed.), *Reproductive Technologies: Gender, Motherhood and Medicine*, Oxford: Polity.
Stanworth, M. (1990), 'Birth Pangs: Conceptive Technologies and the Threat to Motherhood', in M. Hirsch and E.F. Keller (eds), *Conflicts in Feminism*, New York: Routledge.
Strickler, J. (1992), 'The New Reproductive Technology: Problem or Solution?', *Sociology of Health and Illness*, **14**, 111.
Sullivan, D. and R. Weitz (1988), *Labor Pains: Modern Midwives and Home Birth*, New Haven: Yale University Press.
Sykes, G.M. and D. Matza (1957), 'Techniques of Neutralization: A Theory of Delinquency', *American Sociological Review*, **22**, 664.
Taub, N. (1989), 'Feminist Tensions: Concepts of Motherhood and Reproductive Choice', in J. Offerman-Zuckerberg (ed.), *Gender in Transition*, New York: Plenum.
Thorne, B. with M. Yalom (eds) (1982), *Rethinking the Family: Some Feminist Questions*, New York: Longman.
Veevers, J. (1979), 'Voluntary Childlessness: A Review of Issues and Evidence', *Marriage and Family Review*, **2**, 1.
Veevers, J. (1980), *Childless by Choice*, Toronto: Butterworths.
Waller, L. (1992), 'Australia: The Law and Infertility – The Victorian Experience', in S.A.M. McLean (ed.), *Law Reform and Human Reproduction*, Aldershot: Dartmouth.
Wikler, N.J. (1986), 'Society's Response to the New Reproductive Technologies: The Feminist Responses', *Southern California Law Review*, **59**, 1043.

Cases

Planned Parenthood of Southeastern Pennsylvania v. *Casey* 120 L Ed 2d 674 (1992).
Roe v. *Wade* 410 US 113 (1973).
Webster v. *Reproductive Health Services* 109 S.Ct. 3040 (1989).

6 Gamete Donation, Reproductive Technology and the Law

BELINDA BENNETT[1]

The development and availability of the new reproductive technologies have challenged traditional concepts of 'family' while the meaning of 'parent' has been unravelled into its constituent elements. A genetic parent may or may not be a social parent and involved in raising his/her child; a genetic mother is no longer necessarily the gestational mother and neither may be the child's social mother. Of course, the separation of genetic and social parenthood is not unique to the new reproductive technologies. For a variety of reasons, including adoption and divorce, many children have one or more parents to whom they are not genetically related (Charo, 1992–93, p.22). To a large degree, it is the potential for using donated sperm and ova in assisted conception procedures that has opened up new possibilities and that has forced us to rethink the meaning of 'parent' and 'family'.

It is somewhat paradoxical, then, that while the new reproductive technologies have challenged our understandings of parenthood, regulatory responses to reproductive technology have ensured that the families formed with the assistance of this technology conform to the image of the traditional nuclear family. Concern over maintaining the anonymity of gamete donors and the legitimacy of children born as a result of donated gametes, along with rules restricting access to the technologies, have ensured that traditional notions of the family have not been unduly disturbed.

Infertility has been said to affect 10 per cent of couples, although infertility rates appear to vary in different societies (NBCC, 1991, pp.7–8). The use of reproductive technology has now become a popular option for infertile people. Figures published by the National Perinatal Statistics Unit (NPSU) have reported that in Australia and New Zealand there were 15764 live births from IVF and GIFT (gamete intra fallopian transfer) pregnancies from 1979–1993 (Lancaster *et al.*, 1995, tables 51, 79). 295 IVF pregnancies used donated oocytes, while 978 IVF pregnancies used donated sperm (Lancaster *et al.*, 1995, table 29). Clearly, there is considerable demand for the services provided by infertility clinics. The enactment in some Australian states of legislation regulating these services,[2] and the provision of public funding for infertility treatment, indicate government recognition of the legitimacy of using reproductive technology as a means of having a child.

Protecting the Family Secret

Legal discourses have always involved a preoccupation with paternity (Smart, 1987). Paternity of legitimate children has historically been important in assigning ownership of property and securing succession (ibid., p.99). Historically, the children of a marriage were presumed to be legitimate (ibid., p.104), thus creating a link between children and their fathers and ensuring the support of dependent children (ibid., p.105). Indeed, as Smart argues, it was paternity defined through marriage rather than biological realities which structured the father–child relationship (ibid., p.101).

Reproductive technologies have raised new issues of paternity, with the focus once again being on marriage rather than biology. At common law, a woman who gave birth to a child conceived with the use of donated sperm (that is, not her husband's sperm) gave birth to an illegitimate child (Smart, 1987, p.106; Warnock, 1984, para.4.9). Over time, such stigmatization of the child conceived through donor insemination (DI) came to be seen as unfair since DI children were wanted by their parents and DI was seen to assist the creation of nuclear families rather than undermine them (Smart, 1987, pp.106–7). A distinction developed between the 'wanted' DI child and other illegitimate children, who were presumed to be 'unwanted' (ibid., pp.107–8).

Many jurisdictions have now enacted legislation which provides that, if a married woman is artificially inseminated with donated sperm with her husband's consent, there is a presumption that her husband, and not the sperm donor, is the father of any resultant child (Atherton, 1986, pp.375–6; Gamble, 1990, p.132; Otlowski, 1990, pp.[2]–[3]).[3] Enabling the infertile male partner to appear as the father of the DI child is seen as being in the interests of the newly-formed family. For the Warnock Committee, it was regarded as 'consistent with the husband's assuming all parental rights and duties with regard to the child' (Warnock, 1984, para.4.25). In certain circumstances, however, the presumption of paternity may be rebuttable. Since the sperm donor is presumed not to be the child's father, if the woman's husband has not consented to the procedure, if the woman is not married, or if a man's frozen sperm is used posthumously, the issues of paternity become more complex and the child may be left without a legal father (Morgan and Lee, 1991, pp.154–6; Warnock, 1984, para.4.24; Otlowski, 1990, pp.[7]–[10].

The presumption of paternity legislatively introduced in response to DI indicates a need to establish clear relationships between men and children (Dewar, 1989, pp.126–7; Smart, 1987, p.114). However, as Dewar has noted, defining paternity in terms of marriage is a response which 'avoids inquiring into the biological facts altogether' (Dewar, 1989, p.127). The maintenance of secrecy, the presumption of paternity and the anonymity of donors in the DI context facilitate the perpetuation of a fiction which obscures the gap between biological and social paternity. By permitting such a fiction, legal discourses support the notion of the family formed by donation as 'normal' (Haimes, 1990), while the anonymity of the donor ensures that the fiction will not be exposed since the family's 'non-conformity cannot be manifested in the form of a real, living person' (ibid., p.169).

Secrecy, including anonymity of sperm donors, has been one of the hallmarks of DI. This is perhaps unsurprising, given the secrecy historically associated with adoption (Achilles, 1992, pp.28–9; NBCC, 1988; O'Donovan, 1989). Concerns over stigmatizing the DI child and family (Achilles, 1992, p.28; NBCC, 1988, pp.15–16; O'Donovan, 1989, pp.106–7; Rowland, 1983, p.83) and the emotional difficulties of publicly acknowledging male infertility (Achilles, 1992, p.28; NBCC, 1988, p.16; O'Donovan, 1989, pp.106–7; Rowland, 1983, pp.82–3) have all contributed to providing incentives for secrecy in DI. Indeed, some parents may never tell the child about the biological realities of her or his conception (Achilles, 1992, pp.28–31; NBCC, 1988, p.17; O'Donovan, 1989, p.106; Rowland, 1983, pp.81–3). For those parents, their secret is protected by virtue of the presumption of paternity and donor anonymity. For those who do tell, the information able to be passed on to the child may be limited by rules ensuring the anonymity of the donor.

Ova Donors and Surrogate Mothers

The use of donated ova raises many of the same issues that arise in the context of DI. Indeed, the Warnock Committee concluded, 'It is both logical and consistent that the law should treat egg donation in the same way as AID' and recommended 'that egg donation be accepted as a recognised technique in the treatment of infertility' (1984, para.6.6). The Committee made this recommendation after it had concluded that, 'since we have accepted AID and IVF it would be illogical not to accept egg donation, notwithstanding the relatively minor surgical risks to the donor inherent in egg recovery' (1984, para.6.6).

However, it is arguable that there are significant differences between sperm and ova donations. Collection of ova for donation is obviously more difficult than the collection of sperm, since ova are relatively few in number and their collection requires surgical procedures to be performed on the donor (Waller Committee, 1983a, para.2.11). In addition, since ova donors are often women in infertility programmes, there are often differences in the fertility of sperm and ova donors as 'the oocyte donor is likely to be infertile herself while sperm donors are fertile men' (Roach Anleu, 1990, p.45).

While one ought not to assume that women will be unwilling to donate ova (Birke *et al.*, 1990, p.100), it will be undesirable to some women, particularly if the ova are to be used for embryo experimentation (ibid., 1990, p.100; Rowland, 1992, pp.92–3). It is therefore important to assess the circumstances within which the donation takes place, in order to ensure that the consent to donation is real and, in particular, that it is fully informed. Concern has been expressed over the pressure potential donors may feel to donate (Roach Anleu, 1990, p.45; Rowland, 1992, p.92). The Waller Committee noted that 'there may be instances where a woman in the IVF programme cannot be considered as a genuine donor, because of a reluctance to disappoint doctors, scientists and other patients in the programme' (1983b, para.3.24). Accordingly, the Committee recommended that counselling be provided prior to consent to the use of ova and that the consent be given before the procedure to collect the eggs is performed (ibid., para.3.25).

Unlike paternity, maternity has traditionally been of little concern in legal discourses. In part this is due to the fact that, unlike paternity, maternity has not been concerned with the status of children (Roach Anleu, 1990, p.49; Rowland, 1992, pp.268–9; Smart, 1987, p.115). Since paternity was established through marriage (Smart, 1987, pp.103–4), 'the "illegitimate" child, in English and Australian common law, was defined as a child of no one' (Rowland, 1992, p.268). It is only with the development of the new reproductive technologies that maternity has become an uncertain thing (Smart, 1987, p.100).

Like their male counterparts, ova donors are rendered invisible by the circumstances and legal rules surrounding donation. For the ova donor, her role is obscured by legislative provisions in almost all Australian jurisdictions which make provisions as to the maternity of a child conceived artificially such that the birth mother is either to be regarded as or is presumed to be the child's mother (Otlowski,

1990, p.[3]). In New South Wales, there has been no presumption as to maternity, since the legislation only addressed paternity (Atherton, 1986, pp.383–4; Otlowski, 1990, p.[3]) however, when it commences operation, the Status of Children Act 1996 in New South Wales will resolve this anomaly by providing that the birth mother is the legal mother. Legal arrangements ensure that the ova donor, like the sperm donor, is largely invisible to the infertile couple.

The situation is more complex when surrogate motherhood is considered. Where a child is born as a result of artificial insemination in a surrogacy arrangement, the birth ('surrogate') mother rather than the commissioning mother would be the legal mother of the child and, if the surrogate's husband consented to her artificial insemination, there would be a presumption that he, rather than the commissioning father, was the father of the child (Atherton, 1986, p.379; Otlowski, 1990, pp.[5]–[6]). This might be the case even if the commissioning parents had provided both the sperm and the ovum; that is, if the 'surrogate' mother was not the child's genetic mother (Otlowski, 1990, pp.[10]–[13]).

Clearly, presumptions as to parentage make the surrogate mother considerably more visible than the ova donor. However, the language used to describe surrogacy promotes invisibility rather than visibility. Even the use of the term 'surrogate' to denote the birth mother, who is often the genetic as well as the gestational mother, rather than the social mother, ensures that the 'surrogate' is firmly placed outside the family formed by the infertile (commissioning) couple and gives the whole arrangement a commercial sense (Ashe, 1988, p.528; Finley, 1989, p.888). As Pateman has argued, 'The qualifier "surrogate" indicates that the point of the contract is to render motherhood irrelevant and to deny that the "surrogate" is a mother' (1988, p.212).

Identifying the Gamete Donor

The anonymity of donors in the new reproductive technologies raises important issues about the rights and interests of the various parties involved: the donor, the recipient couple and the child born as a result. Anonymity of the sperm donor is generally regarded as being in the interests not only of the infertile couple, but also of the donor himself. The anonymity is often justified in terms of the donor's right to privacy and freedom from parental obligations towards the DI child, or inheritance claims by the child (NBCC, 1988, p.19; Rowland, 1983, p.85). Yet, as Gamble argues, the identification of the donor as the child's parent would not necessarily lead to the imposition of parental obligations on the donor since the courts are now primarily concerned with the child's best interests, rather than parental rights (Gamble, 1990, p.142). The donor's fear of the imposition of parental obligations must now be discounted as the result of legislative changes which presume that the sperm donor is not the child's legal father (ibid.).

The factors motivating sperm donors to donate are important, since it is often argued that potential donors will not donate if they are identifiable (NBCC, 1988, p.15; Warnock, 1984, para.4.22). Sperm donors appear to donate primarily for altruistic reasons (Achilles, 1992, p.21; Handelsman *et al.*, 1985), although other reasons, such as acquiring knowledge of their fertility, a desire to procreate or financial considerations may also be relevant (Achilles, 1992, p.21; Handelsman *et al.*, 1985). Yet there is relatively little information about the willingness of sperm donors to be identified. In one study, 67 per cent of donors opposed disclosure of identifying information to the DI child (Handelsman *et al.*, 1985), while in another study, 42 per cent indicated a willingness to donate if their name was given to the infertile couple, and 60 per cent did not mind being contacted by their DI child when the child was over the age of 18 (Rowland, 1983; for discussion of these and other studies, see Achilles, 1992, p.22; NBCC, 1988, p.20). The long-term effect of sperm donors being identifiable appears unclear (Achilles, 1992, pp.22–3).

While the benefits of donor anonymity are understandable from the perspective of the infertile couple and the donor, and the reasons motivating donors are certainly important to discussions of donor identification, it is important to remember the point of view of the DI child. Annas suggests that the interests of the donor have been placed above those of the DI child (Annas, 1980). The interests that the infertile couple and the donor may have in maintaining anonymity and secrecy and the interests that the child may have in knowledge of the fact of DI and identification of the donor raise many issues similar to those raised in discussions about adoption (Haimes, 1988; NBCC, 1988; O'Donovan, 1988). While there are both similarities and differences between adoption and assisted conception, the knowledge acquired from experiences with adoption does appear highly relevant to the new reproductive technologies (Haimes, 1988, pp.47–9). These new technologies present us with many old and familiar issues, albeit in a slightly different form. Indeed, as Haimes has pointed out, 'in adoption the dominant way of thinking *used to be* what the current thinking is now on artificial reproduction' (ibid., p.49).

Experience with adoption has demonstrated the desirability for honesty within the family and that secrecy about a child's genetic origins may do harm to the relationship between parents and their child (Haimes, 1988, pp.50–51; NBCC, 1988, pp.4–5; O'Donovan, 1988, p.37). Certainly, experience with adoption would tend to suggest the child may have a strong interest in acquiring knowledge of her or his genetic origins (Ley, 1992; O'Donovan, 1988). Adopted children have been said to experience 'genealogical bewilderment' or confusion about their origins (Sants, 1964; NBCC, 1988, p.5) and relinquishing mothers to experience a sense of loss for many years after the adoption (NBCC, 1988, pp.7–8; NSWLRC, 1992, para.2.16). For the child whose genetic parent is a donor, there may be a similar interest in having knowledge of genetic origins (Ley, 1992; NBCC, 1988, pp.17–18). Furthermore, the interest that a DI child may have in knowledge of genetic parentage goes beyond a search for family links. Knowledge of family history of medical conditions can be very important and its importance is only likely to increase as our knowledge of genetics grows (O'Donovan, 1988, pp.29–30). Yet, even if a child is aware that one of her or his parents is a donor, it may only be possible to gain access to non-identifying information about the donor. While this situation may seem justified in terms of the interests of infertile couples and donors outlined above, it does leave reproductive technology in a somewhat anomalous position when compared to the current trend towards increasing access to information for adoptees.

Government committees dealing with DI have recognized the need for openness and information in donor programmes. Although the Warnock Committee stated that 'there is a need to maintain the absolute anonymity of the donor' (1984, para.4.22), it also stated that, at the age of 18, the DI child 'should have access to the basic information about the donor's ethnic origin and genetic health' (ibid., para.4.21). In Australia there have been a number of reports on various aspects of reproductive technology.[4] In Victoria, the Waller Committee supported 'honesty and integrity within the family' (1983b, para.3.37) and recommended counselling for the infertile couple to 'make it as easy and natural as possible for them, in their family, to tell their child about her or his origins' (ibid., para.3.35). The Waller Committee recommended that it 'be unlawful to use donor gametes in IVF in such a way as to confuse those concerned about the genetic background of any child born' (ibid., para.3.37). Accordingly, the Committee recommended the prohibition of mixing sperm or transferring embryos from more than one source (ibid.) and also recommended the maintenance of a register of information about donors (ibid., para.3.32). The Family Law Council's Report also advocated openness and honesty (1985, para.6.3.10) and recommended statutory provisions that a child under 18 years be allowed access to non-identifying information and that access to identifying information be available to adults (ibid., para.6.3.11). The Report recommended that the infertile couple receive counselling 'as to the importance to their child of honesty, openness and information as to their family origins and conception' (ibid., para.6.3.12) and that gamete donors be counselled on 'the importance to the child/adult of information on origins, and of the implications of later access to such information' (ibid.).

While accepting the desirability of 'openness, integrity and honesty in all relationships' (NSWLRC, 1986, para.13.16), the New South Wales Law Reform Commission in its 1986 Report, *Human Artificial Insemination*, decided there was no justification for deciding that DI was such a special case that honesty and openness should be legislatively enforced (1986, para.13.16). As the Commission stated, 'parents may be honest and open with their children and yet decide that it is not in the children's interests to be given all information regarding their origins' (ibid., para.13.9). In the Commission's view, there were significant differences between adoption and DI, since the DI child is generally raised by her or his biological mother and her consenting husband (ibid., paras.13.4, 13.17) and Australian reports which relied on an analogy between adoption and DI had failed to address this difference (ibid., para.13.17). The Commission recommended that there should be no right of access to identifying information and that such information should be released by a record keeper only if 'the subject of the information formally consents' (ibid., para.13.23). However, the Commission did recommend the enactment of a statutory entitlement allowing access to non-identifying information where the applicant showed 'good cause' (ibid., para.13.23). In its 1988 Report on *in vitro* fertilization, the Commission recommended that IVF children, gamete donors and others be granted access to non-identifying information if they are able to show 'good cause' and with the agreement of the record keeper or the proposed statutory authority (NSWLRC, 1988, Recommendation 30). The Commission recommended that there should be no right of access to identifying information about a party to IVF and that such information could only be divulged in certain limited circumstances (ibid., Recommendation 31). While the Commission's recommendations did not allow a right of access to identifying information, the Commission acknowledged the trends concerning access to information in adoption and 'the likelihood that at a future time the perception of the best interests of the child may alter' (ibid., para.5.59) and recommended that the proposed legislation be subject to review (ibid., Recommendation 32). More recently, the Commission has again opened the question of access to information on reproductive technology. As part of its review of the Adoption of Children Act 1965 (NSW) the Commission has surveyed the issues raised by surrogacy and reproductive technology in the context of adoption and adoption legislation (NSWLRC, 1993; 1994).

The former National Bioethics Consultative Committee (NBCC) also considered access to information in its 1989 report on reproductive technology. Like other committees, the NBCC expressed support for honesty in relationships (1989, p.25). The Committee recommended that information and counselling be given to donors and the infertile couple prior to entering and during the donation programme (ibid., p.32), with the parties giving formal consent to conditions for gaining access to information when entering the programme (ibid.). Under the NBCC's recommendations, any person with a legitimate interest could gain access to non-identifying information upon written application to the relevant registry (ibid.). In relation to identifying information, the Committee felt that community views were changing but recognized that little research had been done on the attitudes of (potential) users of donor programmes (ibid., p.25). The Committee recommended the introduction of a short-term dual system supported by 'Educational programs, focusing on the desirability of openness and honesty within donor gamete programs' (ibid., p.25). Under the proposed dual scheme, gamete donors and social parents would choose one of two options prior to entering the programme. Under option 1, a person with a legitimate interest could make a written application for identifying information after the child had reached the age of majority. Option 2 contained the additional requirement that the person about whom the information was sought consented to the information being made available and that, if information was sought about offspring, the consent of the child's social parents was required (ibid., p.32). By vesting the authority to consent in the social parents, the Committee acknowledged that the child might not have been told about her or his conception and 'if the consent was sought from the offspring, that may be the first awareness the offspring has of these circumstances' (ibid., p.27). The NBCC also recommended that the operation of the proposed dual system be monitored and an evaluative review conducted after five years (ibid., p.32).

Despite widespread consideration of the legal implications of the new reproductive technologies in Australia, only Victoria, South Australia and Western Australia have enacted legislation regulating the technologies, although Victoria, Queensland, South Australia, Tasmania and the Australian Capital Territory have enacted legislation dealing with surrogacy. Victoria, South Australia and Western Australia each require that particulars relating to participants in assisted conception be recorded.[5] Each of these states also expressly provide for access to non-identifying information about parentage and in South Australia and Western Australia for access to identifying information in limited circumstances.[6] The new Infertility Treatment Act 1995 (Vic.) will, when the relevant provisions commence operation, permit access to identifying information about offspring and parentage in certain circumstances.[7] Guidelines issued by the National Health and Medical Research Council in Australia have also indicated the importance of knowledge of parentage:

> Children born from the use of ART procedures are entitled to knowledge of their biological parents. Any person, and his or her spouse or partner, donating gametes and consenting to their use in an ART procedure where the intention is that a child may be born must [...] be informed that children may receive identifying information about them. (NHMRC, 1996, para. 3.1.5).

Access to Treatment

Rules determining eligibility for access to infertility treatment programmes have a gatekeeping role which operates in addition to financial, geographic and cultural factors in influencing access (NBCC, 1991). Restricting access to married heterosexual couples ensures that the final products – couple plus child(ren) – match the structure of the traditional nuclear family. In Canada, the Royal Commission on New Reproductive Technologies recommended that

> Access to IVF treatment be determined on the basis of legitimate medical criteria, without discrimination on the basis of factors such as marital status, sexual orientation, or economic status. (Royal Commission on New Reproductive Technologies, 1993, p.554).

This position stands in stark contrast to that of the Warnock Committee in Britain in the 1980s. The Warnock Committee expressed the view that DI is 'a legitimate form of treatment for those infertile couples for whom it might be appropriate' (1984, para.4.16) and that 'as a general rule it is better for children to be born into a two-parent family, with both father and mother' (ibid., para.2.11). This concern for the welfare of the child appears in s.13(5) of the Human Fertilisation and Embryology Act 1990 (UK):

> A woman shall not be provided with treatment services unless account has been taken of the welfare of any child who may be born as a result of the treatment (including the need of that child for a father), and of any other child who may be affected by the birth.[8]

In Victoria, South Australia and Western Australia, access to DI, IVF and other forms of reproductive technology is limited to married couples (although de facto couples of long standing have access in certain circumstances) who are infertile or who are at risk of passing on a genetic condition to a naturally conceived child.[9]

It has been argued that the rules governing eligibility for treatment appear largely to ignore the reproductive rights of single and lesbian women (Cooper and Herman, 1991; Kritchevsky, 1981; Note, 1985). It may well be preferable for a child to be raised with her or his father, provided the home is a happy one. Yet, while the Warnock Committee noted that 'many believe that the interests of the child dictate that it should be born into a home where there is a loving, stable, heterosexual relationship' (1984, para.2.9), Golombok and Rust (1986, p.185) point out that the Warnock Report made no comment 'about the many children who are born into non-loving and unstable heterosexual relationships'. Furthermore, in these days of high divorce rates and single-parent families, many children already have limited contact with their fathers. Golombok and Rust (1986, p.183) ask, 'Is it really sensible to suppose that the one and a half million or so children who are growing up in Britain today without fathers will be damaged by this experience?'

Clearly, in the context of providing access to DI to lesbian women, there are concerns over the non-conformity of lesbian couples. There may be beliefs that such couples do not constitute a family, that they are 'deviant' or that they are not biologically infertile and therefore should be ineligible for treatment (discussed in Cooper and Herman, 1991, pp.57–8 and Somerville, 1982, pp.131–3). There may also be concerns that parental homosexuality may have adverse effects on a child raised in a lesbian household (discussed in Cooper and Herman, 1991, pp.54–5 and Somerville, 1982, p.133). Under Victoria's Infertility (Medical Procedures) Act 1984, it is an offence for anyone other than a medical practitioner to perform artificial insemination (s.17(1)). Sperm donations arranged on an informal basis, such as could be arranged between friends or acquaintances, may create further problems for the woman concerned. Since she would not have the benefit of donor anonymity, the possibility exists that the sperm donor could claim paternity and seek parental rights such as access (Craig, 1990, p.2; Gamble, 1990, pp.139–40). While the donor may not have a very strong claim in terms of the child's best interests, if the claim rests purely on the fact of genetic paternity, his position may be much stronger if a continuing relationship with the child can be established (Gamble, 1990, p.139).

There are no easy answers to the issue of infertility programmes for single and lesbian women. In some jurisdictions, however, current rules governing access to infertility programmes operate so as to reinforce the notion of the traditional nuclear family as the normal family structure, thus limiting reproductive options. As Roach Anleu has argued: 'Only certain people – excluding single, lesbian, divorced women – have access to the technologies and are able to exercise the *choice* of whether or not to participate' (1993, p.32).

My Own Child

Being a parent and having a genetically related child are of course not synonmous. There are a variety of ways in which individuals can act as parent to a child to whom they are not genetically related. Adoption is one example, while divorce and remarriage or cohabitation present other examples (Charo, 1992–93, p.2). Yet, for those who wish to have a child, there will often be the wish to have a child of their own. The idea of having a genetically related child will be something quite special.

One of the great advantages of reproductive technology, and perhaps one of the reasons for its great popularity, is that it allows infertile couples to have a child of their 'own' (Overall, 1987, pp.145, 150). The child conceived through reproductive technology can be the genetic child of at least one, and often both, of her or his social parents. Indeed, even if donated gametes are used, the presumptions as to parentage ensure that the child will pass as the child of both members of the couple. Obviously, this has enormous appeal for the infertile couple. With the help of some technological assistance at the conception, the child is 'theirs' in the same sense that a naturally conceived child is the child of her or his parents (ibid., pp.143–51). The parents may experience satisfaction or even joy at knowing that the child is their biological child, in watching the child grow and in seeing the development of family characteristics such as appearance (ibid., p.154). For women there may be a wish to experience the biological and nurturing aspects of mothering (ibid., p.152), while men in particular may feel a sense of importance in being genetically related to the child (ibid., p.151; Gaze, 1992, p.46). Clearly, many of these factors may motivate infertile couples to seek the assistance of reproductive technology.

It is also important not to underestimate the social pressures on couples to have a child that is genetically theirs. Given the value placed on fertility in our society, in which women are valued as mothers and which often associates fertility with virility (NBCC, 1988, p.16; Rowland, 1983, p.82), infertility may have a serious impact on the self-esteem of infertile women and men (Roach Anleu, 1993). The experience of infertility may be traumatic. It may cause a crisis in the life of infertile individuals or couples (Need, 1982, p.8; Oke and Aitken, 1982) and may lead to feelings of guilt, depression and isolation (Need, 1982, p.9; Oke and Aitken, 1982).

While some feminists have been critical of the new reproductive technologies (for discussion, see Charlesworth, 1995), it is also important to recognize the autonomy of women and men who decide to use the technologies and the ability of these individuals to make meaningful choices (Roach Anleu, 1993). It is important to ackowledge the interests of infertile women and couples in the use of the new reproductive technologies to achieve a pregnancy and to accept their interest in having a genetically related child if possible (Sandelowski, 1990). Genetic links are important to us. They play an important role in shaping our sense of identity (O'Donovan, 1988) and they have strong social and cultural significance (Charo, 1992–93). It is for these reasons that the potential of reproductive technology to offer hope in the face of crisis cannot be underestimated. Yet at the same time it is also important to evaluate critically the meaning of parenthood promoted by the use of reproductive technology as a solution to infertility, and the elevation of genetic over social parenting inherent in the technologies (Overall, 1987, p.151; Gaze, 1992, pp.46–7).

Rethinking the Family

As the discussion above shows, the use of donated gametes has been surrounded by secrecy. The presumption of paternity for the husband who consents to his wife's artificial insemination, as well as the anonymity of the sperm donor, ensure that the husband's infertility is hidden from general knowledge, and perhaps even from the child, unless the couple decide to disclose the matter themselves. The inability to obtain identifying information about the donor, and the general gap between the treatment of adoption and the use of donated gametes, further obscure the infertility. These factors, as well as the rules concerning eligibility for access to infertility programmes, make it clear that legal regulation of reproductive technology operates in such a way as to obscure the manner in which the family with artificially conceived children was formed, thus reinforcing its apparent normality (Haimes, 1990; O'Donovan, 1988, p.35).

While it would be premature, in the absence of further research, to argue for a right of access to identifying information on gamete donors, or to argue that the state has a duty to provide such information (for discussion, see NBCC, 1989, p.45; O'Donovan, 1988, pp.41–2), legal responses to reproductive technology do raise a number of questions about our conceptualizations of the family. The apparent need of infertile couples to ensure that their family appears 'normal' (Haimes, 1990; O'Donovan, 1988, p.35), when the definition of 'normal' appears to mean a heterosexual couple who are genetically related to their child(ren), is indicative of the narrowness of these conceptualizations.

Certainly, one cannot criticize infertile couples for wishing to use assisted conception techniques in order to help them to form a family in which their child is, to the extent possible, genetically related to her or his parents. Nor can infertile couples be criticized for wanting to maintain their privacy in relation to their child's conception. After all, the privacy of the family is still a very strong social norm, particularly on matters concerning reproduction. So, while we must respect the rights and decisions of infertile couples and individuals, we must also be wary of legal responses which reinforce secrecy and potentially make it difficult for children born as a result of assisted conception techniques to discover the identity of their genetic parents. We must also be wary of discourses surrounding the new reproductive technologies which seem to define the family *only* in terms of the nuclear family. There are, after all, many families today that do not conform to this mould. Claims by gay couples to be seen as family (Cossman, 1994) have joined rising divorce rates and increasing numbers of single-parent families in their challenge to the nuclear family and the idea that it is the norm. Furthermore, with the new reproductive technologies we are increasingly facing claims between different categories of parents as the courts and legislatures address issues such as surrogacy, disposition of frozen embryos and the availability of information about gamete donors (Charo, 1992–93). Rather than trying to decide who is, or is not, a child's parent we could, as Charo suggests, recognize that a child may have more than two biological parents (1992–93, p.20).

What is clear is that the family structures formed through reproductive technology are limited by legal regulations which rely on a traditional image of the nuclear family. The challenge presented by reproductive technology must surely be to respect the reproductive rights of the infertile to access to reproductive technology, while critically evaluating and seeking to transcend the narrow confines of the definition of 'family' within which reproductive technology operates.

Postscript

A number of recent cases in Australia have challenged restrictions limiting access to reproductive technology to married women. These cases have sparked public debate over access to reproductive technology. It is possible that there may be some changes in the law in response. For discussion of these recent trends see Jenni Millbank, '"We're Not a Hot Bread Kitchen": Discrimination and Fertility Services' (1997) *Alternative Law Journal* (forthcoming).

Notes

1 I wish to thank Iain Stewart for his helpful comments. An earlier version of this paper was published in *Law in Context*, **11**, 1993, p.41.
2 Infertility (Medical Procedures) Act 1984 (Vic.); Reproductive Technology Act 1988 (SA); Human Reproductive Technology Act 1991 (WA). It should be noted that the Victorian Infertility (Medical Treatment) Act 1984 will be replaced by the Infertility Treatment Act 1995 (Vic.). At the time of writing the main parts of the new Act had not commenced operation. The National Health and Medical Research Council has released, *Ethical Guidelines on Assisted Reproductive Technology* (Canberra, Australian Government Publishing Service, 1996) which will provide guidance in those states without legislation in this area.
3 Artificial Conception Act 1984 (NSW); Status of Children Act 1974 (Vic.); Family Relationships Act 1975 (SA); Status of Children Act 1974 (Tas.); Status of Children Act 1978 (Qld); Artificial Conception Act 1985 (WA); Artificial Conception Act 1985 (ACT); Status of Children Act 1978 (NT); Family Law Act 1975 (Cth), s. 60B. The Status of Children Act 1996 (NSW) will replace the Artificial Conception Act 1984 (NSW) when it commences operation.
4 For discussion of these reports and others, see Roach Anleu (1990, pp.41–4); Roach (1989).
5 Infertility (Medical Procedures) Act 1984 (Vic.), s.19; Reproductive Technology Act 1988 (SA), s.13(3); Reproductive Technology (Code of Ethical Clinical Practice) Regulations 1995 (SA), cl.28; Human Reproductive Technology Act 1991 (WA), ss.44, 45. The new Infertility Treatment Act 1995 (Vic.) will also require certain records to be kept: Infertility Treatment Act 1995 (Vic.), ss.62–7.
6 Infertility (Medical Procedures) Act 1984 (Vic.), ss. 20, 23; Reproductive Technology (Code of Ethical Clinical Practice Regulations 1995 (SA), cl28; Human Reproductive Technology Act 1991 (WA), s.46(3). The Infertility Treatment Act 1995 (Vic.) will also permit access to non-identifying information: Infertility Treatment Act 1995 (Vic.), ss.74–80.
7 Infertility Treatment Act 1995 (Vic.), ss.74–80.
8 Morgan and Lee (1991, pp.141–8, 194); for a discussion of the history of this section, see Cooper and Herman (1991, pp.46–7).
9 Infertility (Medical Procedures) Act 1984 (Vic.), ss.10(3), 11(3), 12(3), 13(3), 13A(3); Reproductive Technology Act 1988 (SA), s.13(3)(b); Human Reproductive Technology Act 1991 (WA), s.23. The new Victorian Act will also limit access to infertility treatment to married couples: Infertility Treatment Act 1995 (Vic.), s.8. For discussion of the legislative provisions dealing with access to treatment, see Skene and Szwarc (1991, p.6). For recent developments see Postscript.

References

Achilles, Rona (1992), *Donor Insemination: An Overview*, Ottawa: Royal Commission on New Reproductive Technologies.
Annas, George (1980), 'Fathers Anonymous: Beyond the Best Interests of the Sperm Donor', *Family Law Quarterly*, **XIV**, 1.
Ashe, Marie (1988), 'Law-Language of Maternity: Discourse Holding Nature in Contempt', *New England Law Review*, **22**, 521.
Atherton, Rosalind (1986), 'Artificially Conceived Children and Inheritance in New South Wales', *Australian Law Journal*, **60**, 374.
Birke, Lynda, Susan Himmelweit and Gail Vines (1990), *Tomorrow's Child: Reproductive Technologies in the 90s*, London: Virago Press.

Charlesworth, Max (1995), 'Whose Body? Feminist Views on Reproductive Technology', in P.A. Komesaroff (ed.), *Troubled Bodies: Critical Perspectives on Postmodernism, Medical Ethics and the Body*, Melbourne: Melbourne University Press, pp.125–41.

Charo, R. Alta (1992–3), 'And Baby Makes Three – or Four, or Five, or Six: Redefining the Family After the Reprotech Revolution', *Wisconsin Women's Law Journal*, **7**, 1.

Committee of Inquiry into Human Fertilisation and Embryology (Chair: Dame Mary Warnock) (1984), *Report*, London: Her Majesty's Stationery Office.

Committee to Consider the Social, Ethical and Legal Issues Arising from In Vitro Fertilization (Waller Committee) (1983a), *Issues Paper on Donor Gametes in IVF*, Melbourne.

Committee to Consider the Social, Ethical and Legal Issues Arising from In Vitro Fertilization (Waller Committee) (1983b), *Report on Donor Gametes in IVF*, Melbourne.

Cooper, Davina and Didi Herman (1991), 'Getting "the Family Right": Legislating Heterosexuality in Britain, 1986–1991', *Canadian Journal of Family Law*, **10**, 41.

Cossman, Brenda (1994), 'Family Inside/Out', *University of Toronto Law Journal*, **44**, 1.

Craig, Sue (1990), 'Issues Associated with Accessing Reproductive Technology Programs for Single Women and Gay Couples/Individuals', in National Bioethics Consultative Committee (ed.), *Access to Reproductive Technology: Workshop Proceedings*, 6–1, Australia.

Dewar, John (1989), 'Fathers in Law? The Case of AID', in R. Lee and D. Morgan (eds), *Birthrights: Law and Ethics at the Beginnings of Life*, London and New York: Routledge, pp.115–31.

Family Law Council (1985), *Creating Children: A Uniform Approach to the Law and Practice of Reproductive Technology in Australia*, Canberra: Australian Government Publishing Service.

Finley, Lucinda (1989), 'Breaking Women's Silence in Law: The Dilemma of the Gendered Nature of Legal Reasoning', *Notre Dame Law Review*, **64**, 886.

Gamble, Helen (1990), 'Fathers and the New Reproductive Technologies: Recognition of the Donor as Parent', *Australian Journal of Family Law*, **4**, 131.

Gaze, Beth (1992), 'Controlling Medical Science: Reproductive Technology, Infertility and the Position of Women', *Law in Context*, **10**, 29.

Golombok, Susan and John Rust (1986), 'The Warnock Report and Single Women: What About the Children?', *Journal of Medical Ethics*, **12**, 182.

Haimes, Erica (1988), '"Secrecy": What Can Artificial Reproduction Learn From Adoption?', *International Journal of Law and the Family*, **2**, 46.

Haimes, Erica (1990), 'Recreating the Family? Policy Considerations Relating to the "New" Reproductive Technologies', in Maureen McNeil, Ian Varcoe and Steven Yearley (eds), *The New Reproductive Technologies*, Basingstoke: Macmillan, pp.154–72.

Handelsman, David, Stewart Dunn, Ann Conway, Lyn Boylan and Robert Jansen (1985), 'Psychological and Attitudinal Profiles in Donors for Artificial Insemination', *Fertility and Sterility*, **43**, 95.

Kritchevsky, Barbara (1981), 'The Unmarried Woman's Right to Artificial Insemination: A Call For an Expanded Definition of Family', *Harvard Women's Law Journal*, **4**, 1.

Lancaster, Paul, Esther Shafir, Jishan Huang (1995), *Assisted Conception Australia and New Zealand 1992 and 1993*, Sydney: AIHW National Perinatal Statistics Unit.

Ley, Pauline (1992), 'Reproductive Technology – What Can We Learn From Adoption Experience?', in Phillip Swain and Shurlee Swain (eds), *To Search for Self: The Experience of Access to Adoption Information*, Sydney: Federation Press, pp.100–10.

Morgan, Derek and Robert Lee (1991), *Blackstone's Guide to the Human Fertilisation and Embryology Act 1990: Abortion and Embryo Research, the New Law*, London: Blackstone Press.
National Bioethics Consultative Committee (1988), *Access to Information: An Analogy Between Adoption and the Use of Gamete Donation. Background Paper and Appendix to the National Bioethics Consultative Committee Report: Reproductive Technology: Record Keeping and Access to Information; Birth Certificates and Birth Records of Offspring Born as a Result of Gamete Donation*, Australia.
National Bioethics Consultative Committee (1989), *Reproductive Technology: Record Keeping and Access to Information; Birth Certificates and Birth Records of Offspring Born as a Result of Gamete Donation*, Australia.
National Bioethics Consultative Committee (1991), *Access to Reproductive Technology: Final Report for the Australian Health Ministers' Conference*, Australia.
National Health and Medical Research Council (NHMRC) (1996), *Ethical Guidelines on Assisted Reproductive Technology* (Australian Government Publishing Service, Canberra).
Need, Jillian (1982), 'Psychological Aspects of Infertility: How the Medical Profession Sees Treatment Affecting People', in P. Harper and J. Aitken (eds), *A Child is Not the 'Cure' for Infertility: Workshop on Infertility*, Melbourne: Institute of Family Studies, pp.8–11.
New South Wales Law Reform Commission (NSWLRC) (1986), *Report: Artificial Conception – Human Artificial Insemination*, Sydney (LRC 49).
New South Wales Law Reform Commission (NSWLRC) (1988), *Report: Artificial Conception – In Vitro Fertilization*, Sydney (LRC 58).
New South Wales Law Reform Commission (NSWLRC) (1992), *Report: Review of the Adoption Information Act 1990*, Sydney (LRC 69).
New South Wales Law Reform Commission (NSWLRC) (1993), *Review of the Adoption of Children Act 1965 (NSW)*, Sydney (Issues Paper 9).
New South Wales Law Reform Commission (NSWLRC) (1994), *Review of the Adoption of Children Act 1965 (NSW)*, Sydney (Discussion Paper 34).
Note (1985), 'Reproductive Technology and the Procreation Rights of the Unmarried' *Harvard Law Review*, **98**, 669.
O'Donovan, Katherine (1988), 'A Right to Know One's Parentage?', *International Journal of Law and the Family*, **2**, 27.
O'Donovan, Katherine (1989), '"What Shall We Tell the Children?" Reflections on Children's Perspectives and the Reproduction Revolution', in R. Lee and D. Morgan (eds), *Birthrights: Law and Ethics at the Beginnings of Life*, London and New York: Routledge, pp.96–114.
Oke, Kay and Jan Aitken (1982), 'The Implications of IVF for the Individual', in M. Brumby (ed.), *Proceedings of the Conference: In Vitro Fertilization: Problems and Possibilities*, Melbourne: Monash Centre for Human Bioethics, pp.67–71.
Otlowski, Margaret (1990), 'NBCC Consultancy Report: Legal Parentage', in National Bioethics Consultative Committee, *Discussion Paper on Surrogacy 2 – Implementation*, Australia, Appendix 2, [No page numbers in original Appendix].
Overall, Christine (1987), *Ethics and Human Reproduction: A Feminist Analysis*, Boston: Allen & Unwin.
Pateman, Carole (1988), *The Sexual Contract*, Oxford: Polity Press.
Roach, Sharyn L. (1989), 'Donor Gametes, Record Keeping and Access to Information: An Analysis of Australian and Selected Overseas Reports', in National Bioethics Consultative Committee, *Reproductive Technology: Record Keeping and Access to Information; Birth Certificates and Birth Records of Offspring Born as a Result of Gamete Donation*, Australia, Appendix 4.
Roach Anleu, Sharyn (1990), 'New Procreative Technologies, Donor Gametes and

the Law's Response: Developments in Australia', *Australian Journal of Social Issues*, **25**, 40.
Roach Anleu, Sharyn (1993), 'Reproductive Autonomy: Infertility, Deviance and Conceptive Technology', *Law in Context*, **11**, 17.
Rowland, Robyn (1983), 'Social and Psychological Consequences of Secrecy in Artificial Insemination by Donor', in A. Cushan (ed.), *Proceedings of the Conference: Adoption and AID: Access to Information?*, Melbourne: Monash Centre for Human Bioethics, pp.79–91.
Rowland, Robyn (1992), *Living Laboratories: Women and Reproductive Technologies*, Sydney: Sun.
Royal Commission on New Reproductive Technologies (1993), *Proceed With Care: Final Report of the Royal Commission on New Reproductive Technologies* (Ottawa).
Sandelowski, Margarete (1990), 'Fault Lines: Infertility and Imperiled Sisterhood', *Feminist Studies*, **16**, 33.
Sants, H.J. (1964), 'Genealogical Bewilderment in Children With Substitute Parents', *British Journal of Medical Psychology*, **37**, 133.
Skene, Loane and Josef Szwarc (1991), 'Access to Reproductive Technology Programs: Discrimination Aspects', in National Bioethics Consultative Committee, *Access to Reproductive Technology: Final Report for the Australian Health Ministers' Conference*, Australia, Appendix 2.
Smart, Carol (1987), '"There is of Course the Distinction Dictated by Nature": Law and the Problem of Paternity', in M. Stanworth (ed.), *Reproductive Technologies: Gender, Motherhood and Medicine*, Minneapolis: University of Minnesota Press, pp.98–117.
Somerville, Margaret (1982), 'Birth Technology, Parenting and "Deviance"' *International Journal of Law and Psychiatry*, **5**, 123.

7 Life After Death? Legal and Ethical Considerations of Maintaining Pregnancy in Brain Dead Women

SARAH ELLISTON

Introduction

Since the late 1970s an increasing number of brain dead or comatose women have been, in the words of some members of the medical profession, 'aggressively managed' in order to maintain their pregnancies for as long as possible. The stated goal has been to maximize the chances of survival for the fetus. A variety of justifications has been offered for these forms of management: the wishes of the woman's next of kin, her partner, her presumed wishes, a matter of clinical judgement, the interests of the fetus or the state interest in the preservation of the fetus.

Recent developments in professional and legal guidelines in a number of jurisdictions suggest that the maintenance of pregnancy in such women should be mandatory, to the extent that even her own previously expressed wishes, such as advance directives, may be overruled. In other jurisdictions, the position is less clear and requires principled resolution. It will be argued here that, as a general proposition, continuing to 'treat' a corpse in the interests of any third party, actual or potential, is a grave invasion of the pregnant woman's autonomy. This is an issue requiring close consideration as it illustrates the manner in which the reproductive capacity of women is invoked in order to deny them the right to control their bodies, or to give others the power to control women's bodies without their agreement.

The aim of this chapter is to explore the legal and ethical issues surrounding the maintenance of pregnancy in brain dead women. Three models of the relationship between the pregnant woman and her fetus will be discussed in order to examine whether they provide a legal or ethical basis on which such pregnancies may be maintained. At present there is considerable academic interest in the way in which it is appropriate to view the relationship between a pregnant woman and her fetus. Attempts are being made to move away from the polarized arguments, seen perhaps most clearly in the continued acrimonious debates over abortion, in which the pregnant woman and her fetus are set up as adversaries. New ways of analysing the period of pregnancy, however, have more than mere academic value. Utilizing other models enables us to consider critically situations that have already arisen in practice and that may well arise with increased frequency in the future.

Which, if any, of the potential models is thought to be most appropriate may, as with many moral judgements, largely depend upon the value systems of the individual and the society and culture in which they live. However, I endeavour to explain and justify my own response in the hope of initiating further discussion of these issues.

Surprisingly little attention has been paid to post mortem pregnancies in the UK, although it has provoked more debate in other jurisdictions.[1] It will be argued below that, although continued support may be justified, its sole justification comes from what the pregnant woman has already said she would wish or from a coherent and thorough attempt to assess what she would have wanted. In my view, interventions outside this framework are unjustified and amount to a devaluing of, and a disrespect for, pregnant women by treating them as mere fetal containers, whose bodies can be legitimately used after their deaths as a means of support for the fetus. Such treatment would be to equate the support given to the fetus by the woman as akin to technological support and would disregard the status of the woman as an autonomous actor during her life and particularly during pregnancy. It would also conceptualize pregnancy merely as a 'condition' rather than as including the intention to parent which is generally part of a pregnancy, especially one which has been maintained to the point at which the fetus could be saved.

The Diagnosis of Brain Stem Death

Reports of attempts to maintain pregnancies in brain dead and comatose women have been filtering into medical journals and newspaper reports for some time (see note 1). The cases of pregnant women in coma are undoubtedly of concern, but will not be considered here since they pose rather different problems. This is due to the widespread acceptance that a distinction exists in both medical and legal terms between the patient who is diagnosed brain dead (or brain stem dead) and the patient who is severely brain damaged and has no prospect of recovery, but is still regarded as being alive, albeit comatose. This approach leads to important differences in the ways in which the body may be treated.

A diagnosis of death has consequences which must be considered in general terms before a consideration of the dead pregnant woman can begin. Although no legal definition of death has been given by the UK courts, they appear prepared to rely upon the current clinical definition of brain stem death. However, it is worth mentioning that the UK courts considering the question of the lawfulness of withdrawal of treatment from the brain dead have done so primarily in the context of whether the withdrawal of treatment would constitute a *novus actus interveniens*, breaking the chain of causation from a criminal assault that led to the patient lapsing into coma and brain death. In these cases, the courts were not prepared to hold that the withdrawal of artificial ventilation was sufficient to constitute a new act which would absolve the original perpetrator from criminal responsibility for the death of their victim (*R* v. *Malcherek, R* v. *Steel*).[2] The conclusions of these cases were, therefore, open to interpretation since they focused on the criminal law rather than directly on what constitutes death for legal purposes.

Of greater interest is the case of *Re A*, concerning the cessation of ventilation of a brain stem dead child. A consultant paediatric neurologist had made a preliminary diagnosis of brain stem death on 21 January 1992 after applying the criteria recommended by the Conference of the Royal Colleges and Faculties of the UK.[3] This diagnosis was confirmed by a colleague the following day. The judge in the case, Johnson J, stated that he had 'no hesitation at all in holding that A has been dead since Tuesday ... January 21'. In addition, he held that he had jurisdiction 'to make a declaration that A is now dead for all legal, as well as medical, purposes', thereby supporting the view that the legal approach to the definition of death is reliant upon the medical definition. Unless the patient fulfils these criteria she is deemed to be alive and must be treated accordingly (see *Airedale NHS Trust* v. *Bland*).

However, the criteria for brain stem death are not universally accepted and have been subjected to trenchant criticism (Singer, 1995). Furthermore, in some countries, most notably Japan, these criteria have not been adopted as a means of deciding that the patient has died, and patients who would be declared dead in the UK are routinely maintained on artificial support. While there is ample room for debate over whether it is appropriate to maintain patients in general in this way, the fact remains that this is not the practice adopted in the UK and that, unless the criteria for brain stem death are changed, their application, and consequences of diagnoses based on them, ought to be consistent. Moreover, and critically for the purposes of this discussion, it must be borne in mind that existence after brain death cannot be maintained indefinitely.

The Brain Dead Pregnant Woman

It could be argued that, once the woman is declared dead, any steps possible should be taken to attempt to maintain her pregnancy for the time necessary to maximize the chances of survival and delivery of the fetus. Some might see this as being in accordance with the interests of society by showing respect to the fetus and the value owed to it.[4] This might also reflect the wishes of relatives, who may feel there is some comfort to be gained by attempting to bring life forth after death and that the successful delivery of a child would salvage something from the tragic loss of their loved one.

From the reported cases, it does indeed seem that the wishes of relatives, and those of the woman's partner, have often been appealed to as a justification for continuing support of the brain dead woman's body, even although in law these wishes have no standing. However, even in the absence of their agreement, medical staff have still been prepared to continue treatment and, indeed, in the words of one doctor, 'to sin bravely'. This is itself an interesting comment, since it suggests that the doctor was fully aware that what they were proposing to do was by no means beyond criticism. There are wide-ranging ethical and legal implications of adopting such an approach which need to be carefully evaluated.

Before considering a proposed framework for determining whether support should continue, it is necessary to discuss the justification that appears to be at least implicit in the reported cases, the question of whether the fetus itself is an 'other' – a patient to whom a duty is owed. In this case the duty would be to attempt to maintain the pregnancy to allow a child to be born. It is in exploring this issue that the three possible models of viewing the relationship between the woman and her fetus will be considered. These models, or variations upon them, can be extracted from the literature concerning pregnancy and merit fuller discussion than is possible here. A useful discussion on them and their consequences can be found in Seymour (1995, esp. pp.46–57) and the classification of the three models set out in that report has been adopted below. For the purposes of my argument, only a brief outline of each of the models will be presented.

Three Models for Viewing Pregnancy

Separate Entities Model

This view treats the fetus as an independent entity, whether from conception or from some later stage of development. Central, though, is the idea that the fetus should be accorded some rights prior to birth. The scope of such rights is itself a matter of debate, but a chief assertion is that the fetus has a right to life – a right to be born. This terminology is also adopted in the abortion debate and is used to support the view that the fetus is an unborn child, merely separated from the rest of the community by being within the womb of its mother. It is often further contended that the interest of the fetus in being born should take precedence over any other consideration, even the views of the pregnant woman herself.

Single Entity/Part of the Woman's Body Model

According to this model, the fetus should be regarded as no more than a part of the woman's body before it is born. The single entity is the woman.

Indivisibly Linked Model

The proposition here is that the woman and her fetus cannot be regarded as a unified entity. Instead, they are regarded as having separate but intimately connected identities. The conclusion that follows would be that the pregnant woman, as the only entity who can act as an autonomous agent, is accorded the ability to make decisions for herself and also on behalf of her fetus.

Having outlined the three models, it is now possible to seek to apply them to the situation of the brain dead pregnant woman and to consider what the consequences of doing so would be.

Application of the Three Models to the Brain Dead Pregnant Woman

Separate Entities

If this model is adopted in relation to the brain dead pregnant woman, it would suggest that the prime consideration of medical staff ought to be to take whatever steps will maximize the chances of a successful delivery of her fetus. This would be the case whether or not the woman had expressly stated, in anticipation of her death during pregnancy, that she would not wish her body to be treated in this way.

There appears to be some support for this approach in the UK. The Scottish Law Commission (SLC) have recently, 1995, considered the question of the treatment of incapacitated adults and concluded that refusal of treatment which will endanger the life of another 'adds another dimension the effect of which ought to outweigh patient autonomy' (SLC No. 151, para. 5.57). If this is applied to a pregnancy and is used to justify intervention, it will need to accord the fetus status as an 'other'. This would be to fly in the face of the law as currently interpreted and applied. In addition, the SLC recommend that 'An advance refusal of treatment by a female patient should be ineffective to the extent that it refuses treatment which if not given would endanger the life of a foetus, aged 24 weeks or more, which she is carrying' (Recommendation 73 and Clause 40 (7) (d) of the appended draft bill, The Incapable Adults (Scotland) Bill (proposed by the SLC) SLC Report 216(6)). These comments appear to have been made in the context of a refusal of treatment where the woman is still alive, but it must be doubted whether the fact that the woman has been declared dead would alter these conclusions. In any event, their recommendation, if adopted, would appear to be wide enough to cover a refusal of treatment where the woman had in fact died.

However, to argue that a woman's advance refusal of treatment is endangering the life of her fetus is not the end of an argument, but the beginning. If it is to have any significance, further arguments must follow: that the life of the fetus ought not to be endangered and that steps should be taken to avoid such endangerment. Crucial to the SLC recommendation is the apparent willingness to hold that the fetus is an 'other' who has an interest in the preservation of its life and presumably in achieving an independent existence by being delivered. The use of the terminology of 'the unborn child' suggests that views expressed in this report (SLC Report 214(6)) were indeed based upon the conceptualization of the fetus as an entity with an existence and with interests separate from those of the woman.

But this presents an immediate problem, since the fetus is not an 'other' in UK law. The fetus has been deemed to have no legal personality . The effect of this is that, since the fetus has not been legally accorded the status of a person, it has no legal rights or interests until it is born. A fetus cannot be made a ward of court and a man cannot prevent a woman from seeking a termination of her pregnancy either as the potential father or as a representative of the fetus (*Paton* v. *Trustees of the British Pregnancy Advisory Service*, *C* v. *S*, *D* v. *Berkshire*

County Council, Re F (In Utero)). The fetus gains legal personality only when it has achieved an independent existence by being born.

For these reasons, to suggest that it would be legitimate to continue interventions upon a pregnant woman because this would be in the interest of the fetus would be fundamentally to alter the position of UK law by according interests to the fetus while still within the body of a woman. In fact, the SLC drew support for their recommendation from the one UK case regarding a non-consensual Caesarean section performed upon a competent pregnant woman (*Re S (Adult: Refusal of Medical Treatment)*). In *Re S*, the decision of the court was to authorize the operation without her consent because it was 'in the vital interests of both the mother and the unborn child'. The balance in this case was struck in favour of medical intervention and against the autonomy of the pregnant woman, but this case has attracted wide condemnation on grounds of legal principle, as well as on ethical, professional and pragmatic grounds (Mair, 1996). In any event, authorizing such an intervention was contrary to existing law and the judgement ought not to be followed. In the only other judicial comment on this issue by the courts, Lord Donaldson stated that the only possible circumstance in which the refusal of consent to treatment by a competent patient could be overruled was where that patient was a pregnant woman (*Re T (Adult: Refusal of Medical Treatment)*). This statement was an *obiter dictum* made without consideration of any authority and appears to be at best of dubious standing, for the reasons given earlier.

So far, the separate entities model would unequivocally seem to indicate that treatment cannot be imposed upon a pregnant woman simply because of the pregnancy because she, and only she, is an entity for legal purposes and her rights to bodily integrity will (apart from the occasional aberration) be respected. But can it be argued that, once the woman is dead, the situation changes? It might, for example, be said that different interests are now at stake. The woman, being dead, could be seen to have no interests, while society might have an interest in saving the fetus and the fetus might have an interest in being born.

Society may well have an interest in the fetus, but it also has an interest in reassuring those who are currently alive that they will be treated in a dignified manner after their death. In fact, specific crimes deal with mishandling or maltreatment of corpses for this very reason. Unless there is a more compelling reason available, the fact that the woman has died should have no place in reducing the respect to which she is entitled, even after death. The possible source of this additional reason might be found in the interest, possibly attributable both to the state and to the fetus, in a live birth. But given what has just been said, this would only be a trumping interest if there was something about the status of the fetus that changed as a result of the woman's death. Manifestly, this does not occur. The position of the fetus has not altered at all. It is no more a legal person than before her death.

Any attempt to justify continued interventions upon the corpse of a pregnant woman based on the separate interests of the fetus in surviving and being born opens the floodgates to restrictions upon the personal freedom of choice and bodily integrity of women. Mandating support of pregnancies where the woman is dead would be to permit the use of her body as a piece of equipment, truly equating her with an incubator. Furthermore, the conclusion would be that her body, unlike the body of anyone else, could be subject to grave intrusions and aggressive management in order to benefit a legal non-person. This would be an extraordinary conclusion to reach, given that the state is not ordinarily empowered to demand the use of a corpse, even where to do so would be to benefit existing legal persons. This question, chiefly connected with the use of corpses for medical purposes under the Human Tissue Act 1961 (UK), will be dealt with in greater detail below.

The Single Entity Model

The single entity model has attractions for those concerned about the non-consensual artificial support and 'aggressive management' of pregnancy in brain dead women. If this model were followed, any interventions upon a pregnant woman should cease upon her death, because the fetus is regarded as no more than another of her organs or collection of tissues and its somatic death should be allowed to follow on from the death of the woman. This would involve treating the pregnant woman in exactly the same way as any other patient who was declared brain dead, and would have the same outcome, no matter the age of the fetus.

However, this model is problematic for a number of reasons. As Seymour (1995) notes, it has been largely discredited on a number of cogent grounds. First, the fetus has a distinct genetic make-up. Although it is contained within the body of the woman and is dependent upon nutrients supplied by her for its growth and development, unlike any part of her body it has a unique genetic constitution. It is therefore unrealistic to speak of the fetus as being, on a genetic level, a mere part of the pregnant woman's body (Kluge, 1988, King, 1979). Secondly, the fetus is also physiologically distinct, having, a short time after conception, its own circulatory system and having developed its own set of organs. It seems highly counter-intuitive, if not inaccurate, to speak of a fetus as merely being a part of the woman's body. Thirdly, it has also been suggested that the single entity model does not accord with pregnant women's own views of the fetus. Failing to give recognition to their perception of the fetus would indeed be to devalue women's fundamental experiences of pregnancy (Nelson, 1994). While such views may need to be treated with caution, since as has been suggested by Duden, amongst others, we may experience what we are taught or expected to experience (Duden, 1993), to ignore them would be to disrespect the views of the pregnant woman, something that has arguably happened all too often.

Thus, like the first model, the single entity approach fails to allow for a flexible and individualistic approach to the experience of pregnancy. If the fetus is no more than a part of the woman's body, no allowance can be made for a woman's wish to be maintained in the event of death to give her fetus a chance of survival. The single entity model has also not found favour with the law. Instead, the legal approach has been in accordance with the third model, namely to view the pregnant woman and her fetus as separate but connected entities.

The Indivisibly Linked Model

This model allows the fetus to be accorded significance greater than merely being a part of the woman's body, yet does not insist that it has a right to the continued support of the woman's body, even after her death. Unlike the previous models, there is the possibility of taking the woman's views and wishes into account and, indeed, holding them to be determinative. This model does not demand that in all cases support must be ceased or that in all cases it must continue, but has the capacity to recognize the pregnant woman's unique relationship with her fetus and gives primacy to her perception of her role in supporting the fetus until birth.

This approach avoids ascribing rights to the fetus which might otherwise lead to the potential for conflict where the wishes and needs of the woman regarding treatment can be viewed as being detrimental to it. There has been increased awareness of the potential for such conflicts, which are often described as maternal/fetal conflicts, although perhaps it might be more accurate to describe them as being between pregnant women and health carers or lawyers. UK law has so far resolved any conflicts by regarding the fetus as having only the potential to acquire rights and be owed duties in the womb. Such rights and duties cannot take effect until the child has been born alive. Thus a child can acquire property rights that were created prior to birth or recover damages for prenatal injury, but these rights are wholly contingent upon live birth and no legal action can be raised in connection with them on behalf of a fetus. Similarly, criminal actions may be founded upon injuries suffered by the fetus, but these also depend upon the fetus having been delivered alive.

The law thus takes account of the needs and interests of the born child, but does not prioritize them over those of the woman, either before or after birth. The standing of the woman is unaffected by the fact that she is carrying a fetus, and her agreement to, or refusal of, treatment will be respected in the same way as would be that of a non-pregnant woman or a man. Given that the status of the fetus does not change after the death of the woman, this model offers the benefits of flexibility and is also consistent with the existing UK legal approach to pregnancy. In addition, it would allow the established legal framework concerning medical interventions after death to be applied to the brain dead pregnant woman. It is to this framework that I will now turn.

The Framework for Determining the Acceptability of Medical Interventions after Death

The framework proposed here for determining the acceptability of continued medical support of the brain dead pregnant woman is based upon the previously expressed wishes or views of the individual, either in the form of an advance directive or by the use of a substituted judgement. A useful analogy here is with the UK approach to medical uses of the corpse for organ donation, research and education, which is set out in the Human Tissue Act 1961 (HTA 1961).

Advance Directives

The system of consenting in advance to medical uses of the body under the HTA 1961 in the first instance rests on the individual particularizing what they are and are not willing to consent to either in writing or orally in the presence of two or more witnesses during their last illness (s.1(1)). Although not often considered in such terms, this can be viewed as an example of an advance directive, in that it explains the individual's wishes concerning the use or disposal of their corpse. The law permits a statement in favour of organ donation to be made, although it does not require that this is followed, primarily for practical reasons. But, more relevantly for our purposes, the law is entirely clear that any evidence of a refusal must be followed. In other words, an objection to organ donation, once established, absolutely precludes organ removal. This is so regardless of the perceived good, in terms of benefiting other members of society, that might follow from using the body or parts of it for organ donation, medical education or research.

The primary reason for legally requiring that viable organs, which could save lives, must be destroyed if an objection has been raised is the respect for the primacy of autonomy in matters relating to medical treatment during life which extends to medical interventions after death. In addition, there is profound unease at the thought of treating the dead merely as repositories of organs or training material. The corpse has a tremendous symbolic significance. The importance of the ritual surrounding death has a bearing on the manner in which people live their lives and it is generally regarded as unacceptable that people should live in the knowledge that their bodies may be used after death in a manner that is contrary to their beliefs and values. This is no less true of the pregnant woman.

Moreover, a commonly held argument in favour of respecting a deceased's wishes is based on altruism. In other words, while it might be viewed as desirable that people allow their corpse to be used after their deaths to help others, this should be a matter of choice, not one which society has a right to demand. It is for these reasons that the UK, like many other countries, has retained a system of 'opting in' to organ donation rather than 'opting out' or state requisition of corpses, despite continued debate over the advantages to be gained from permitting the sale of organs or their compulsory or automatic removal.[5] Social utility is not permitted, in this situation, to triumph over the autonomy of the individual, such autonomy including within in it the freedom to choose to act in a manner that may be regarded as selfish or altruistic.

These reasons provide the justification for holding that, where an individual has consented to the use of her body for the purposes specified under the HTA 1961, her wishes ought to be respected. More importantly, however, the same respect is due to her advance refusal. Theoretically, there need in fact be no limits placed on the individual's decisions about the use to which their body may be put, except where there is reason to believe that they would detrimentally affect society as a whole. For example, although UK law has not expressly considered the legality of continued ventilation of the almost dead for transplantation purposes, it is worth noting that, despite Kantian and general libertarian philosophies which would prohibit the use of the person as a means rather than an end in themselves, it could also be plausibly argued that the opportunity for altruism presented by an advance agreement to artificial prolongation of life for the purposes of organ donation would neither breach the Kantian imperative nor violate the autonomy of the individual.[6] What is critical to the above argument, of course, is that there is clear evidence as to what the individual would choose and that they have granted permission for certain things to be done after death. Generally, however, the law may have to rely on less concrete evidence.

Substituted Judgement

In the absence of the individual having expressed their wishes in the manner required by s.1(1) of the HTA 1961, the presumption is that the corpse cannot be used for medical purposes. The person lawfully in possession of the body may not authorize its use unless, having first made reasonable enquiries, 'he has no reason to believe that the deceased had expressed an objection to his body being so dealt with, and had not withdrawn it' (s.1 (2) (a)). Enquiries must obviously be directed to those who knew the individual and in the vast majority of cases this is likely to be his or her relatives. However, relatives are not empowered to consent where the individual is known to have had objections (although s.1 (2) (b) does give a surviving spouse or any surviving relative a right of veto over the individual's consent). In effect this is a form of substituted judgement, since it relies on evidence being given as to what it is believed the deceased individual would have wanted.

Application of the Framework to the Brain Dead Pregnant Woman

A similar framework could usefully be applied in any situation where some continued or novel intervention is proposed in respect of a person who is legally dead. Adoption of a framework based on a combination of advance directives and substituted judgement would lead to a consistency of approach to the dead and would allow the living to determine what shall be done with their bodies after death.

Advance Directives

If a woman, while competent and with adequate information, agrees to support being given in the event of her death in order to enable her fetus to develop and be delivered, it would be consistent with the general legal position regarding treatment of the deceased to honour her wishes. Competent pregnant women are permitted to choose to undergo risky procedures (such as ex-utero fetal therapy) for the benefit of their fetuses, even though there is no legal compulsion on them to do so. There seems to be no reason in principle why a woman could not similarly choose to act altruistically towards her fetus by sanctioning the continuation of her pregnancy and the necessary medical support of her body after death in order to allow, if possible, the fetus to become a person. The most effective way of a woman expressing her views as to continued treatment to maintain her pregnancy would be in the form of an advance directive. This would alert medical staff to her wishes and should ensure that they respect her clearly stated wishes.

The British Medical Association (BMA) has expressed its support for advance directives, although it does not feel that they should be legally binding, provided that they comply with certain criteria designed to ensure that the wishes expressed do represent the free and informed wishes of the competent individual (BMA, 1995). Advance directives are also supported by the Law Commissions of England and Wales and of Scotland, by the House of Lords Select Committee on Medical Ethics and the UK government. However, it must be said that the position of the pregnant woman may be complicated by the stage of her pregnancy and an assessment of whether or not what she asks for would, in fact, amount to futile treatment. Once again, the critical issue is the respect that is given to a refusal of treatment rather than what is done with an advance consent.

The legal validity of advance directives has yet to be directly tested by the UK courts; however if it is accepted that a Jehovah's Witness may refuse blood transfusions by carrying a card refusing consent to such treatments, then, provided that the advance refusal was made when the person was competent and in possession of adequate information, there would seem in principle to be no reason to doubt their validity (*Malette* v. *Shulman, Re T (Adult: Refusal of Medical Treatment)*). Guidelines regarding the making of advance directives are contained in the BMA Code of Practice, April 1995. The person with primary responsibility for determining whether treatment should be instituted or continued during life is the patient herself. Only she is in a position to assess the impact of medical treatment upon herself, in the light of her own experience and values. The importance of this argument is increasingly recognized in relation to the manner of her dying and would appear equally valid in relation to the individual's wishes about what should happen to her body after her death. It is also consistent with the position described above in relation to consent to organ donation and use of the corpse for medical education and research.

Of course, there are difficulties with this approach. First, the number of people making any form of advance directive on medical treatment is small. Secondly, this may be unlikely to be the kind of situation that would be envisaged by those who do, so that the advance directive might not state whether it was intended to apply in the event of pregnancy. Whilst the BMA do encourage more discussion of advance directives, it is possible that medical practitioners would be reluctant to initiate discussion on what a patient would wish to happen if they were to lapse into coma or die, particularly where the patient is already pregnant. This understandable reticence, however, should not blind practitioners to the fact that a failure to initiate discussions on these matters may lead to greater difficulties should such a tragedy occur.

It has also been suggested that the views of a woman as to refusal of treatment may be different if she becomes pregnant and the BMA has advised women of childbearing age to consider this issue. The BMA suggest that a waiver covering pregnancy might be written into an advance directive (BMA, 1995, para. 7.4) Even if it is not clear whether this factor had been taken into account by the woman when she made her advance directive, it should be possible for enquiries to be made as to whether her views on refusal of treatment had changed or were likely to change. To that extent, an advance directive refusing forms of treatment could be disregarded on the basis that it did not in fact represent the view of the pregnant woman in the altered circumstances of her pregnancy. This would not be to act disrespectfully towards the corpse, but would rather respect the autonomy of the individual.

Thirdly, despite the increased support for advance directives in general, there does appear to be some reluctance to respect those made by women if they are pregnant at the time that the advance directive is triggered. The BMA advises that, in this event, legal advice should be sought. While this caution is perhaps understandable, less so is the recommendation by the SLC referred to above, that an advance directive refusing consent to treatment should not be respected if the patient is a pregnant woman. As I have noted, their rationale for this appears to be based on the decision in *Re S*, which is of questionable authority. Clearly, however, their view starts from the presumption that interventions to preserve the fetus ought to be made. It seems likely that they would not oppose the carrying out of an advance directive consenting to such interventions.

The present analysis proceeds from the opposite standpoint, that treatment ought not to be given *against* the wishes of the woman. This discussion has exposed no valid justification for overruling a woman's wish not to be treated even if she is pregnant, although, as with all advance directives, there is a need to consider whether the directive was intended to apply in the precise circumstances that have arisen. Of course, this is not to ignore the potential of the fetus, nor to deny that others may have an interest in seeing that potential fulfilled. But, on strict legal principle, the fetus cannot trump the expressed wishes of the competent woman, even if those wishes are not effectuated until after her death. Where other advance statements are made, the question of the welfare of others, even existing legal persons, is not raised. There can, therefore, be no obvious justification for using the interests of others in these circumstances, and even less justification for treating the perceived interests of non-others as sufficient to override the intention of the person making the declaration.

Substituted Judgement

However, even though the use of advance directives represents a way forward, it remains likely at least in the near future that reliance may have to be placed on substituted judgement instead. Two forms of substituted judgement are possible – substituting what the reasonable pregnant woman would want in the circumstances or what that particular pregnant woman would have wanted. The first form has the danger of placing particular emphasis on societal judgements about motherhood and runs the risk of simplistically assuming that all women would of course agree that any possible steps should be taken to preserve the health of the fetus and to ensure that it is delivered. This assumption is, however, open to challenge (Nelson, 1994).

The second form is potentially more attractive since this focuses attention on the individual woman rather than deeming her to be a member of a group with particular aims and aspirations. It is true that many pregnant women would choose to take steps to ensure that their fetuses are delivered alive and healthy where possible and will undergo many risks to their own health and even lives, but this is not necessarily true for all women. Some women may, for example, focus more upon the parenting relationship and the fact that pregnancy was embarked upon with the view to playing an active caring role in a child's life. Where that parenting role cannot be fulfilled there may be strong arguments against the maintenance of the pregnancy. This view sees pregnancy as a purposive activity and is indeed the attitude adopted by the courts in other contexts where fitness to be a parent rather than a mere passing on of genetic identity is considered crucial (for example, in the sterilization of mentally impaired women and in access to infertility treatment).

Also interesting in this regard is the point that people may have an interest in not becoming parents. A notorious example is provided by the American case, *Davis* v. *Davis*, where a man's interest in not becoming a parent was weighed against a woman's interest in seeing embryos which had been frozen for her infertility treatment used in the treatment of other couples. The court focused on the importance of the parenting role and decided in favour of the man, Junior Davis. Again, perhaps this could be distinguished from the situation of a brain dead pregnant woman, in the sense that Junior Davis would know and have continuing knowledge that he might be a parent, with no active role in the upbringing of his child, whereas the same could not be said of the dead woman. However, it should be noted that it was unclear whether Junior Davis would in fact be informed of a successful pregnancy using the embryos to which he had donated half the genetic material. The perceived harm to him was in knowing that there was a possibility that this could occur. Moreover, this case also demonstrates that a deliberate action (for example, donating sperm and eggs or becoming pregnant) chosen in one situation may ultimately lead to an undesired outcome when circumstances change.

Thus a woman who deliberately becomes pregnant with the intention of rearing that child might legitimately feel that the meaning would go out of the pregnancy if she were unable to fulfil her parenting role. Even if she chooses to continue to carry the child when parenting is a probability, she might still legitimately prefer that her pregnancy is not continued when that role cannot be achieved. If knowledge of a possibility of becoming a parent without a parenting role is sufficient to prevent embryos being used to establish a pregnancy, would there really be any reason for distinguishing the situation of a fetus in a brain dead woman? Such a distinction could only be legitimately drawn if the fetus is accorded independent status, which, as I have argued, is not tenable. In addition, the woman's desire not to have a child after her death may be strengthened by the fact that, in order for this to happen, numerous invasive techniques must be performed upon her body.

These arguments suggest that individuals may have an interest in not becoming parents. If this is accepted, is there a danger that a man might claim an interest in not becoming a father where his partner is pregnant, and thereby acquire a right to demand that the pregnancy be terminated? This unfortunate outcome is avoided by focusing once more on the autonomy of the individual woman and her right to control her own body. A pregnancy can only be terminated by intervening in the woman's body by procuring an abortion or producing a miscarriage. To allow a man's interest in not becoming a father to trump the woman's right to control her own body would clearly be detrimental to the view that women do not lose their status as autonomous actors by becoming pregnant.

Of course, relying upon the evidence of others as to the likely views of the now dead woman presents a danger that her views might have been misunderstood or be misrepresented. This danger, however, also exists in relation to organ donation and would certainly, as in decisions about withdrawing life-sustaining treatment, require the evidence to be rigorously tested (*In Re Quinlan; Cruzan* v. *Director, Missouri Department of Health*). Despite this obvious problem, it at least allows the canvassing of opinion as to what that individual would have wanted and makes this the focus of attention rather than what others feel would be the benefits of such treatment.

In the event of conflicting evidence given by relatives or the absence of any information regarding what the woman's likely views would have been, I would suggest that pregnancy ought not to be maintained. The sole reason for allowing interventions under the proposed framework is to permit the views of the woman to be followed. There is no basis for doing this in the absence of clear evidence that maintenance is what the woman would have wanted. As already argued, to act otherwise would not be to accord primacy to the wishes of the woman but to bring about a birth in the interests of the fetus. Proceeding on these grounds is, in my view, legally and ethically untenable, particularly since her previous interest in maintaining the pregnancy was arguably intimately linked to parenting – something of which she is now irrevocably incapable.

Further Considerations

There are a host of other relevant issues which might suggest that maintaining a pregnancy might not be the optimal outcome. Such considerations might concern the best use of scarce resources and the question of futility. Primarily, such issues would be concerned with the ability of the health carers to maintain the pregnancy, the facilities available and the viability of the fetus. Thus it could be argued that, if there were another patient who might have a prospect of recovery if given the intensive care treatments being directed towards the dead woman, resources might be more effectively allocated by diverting care towards that other patient. This approach would necessitate adopting the view that the fetus was not itself a patient, since it could arguably be unethical to remove care already instituted simply because another patient might have a better prospect of recovery by receiving it.

Similarly, the continued use of intensive care facilities would almost certainly be deemed to be futile where there was no realistic prospect of being able to maintain the pregnancy until the fetus reached a stage of development consistent with an ability to lead an independent existence. To attempt to maintain a pregnancy where the fetus was not viable would be futile in that, although the fetus might be able to survive for some time, the aim of continued treatment (to deliver a live child) could not be achieved. Of course, it could be suggested that this would amount to beneficial research by providing an opportunity to monitor the development of the fetus in a way otherwise impossible and to experiment with combinations of treatment that might help to ensure survival of fetuses that are at present non-viable. However, this is also to experiment on the woman and, no matter what benefits might be derived from it, potential advances in fetal medicine are no justification for using women (even after death) as experimental objects without their consent. In any event, those who would wish to maintain the pregnancy in the absence of an agreement are those who believe that the fetus should be treated as a separate entity. From this moral position, it would be even less ethical to continue with a non-viable pregnancy since this would also add fetal experimentation to the unethical experimentation on the woman.

A test of viability has already been proposed, albeit not in the context of according primacy to the wishes of the woman. The SLC put the point as follows:

> This pre-supposes that the foetus is viable when the treatment is under consideration. The Abortion Act 1967 (as amended by s.37 (10) of the Human Fertilisation and Embryology Act 1990) prohibits the abortion of a foetus aged 24 weeks or more save in exceptional circumstances. We would adopt this time limit as the test for viability since the public policy considerations in advance refusals and abortions are similar. (SLC Report 214 (b), para. 5.58)

The point chosen by the SLC is based, not on an individual consideration of the viability of that particular fetus, but on the time limits set upon abortion which represent a cut-off point in relation to a woman's ability to seek a termination of pregnancy on particular grounds. Although the SLC suggested that the policy considerations concerning abortion and advance refusals of treatment are similar, this view is suspect as again deriving from their interpretation and reliance upon *Re S*.

The BMA Code of Practice is also alert to the uncertainty that surrounds this area and recommends in para 10.5 that 'If a mentally incapacitated and clearly pregnant woman presents with an apparently valid advance directive refusing treatment, legal advice should be sought. The courts may consider the advance refusal ineffective if withholding treatment endangers *an otherwise viable fetus*' (emphasis added).

The meaning of viability expressed in these statements is not clear. Is it to be assessed at the point of treatment, or is it sufficient that the fetus may be brought to viability by continued treatment? Either way, in my view, the important consideration remains the wishes of the woman.

Conclusions

Whilst there are undoubtedly problems arising from the suggested use of advance directives and substituted judgements tests which need further and detailed consideration, it is suggested that they do provide a more justifiable and intellectually coherent means of resolving the painful question of what should be done in the situations considered above. What is not justifiable is the present ad hoc approach to these cases. In the absence of clarity, medical staff may find themselves torn between respect for the dead woman and the wishes of her relatives. Alternatively, they may feel that they must act in order to serve the interests of the fetus. However, although medical opinion is crucial in determining what is clinically possible, it ought not to determine what is legally permissible. Despite the fact that medical practice is increasingly becoming the touchstone for the legality of treatment in difficult areas, such as the withdrawal of treatment from patients in persistent vegetative states, we should be extremely careful before giving legal authority to actions simply because that is what doctors do or feel that they ought to do. Whether or not the framework suggested above provides the best solution, the issues involved require urgent attention since, with the increased ability of medicine to support the critically ill, such cases are bound to arise with greater frequency in the future.[7]

Notes

1 The following articles are of considerable interest in this regard: T.A. Shannon, 'Keeping Dead Mothers Alive During Pregnancy: Ethical Issues', in Shannon (ed.), *Bioethics*, 4th edn, Mahwah, NJ: Paulist Press, 1994. W.P. Dillon, R.V. Lee, M.J. Tronolone, S. Buckwald and R.J. Foote, 'Life Support and Maternal Brain Death During Pregnancy', JAMA, **248**, (9), 1089–91, (1992); D.R. Field, E.A. Gates, R.K. Creasy, A.R. Jonsen and R.K. Laros Jr., 'Maternal Brain Death During Pregnancy: Medical and Ethical Issues', JAMA, **260**, (6), 816–22, (1988); Commentary on previous article, JAMA, **261**, (12), 1729, (1989); C. Anstotz, 'Should a Brain-Dead Pregnant Woman Carry Her Child to Full Term?' The case of the Erlanger Baby', *Bioethics* **7**, (4), 1993, 340–50; J.M. Jordan III, 'Incubating for the State: The Precarious Autonomy of Persistently Vegetative and Brain-Dead Women', *Georgia Law Review*, **22**, 1988, 1103–65; R. Veatch, 'Maternal Brain Death: an Ethicist's Thoughts', *JAMA*, **248**, (9), 1102–3 (1982).

2 *R* v. *Malcherek* per Lord Lane CJ: 'Where a medical practitioner adopting methods which are generally accepted comes bona fide and conscientiously to the conclusion that the patient is for practical purposes dead, and that such vital functions as exist – for example, circulation – are being maintained solely by mechanical means, and therefore discontinues treatment, that does not prevent the person who inflicted the initial injury from being responsible for the victim's death. Putting it another way, the discontinuance of treatment in those circumstances does not break the chain of causation between the initial injury and the death.'

3 See Statement issued by the Honorary Secretary of the Conference of the Medical Royal Colleges and Faculties of the UK on 11 October 1976, *BMJ*, ii, 1187–8, (1976). See also Working Party on behalf of the Health Department of Great Britain and Northern Ireland, 'Cadaveric Organs for Transplantation: a code of practice including the diagnosis of brain death', London: DHSS, (1983), which incorporates papers on Diagnosis of Brain Death and Diagnosis of Death by the Conference of the Medical Royal Colleges and Faculties in the UK.

4 See, for example, the sentiments expressed in the Warnock Report: *Report of the Committee of Inquiry into Human Fertilisation and Embryology*, Cmnd 9314, July 1988.
5 For further discussion and debate on these points, see The King's Fund Institute Report No. 18, *A Question of Give and Take: Improving the Supply of Cadaveric Organs for Transplantation*, London: The King's Fund Institute, 1994.
6 This argument is proposed by S.A.M. McLean in 'Transplantation and the "Nearly Dead": The Case of Elective Ventilation', ch. 8 in S.A.M. McLean (ed.), *Contemporary Issues in Law, Ethics and Medicine*, Dartmouth:Aldershot, 1996.
7 I am indebted to Professor S.A.M. McLean and to Dr K. Petersen for their invaluable assistance in the preparation of this chapter.

References

British Medical Association (1995), *Advance Statements About Medical Treatment: Code of Practice with Explanatory Notes*, April, London: BMJ Publishing Group.
Duden, B. (1993), *Disembodying Women: Perspectives on Pregnancy and the Unborn*, Cambridge, Mass. and London: Harvard University Press.
King, P.A. (1979), 'The Juridical Status of the Fetus: A Proposal for the Legal Protection of the Unborn', *Michigan Law Review*, **77**, 1660.
Kluge, E-H.W. (1988), 'When Caesarian [sic] Section Operations Imposed by a Court are Justified', *Journal of Medical Ethics*, **14**, 208.
Mair, J. (1996), 'Maternal/Foetal Conflict: Defined or Defused?', in S.A.M. McLean (ed.), *Contemporary Issues in Law, Ethics and Medicine*, Aldershot: Dartmouth.
Nelson, H.L. (1994), 'The Architect & the Bee: Some Reflections on Postmortem Pregnancy', *Bioethics*, **8**(3), 267.
Scottish Law Commission Report: *Report on Incapable Adults*, Cm. 2962 (Scot. Law Com. No. 151) Scottish Law Commission, September 1995.
Seymour, J. (1995), *Fetal Welfare and the Law: A Report of an Inquiry Commissioned by the Australian Medical Association*, Canberra: Law Faculty of the Australian National University.
Singer, P. (1995), *Rethinking Life and Death: the Collapse of Our Traditional Ethics*, Oxford: Oxford University Press.

Cases

Airedale NHS Trust v. *Bland* (1993) 1 All ER 821.
C v. *S* [1988] QB 135, [1987] 1 All ER 1230 , [1987] 2 WLR 1101.
Cruzan v. *Director, Missouri Department of Health* (1990) 110 S Ct 2841 (US Sup Ct).
D v. *Berkshire County Council* (1987) 1 All E.R. 20.
Davis v. *Davis* (1992) 842 SW 2d 588 (Tenn Sup Ct).
Malette v. *Shulman* (1990) 67 DLR (4th) 321 (Ont. CA).
In Re Quinlan 70 NJ 10, 355 A 2d 647 (1976).
Paton v. *Trustees of the British Pregnancy Advisory Service* [1979] QB 276, [1978] 2 All ER 987.
Re A [1992] 3 Med LR 303 (Fam D).
Re F (In Utero) (1988) 2 All ER 193, 2 WLR 1288.
Re S (Adult: Refusal of Medical Treatment) [1992] 4 All ER 671, (1992) 9 BMLR 69.
Re T (Adult: Refusal of Medical Treatment) [1992] 4 All ER 649, (1992) 9 BMLR 46 (CA).
R v. *Malcherek*, *R* v. *Steel* [1981] 2 All ER 422, [1981] 1 WLR 690 (CA).

United Kingdom Legislation

Human Tissue Act 1961.

8 Letting Die or Assisting Death: How Should the Law Respond to the Patient in a Persistent Vegetative State?

SHEILA A.M. McLEAN

> Death and dying are issues which in recent years have increasingly become matters of concerned public discussion worldwide ... It is submitted two factors are mainly responsible for this development. First, the process of dying has been shifted from a private setting to the more public setting of health-care institutions, or from the home to the hospital. ... Secondly, advances in medical technology and pharmacology have made it possible to prolong the lives of terminally or otherwise hopelessly ill patients who have little (or no) hope of a cure. (Giesen, 1990, pp.82–3)

Introduction

The quotation that begins this chapter emphasizes the double-edged sword which is modern, high-technology medicine. On the one hand, many lives are saved which, perhaps even 20 years ago, would have been lost. On the other, however, some are reduced to mere existence which can sometimes be maintained indefinitely, but which lacks quality, perhaps even consciousness. The aims of those who developed the technology were to meet the needs of the former group. The value to individuals and the community of the capacity to save life cannot be underestimated, but the spin-off (often compounded by legal and ethical uncertainties) is that, for some, these same capacities represent a cruel or futile enforcement of mere existence, with all of the consequential distress and despair for families, friends and carers.

The House of Lords was recently required to address such a situation, in the case of *Airedale NHS Trust* v. *Bland*. With the support of Anthony Bland's family, a declaration was sought by the Airedale NHS Trust seeking approval for the withdrawal of life support. Anthony Bland, aged $17^1/_2$ at the time, was seriously injured at a football stadium disaster on 15 April 1989. He never regained consciousness. As a result of the disaster, his lungs were crushed and punctured and the supply of oxygen to his brain was interrupted. He was diagnosed as being in a condition known as persistent vegetative state (PVS), which means that higher brain function is missing, although the brain stem continues to function. For legal purposes, he was not, therefore, dead – indeed, given appropriate management, he might have been able to survive for many years. As Lord Keith poignantly explained his condition, 'Anthony Bland cannot see, hear or feel anything. He cannot communicate in any way. The consciousness which is the essential feature of individual personality has departed for ever' (at p.859).

The human issues in such a case are clear. Those who loved this young man, and those who cared for him in hospital, were unable to grieve in the normal way for what was the irrevocable loss of the personality, if not the body, of their loved one. To watch someone in this situation is inevitably profoundly distressing.

Even more recently, Scotland's highest civil court addressed a similar situation in the case of *Law Hospital NHS Trust* v. *The Lord Advocate and Others* (March 1996). In this case, clinical diagnosis of persistent vegetative state was made in respect of Mrs Janet Johnstone, who had attempted suicide. There was, as in the Bland case, no dispute on the medical evidence as to the existence of the condition. She was described by the Lord President, Lord Hope (Scotland's most senior civil judge) as being 'permanently insensate, and she remains alive only because feeding and hydration are provided to her artificially and because of the nursing care which she continues to receive in the hospital' (transcript, at p.2). And in the Republic of Ireland case *In the Matter of a Ward of Court* (1995) the court upheld an order to authorize the withdrawal of artificial nourishment in the case of a young woman who was described as being 'almost' in a persistent vegetative state.

In all of these cases, the question posed was whether or not, the conclusion having been reached by those who cared for the patients that continued existence was undignified and inappropriate, it would be lawful (as well as humane) to terminate the regime of treatment and care which was keeping them alive. For the purposes of this chapter, we will concentrate only on the two UK courts, since the Irish case seems to have been dealing with different circumstances.

Two values would be served by obtaining an answer to this question from the highest civil courts in the UK: first, a response to the question whether the current law can accommodate medical decisions which result in death;[1] and second, clarification of the legal position of those professionally caring for these patients. The latter question is as much an ethical concern as the former. As the Lord President said in the *Law Hospital* case, medical ethics must take account of the law on these matters, but it is not a sufficient reassurance for the doctor in the present state of the law to be told that his proposed conduct is medically ethical. He is entitled to be told whether his conduct will expose him to the risk of an action of damages for negligence, and he cannot ignore the risk that a prosecution may follow on the ground that his conduct amounted to murder or at least to culpable homicide (transcript, at p.7).

The problem confronting both the Court of Session and the House of Lords, of course, was that, although they could competently pronounce on civil liability, albeit by bringing different legal traditions and principles to bear, neither court was authorized to issue guarantees concerning criminal liability, since they are civil courts. The House of Lords was prepared to provide opinion in this matter, but the Bland judgement was immediately followed by an (unsuccessful) attempt at private prosecution of Anthony Bland's doctor. In Scotland, the position was clarified by the Lord Advocate (Scotland's senior prosecution officer) issuing a policy statement following the judgement in the Court of Session that he would not prosecute any doctor who withdrew artificial nutrition and hydration where such removal had been authorized by the Court of Session. This undoubtedly places the Scottish doctor in a clearer position than his/her colleagues in England and Wales. But, in any event, as Compton J said in *Barber* v. *Superior Court of Los Angeles County*, 'a murder prosecution is a poor way to design an ethical and moral code for doctors who are faced with decisions concerning the use of costly and extraordinary "life support" equipment' (at p.1011).

To return to the *Bland* case, although the tradition of the UK courts in dealing with such sensitive and controversial subjects is to make declarations based on each individual case, rather than purporting to lay down more general guidelines, much was expected of the House of Lords – at least by way of statements of principle which could be taken as forming the basis of some sort of guidance for future conduct. It is the aim of this discussion to seek to highlight what, if any, principles can be identified from this judgement. Comment will also be informed by the more recent Scottish case. By identifying and criticizing the tests used and the principles elucidated it will be argued not only that the courts are inappropriate fora for decisions of this sort, but also that wider, more fundamental and more comprehensively rigorous standards are needed to meet these situations. Before considering the judgements in more depth, however, there are two matters which must be clarified.

The first relates to the condition itself. Questions about treatment of those who are terminally ill, temporarily incapacitated or conscious but incompetent are not the same ones as those raised by PVS. Matters of consent and capacity to give or refuse it are substantially irrelevant where the loss of capacity is absolute and permanent. The legal maxim that the competent adult may refuse or reject treatment arguably is of little help in this situation although, as will be shown in this chapter, some of their Lordships found some source of interest in it. The decisions reached in the cases of Anthony Bland and Janet Johnstone hinged on the accuracy of the diagnosis of PVS and the creation, elucidation or discovery of principles which apply only in such circumstances. Manifestly, therefore, those who do not meet the criteria for PVS are not affected or threatened by them, although the need for accuracy in diagnosis cannot be underestimated. This last comment has particular poignancy given recent reports that two patients who had been diagnosed as being in persistent vegetative state had subsequently 'recovered'.

The second matter relates to the question, doubtless posed by many, as to why the issue of withdrawing life support treatment is ever considered. Is not our law duty-bound to protect and enforce the doctrine of the sanctity of life, and does it not follow from this that someone who is not 'dead' for legal purposes – who is, *ex hypothesi*, alive – must be permitted or assisted to maintain that existence? For some, the fact that the life is mere existence is irrelevant – it is not for doctors or courts to 'play God'. Obviously, there are those who would not endorse such a radical sanctity of life view and, equally obviously, this theological or ethical argument is one which the present writer cannot resolve. In the Bland case, Lord Keith saw no conflict between a decision to withdraw life-sustaining treatment and the doctrine of the sanctity of life:

> In my judgment it does no violence to the principle [of the sanctity of life] to hold that it is lawful to cease to give medical treatment and care to a PVS patient who has been in that state for over three years, considering that to do so involves invasive manipulation of the patient's body to which he has not consented and which confers no benefit to him. (At p.861)

In addition, as Lord Mustill pointed out, 'The interest of the state in preserving the lives of its citizens is very strong, but it is not absolute' (at p.891).

One further matter needs to be attended to before moving on to consideration of the Bland case. Although the British Medical Association (BMA) has recently moved towards at least a recognition of the standing of advance directives (*Bulletin of Medical Ethics*, 1992), there is considerable doubt that they have full legal force in the UK. This point is mentioned because, given legal recognition, the number of people finding themselves in the situation of the family and doctors of Anthony Bland might be reduced, even if only slightly. For some, therefore, full recognition of 'living wills' (hinted at by some of the judges in the Bland case) might so significantly reduce the number of cases as to render consideration of these few remaining cases redundant or at least less urgent. Even those who hold to a strict sanctity of life approach might concede that autonomous and competent choices should be recognized as valid, while at the same time insisting that those who have not made such directives must be kept alive.

However, this view is problematic. Pragmatically, it does not seem likely that a significant number of people who find themselves in PVS would actually have made such an advance directive. Like Anthony Bland, many who suffer the kind of trauma which results in PVS tend to be young and unlikely to have contemplated their own death. It might also be said that, even if a significant number of cases could be dealt with by this mechanism, the remaining cases still require – perhaps even demand – that a sophisticated and compassionate society resolve their individual dilemmas in a principled way. Of course, in the Johnstone case, it might have been argued (although it was not) that Mrs Johnstone's attempt at suicide could be taken to have the equivalence of an advance directive. Since she had attempted to take her own life, might it not be presumed that she had made a statement which should be binding? Of course, this would not be regarded as a strong argument, since it is widely believed that many suicide attempts are not real efforts to end life and the evidence seems to be that many of those whose lives are saved do not go on to repeat the attempt.

The Legal Questions

In the progress of the Bland case, the Court of Appeal, whose judgement was being reviewed by the House of Lords, issued a declaration in these terms:

> That despite the inability of the defendants to consent thereto, the plaintiff and the responsible attending physicians: (1) may lawfully discontinue all life-sustaining treatment and medical support meas-

> ures designated to keep [the defendant] alive in his existing persistent vegetative state including the termination of ventilation, nutrition and hydration by artificial means; and (2) that they may lawfully discontinue and thereafter need not furnish medical treatment [to the defendant] except for the sole purpose of enabling [him] to end his life and die peacefully with the greatest dignity and the least of pain and suffering and distress. (At p.833)

In endorsing the Court of Appeal's judgement, a number of strategies were applied by their Lordships and a number of concerns expressed. None, however, dissented from the view that Anthony Bland should be permitted to die. Rather, a number of, sometimes disparate and sometimes interlocking, tests were formulated which allowed this decision to be reached. This discussion concentrates on a critical analysis of these tests before postulating an alternative.

The Legal Answers

A number of their Lordships gave consideration to what the *competent* person could and could not lawfully do. In judgements which will have given great encouragement to those who despair of the 'medicalization', evident in other cases, of the patient's right to refuse or reject therapy, it was firmly restated that the competent adult can make, as a matter of right, his or her own decision about therapy. Indeed, it was even noted that this decision need not be rational.[2] From the perspective of the PVS patient and even in the face of a considerable number of UK cases which have seemed to many commentators (McLean, 1989; Brazier, 1992; Mason and McCall Smith, 1994) to call such rights into question, this recognition was not, however, irrelevant.

In the same way as courts in the UK have approached questions relating to the sterilization of women with severe intellectual disabilities,[3] so, too, the fact that the competent person has such rights was thought to be a foundation for the argument that, if they are to be valuable, these rights are not inevitably removed by the fact of incompetence. This is illustrated by what was described above as a somewhat tentative endorsement of the validity of advance directives, and also by the genuinely held concern that incompetence should not result in an automatic diminution of human rights.[4]

Lord Browne-Wilkinson, for example, based much of his argument in *Airedale NHS Trust* on the issue of consent. As he says:

> The correct answer to the present case depends on the extent of the right to continue lawfully to invade the bodily integrity of Anthony

> Bland without his consent. If in the circumstances they have no right to continue artificial feeding, they cannot be in breach of any duty by ceasing to provide such feeding. (At p.882)

It can be argued that, although logical in legal theory, this approach takes insufficient account of the fact that, in other circumstances, it would be unlawful to discontinue treatment even when it is not authorized. The critical difference is not, therefore, the question of consent or its absence, but rather the anticipated outcome of continuation/discontinuation. Nevertheless, there is some considerable appeal to this perspective since it does seem to prioritize the rights of the individual – or at least some of their rights.

More contentious, however, are the other approaches adopted. The first of these was the use of what is called the acts/omissions doctrine. Broadly, this would hold that we are responsible for our acts but not for our omissions. I may not kill, but I am under no legal obligation to feed the children of others to save their lives. As a physician I do, of course, have a duty of care towards my patient and, therefore, in strict theory my omission may be as culpable as my act.

In these circumstances, there are very good reasons for not translating the morally dubious distinction between act and omission into law, and the House of Lords recognized the artificiality of the distinction. Lord Lowry, for example, was unwilling to hold that a distinction should be drawn between the doctor who did not offer treatment and the doctor who started it and then felt that it should be abandoned. He said:

> Such a distinction could quite illogically confer on a doctor who had refrained from treatment an immunity which did not benefit a doctor who had embarked on treatment in order to see whether it might help the patient and had abandoned the treatment when it was seen not to do so. (At p.875)

Others in the House of Lords were unhappy with this distinction for other reasons. Lord Browne-Wilkinson argued that the removal of nasogastric feeding should not count as an act, since the tube by itself was not what kept the patient alive. As he said, 'The removal of the tube by itself does not cause the death since by itself it did not sustain life' (at p.881). The doctor who removes the tube cannot therefore be said to have committed the *actus reus* of murder. Logically, it is the removal of food/hydration which is inserted through the tube which causes death or, perhaps more accurately, it is the omission to continue its provision which results in death. However, this begs a fundamental question. In some cases, a patient in this condition may be fed through a tube, not because it is absolutely essential, but rather because (a) better nourishment is provided and (b) it is easier for staff to manage. However, this course of logic invites us towards a conclusion, not that death should be permitted to occur, but rather that manual feeding (which is possible in some cases) should be continued. In other words, all that this argument can do is authorize the removal of artificial feeding, but, if feeding by hand is possible, it does not authorize its discontinuation.

Yet the patients are in precisely the same clinical condition. So, if the broad distinction is dubious, to what extent should we turn our attention to a refinement of this: namely, to what extent should we concede the similarities, but concern ourselves with intention, since, even if there is no critical difference in the establishment of the *actus reus*, does not the *mens rea* of the actor have relevance? In other words, does it matter that the intention of the doctor is benign and not criminal? Doctors are already, with a patient's consent, allowed to perform procedures which would otherwise be criminal offences, and which no consent, in the non-medical setting, would render anything other than criminal. The beneficence of the clinical act is seen as redefining the nature of the act so that consent can obviate criminal liability. Why would this not be a satisfactory way of dealing with this set of circumstances?

The answer is again provided by Lord Mustill. Medical treatment in general stands apart from the criminal law, but 'it is intent to kill or cause grievous bodily harm which constitutes the *mens rea* of murder, and the reason why the intent was formed makes no difference at all' (at p.890). Or, as Lord Browne-Wilkinson put it, 'As to the element of intention or *mens rea*, in my judgement there can be no real doubt that it is present in this case: the whole purpose of stopping artificial feeding is to bring about the death of Anthony Bland' (at p.880). Further doubts about the use of the acts/omissions doctrine were raised by Lord Clyde in the Court of Session, where he said, 'It may well be that the distinction between a positive intervention which causes death and the omission or discontinuance of an act which would have prevented death may provide a sufficient solution but I find greater strength in the submission that if there is in the circumstances no longer a duty to continue with a system of life support there would be no crime committed by the discontinuance of that system' (transcript, p.4).

These are critical points, since they lead inexorably to the next set of considerations used in the judgement. Given that there is no actual legal distinction between act and omission in these circumstances, and given the agreement that the intention is to kill, how could it then be permissible to endorse omissions intended to do precisely that, in a legal system which claims to oppose killing? It is here that other matters are given credibility, taking the act or omission outside the scope of the criminal law and painting the decision with a brush of respectability. From what has been said so far, it is clear that those who would oppose the conclusion in these PVS cases might seem to have strong arguments behind them, arguments which go beyond their own personal attitudes. Nothing that has yet been said actually explains or justifies a decision which ends a life of whatever quality unless there is something other than these considerations which is of direct relevance to the particular circumstances.

A variety of other possibilities spring to mind. For example, might it not be said that it is in the 'best interests' of the person to be allowed to die? Clearly this might be thought to be true in any number of circumstances in which we would still not even contemplate suggesting that the killing (or letting die) was lawful. So we would have to find a way of distinguishing this set of circumstances from others – a way which would satisfy the intuition that in *this* kind of case the behaviour is *not* unlawful.

An immediate objection to the use of 'best interests' is shown by taking another example. I cannot claim that it is in the 'best interests' of a starving, terminally ill and profoundly handicapped relative that they should not live, and therefore refuse to feed them – not, at least without incurring criminal liability. But two arguments are used to differentiate the decision which I might reach from that reached by doctors. The first, or at least the one which can be disposed of first, is that it is both an obligation and a sacred trust of the carers to decide and act in the 'best interests' of their patient. In the Court of Session, the Lord President somewhat refined this notion of 'best interests'. His formulation was as follows:

> The question is whether the continuance of the treatment can be of any benefit to the patient in view of the condition which she has now reached. If it is possible to say that it can be of any benefit to her, then no doubt there is a balancing exercise to be done in order to assess whether it is in her best interests that the treatment should be discontinued. But if it cannot be of any benefit to her – and it is her benefit alone which must be considered in order to decide how the jurisdiction is to be exercised in the light of the medical evidence – then there are no longer any interests to be served by continuing it. (Transcript, pp.32–3)

The introduction of the question of 'benefit' is a welcome refinement of the 'best interests' test, the problems of which will be highlighted below. In agreeing with the Lord President, Lord Milligan explains why the test postulated in this way can be reasonably applied. Expressing 'considerable difficulty' with the use of a 'best interests' test in such cases, he nonetheless concluded that 'such a test can properly be applied in a case such as the present if the matter be viewed negatively, namely that it is not in the best interests of the patient to be kept alive by artificial means where the court is satisfied that the diagnosis is so clear and the prognosis so futile that the ward truly has no interest in being kept alive' (transcript, p.3).

The conclusion, therefore, would be that Anthony Bland, and others in his situation, do not *benefit* from the continuation of treatment, and therefore it cannot be said to be in their 'best interests'. Before looking in more depth at the problems of the more commonly used, unrefined version of the 'best interests' test, it is worth considering its main jurisprudential rival: that of using a substituted judgement test. In such a case, the court (or others) would be invited to reach a conclusion based on what they believe the patient would want were they in a position to speak for themselves. Although one or two references have been made to the possibility of using a substituted judgement test, which would seek to decide as the patient would, if he or she had been able (Hastings Center, 1987), this for some, is a manifest nonsense. In *Re Eve*, for example, the Canadian Supreme Court dismissed it, in non-therapeutic circumstances, as a fallacy. In other words, where the outcome was not clearly of benefit to the individual concerned, this test was completely inappropriate. In the UK, Lord Goff said, in the *Bland* case, that it 'may be of comfort to his relatives if they believe ... that the patient would not have wished his life to be artificially prolonged if he was totally unconscious and there was no hope of improvement in his condition' (at p.873), but that the personality of the person could scarcely be relevant.

Manifestly, as a test, substituted judgement has its flaws. Seldom will we be in a position truly to estimate what a non-competent person would have wanted. In fact, the suicide question has relevance here also. Where a person becomes incompetent as a result of a suicide attempt (as in Mrs Johnstone's case) it remains medically usual and legally permissible in effect to make a substituted judgement that they would prefer to be saved. Our doctors (endorsed by courts) are in fact used to making such assumptions, although they are not always legally endorsed, for example as in the Canadian case of *Malette* v. *Shulman* (it should be noted that this case did not involve a suicide attempt but was concerned with the doctor's ignoring of a competently executed prior declaration by the patient which refused blood transfusion in any circumstance). Nonetheless, even given that such substituted judgements *are* made in certain circumstances, there is a reluctance to engage in the intellectual sophistry which they can entail in most cases. UK courts, therefore, tend to prefer the 'best interests' approach.

However, dismissal of the substituted judgement test does not provide or elucidate the intellectual or moral content of the 'best interests' test. Best interests seems to imply that the person concerned gains, or at least does not lose, by the decisions taken on their behalf. However, as the Hastings Center pointed out, 'Patients who are permanently unconscious are unaware of benefits and burdens' (Hastings Center, 1987, p.19), so how would one go about assessing their 'best interests'? This same report concedes that, in fact, many of the considerations actually at stake in such cases will be concerned with whether

> a reasonable person in the patient's circumstance would find that this benefit [of continuing treatment], as well as the benefits to the patient's family and concerned friends (such as satisfaction in caring for the patient and the meaningfulness of the patient's continued survival) are outweighed by the burdens on those loved ones (such as financial cost and suffering). (Hastings Center, 1987, p.19)

Yet, as Lord Mustill would reply in *Airedale NHS Trust*:

> It seems to me to be stretching the concept of personal rights beyond breaking point to say that Anthony Bland has an interest in ending these sources of others' distress ... By ending his life the doctors will not relieve him of a burden become intolerable, for others carry the burden and he has none ... The distressing truth which must not be shirked is that the proposed conduct is not in the best interests of Anthony Bland, for he has no best interests of any kind. (At p.894)

Lord Mustill notes that the logic of this is also that Anthony Bland has no 'best interests' to be served by being kept alive. In a sense, therefore, the outcome might almost be thought to be morally neutral. Of course, this is not suggested by any of the judgements in the House of Lords, but their efforts to explain the decision to permit Bland's death seem to suggest that the morality of the decision must be found elsewhere than from consideration of the principles we have already considered. None, to date, is entirely satisfactory, for each is open to question. However, there is one very critical move which can be, and is, made which has on numerous occasions apparently been felt to change the value structures within which decisions are taken and to render acceptable what would otherwise not be. This has briefly been referred to already, although not in these terms, and amounts to what we shall call the 'medicalization' of the problem.

If no abstract or disinterested principles can be applied without resorting to sophistry or to a somewhat disingenuous elision of categorization, the option not uncommonly used is to address the context of the event rather than its content. So the morality of actions (or inactions) might be judged not against abstract principles but rather by principles held to apply in specific circumstances, for example in the practice of medicine. Arguably, of course, context should not have determinative standing in respect of judgements concerning such fundamental questions, but there is a tradition in the UK of using the context of medicine as a critical predictor of the ethical, and not just the professional, quality of behaviour. This is achieved in two principal ways: first, by defining what is going on as 'medical' and, second, by then applying to this 'medical' matter the tests routinely used in judging the practices of doctors.

A crucial question, therefore, related to whether or not what was proposed fitted within the medical model, much criticized by many commentators (see Illich, 1985; Kennedy, 1981; McKeown, 1976). One obvious objection to viewing this matter as medical (even given the fact that it occurs in a medical setting) is that nutrition and hydration are natural and not medical matters. Even if they have to be administered artificially by someone who has medical training, surely they are not solely the province of medicine. Mason and McCall Smith (1994) have long held the view that the technical intervention required is sufficient to categorize this as medical, a view apparently endorsed by Lord Keith in the Bland case, who – while arguing that the whole regime and not just nutrition and hydration should be looked at – nonetheless concludes, 'In any event, the administration of nourishment by the means adopted involves the application of a medical technique' (at p.861).

This is so, but, as has been suggested, this is only because so far I, or someone else, have not been shown how to do it. If I could do this, would its administration by a lawyer still render it eligible to be considered as medical? And what of the cases mentioned earlier where the nasogastric tube is at least in part used for the management of the case rather than because it is essential? Would Lord Keith say that, if natural feeding were possible, the feeding should still be stopped and, if not, why not?

An alternative answer was proffered by Lord Goff. Simply put, he states: 'There is overwhelming evidence that, in the medical profession, artificial feeding is regarded as a form of medical treatment' (at p.871). One might well say, so what? Indeed, Lord Goff seems then to concede that this need not be definitive by continuing, 'even if it is not strictly medical treatment, it must form part of the medical care of the patient' (at p.871). Arguably, on the surface, this might look like a major concession and open the possibility of challenge. Unfortunately, however, it results in a relatively similar conclusion, namely that, somehow or another, artificial nutrition and hydration are parts of medical care and therefore fit within the medical model.

The real importance of this is that it leads to the final legal answer. If this is medical treatment then, whatever objections may be raised to the other possible principles which have been discussed, in the tradition of the UK courts the behaviour of the clinician is to be judged by a particular test, the Bolam Test, derived from the case of *Bolam* v. *Friern Hospital Management Committee*. This test, although arguably slightly modified by the subsequent case of *Sidaway* v. *Bethlem Royal Hospital Governors and Others*,[5] effectively says that if a doctor acts in accordance with a practice which is held to be reasonable by a responsible body of medical opinion then he or she cannot be negligent (Brazier, 1992).

The application of this test in routine cases of negligence has many critics (McLean, 1989; Brazier, 1992), but its use as a method of testing the morality of decisions which will result in death must surely be even more suspect. Yet all that has gone before has inevitably led to a situation where, in the majority of judgements, the court has been left with the general principle that medical actions, unless obviously untenable, will be judged by what the profession thinks is 'reasonable'.

This approach has been used in a wide range of other controversial cases, such as the sterilization of women with severe intellectual disabilities, as well as in the more standard negligence situation. Although avoided by the High Court of Australia in *Rogers* v. *Whitaker*, it remains a powerful tool in decision making about clinical practice. But can it really be said to be satisfactory? Even ignoring the doubts already expressed about the use of the medical model in matters concerning the deliberate termination of life, there is little of morality within the Bolam Test itself. Despite the fact that courts claim to reserve to themselves the final decision, it is clear that they generally adhere to the standards required by the Bolam Test. Yet in fact all the Bolam Test does is to balance the behaviour of one doctor against his/her professional colleagues' behaviour. But, for Lord Goff, 'this principle must equally be applicable to decisions to initiate, or to discontinue, life support, as it is to other forms of treatment' (at p.871).

So can we really describe the Bolam Test as a principle? And, even if we can, does it have sufficient moral gravitas to be adequate to meet the conditions of patients whose lives may well be at risk because it is medical practice to do this? Are the problems underlying such cases not infinitely more complex, and considerably more profound, than mere reference to medical opinion can explain or conclude upon? As Lord Browne-Wilkinson said in the House of Lords, 'behind the questions of law lie moral, ethical, medical and practical issues of fundamental importance to society' (at p.877). Surely, society is not content that these matters should simply be defined and concluded upon by reference to what some doctors actually do?

Although it might be tempting to shift the onus from the community to the clinician, this neither reflects well on society nor does any favours to those charged with carrying the moral burden, that is, the doctors and nurses who are responsible for decision making and treatment. As Lord Mustill said, 'the decision is ethical, not medical, and ... there is no reason in logic why on such a decision the opinions of doctors should be decisive' (at p.895). Indeed, this view was expressed in 1991 by the Law Commission Consultation paper *Mentally Incapacitated Adults and Decision-Making: An Overview*, which noted that 'A test developed to deal with matters of clinical judgement is not necessarily the most appropriate one to use in circumstances where the balancing of other interests may be required' (Law Commission, 1991, p.33, paras. 2–24).

The Alternative

On this analysis, there is little real principle in the Bland decision. Despite some excellently argued judgements, their Lordships were thrown back on either using dubious moral propositions or on 'medicalizing' matters of life and death. Few of them were entirely satisfied with this, and Lords Browne-Wilkinson and Mustill made particularly strong pleas for alternatives to be found, as did Lord Milligan in the Johnstone case.

Two main options present themselves. First, it may be thought that an ethics committee framework within the hospital setting could offer a speedy, inexpensive resolution. However, experience of ethical committees in various jurisdictions and used for various purposes does not suggest that this is necessarily the best path. Committees have been shown to be uncertain about their functions, about their powers and about the roles of their membership. In particular, committees which lack statutory definition are likely to function in a legal vacuum. In any event, although undoubtedly the major issues in these cases are ethical, there is sufficient legal content to make this writer at least reluctant to hand over the responsibility of interpreting our laws to non-experts.

The second option is legislation. In a powerful plea for legislative intervention, Lord Browne-Wilkinson put the matter thus:

> it seems to me imperative that the moral, social and legal issues raised by this case should be considered by Parliament. The judges' function in this area of the law should be to apply the principles which society, through the democratic process, adopts, not to impose their standards on society. (At p.879)

This view was echoed by Lord Mustill, who took the debate one step further by also noting that the adversarial process seems inappropriate in issues of this type (at p.889). In the Court of Session, Lord Milligan welcomed what he saw as a start towards framing legislation, but conceded that for the present there is no option but that courts must be involved (transcript, p.2).

Beyond consideration of the role of the judiciary vis-à-vis Parliament are more vital issues which must be grasped, and Parliament surely is the only body capable of so doing. First, we must agree whether or not we want to offer treatment which prolongs existence, but not 'life with meaning', and in which cases. As the Hastings Center Report notes: 'Many medical treatments can sustain vital functioning without being able to reverse the underlying processes that may cause suffering or lead to death' (1987, p.viii). Equally, the failure to provide such treatments is a proxy decision for death, and because it is taken by third parties it is necessary that the community endorse it and that the way in which it is carried out be humane and compassionate, transparent and accountable.

Legislation, if conceding that sometimes this hard decision is appropriate, has the power to do more than merely acknowledge this as fact. It also has the capacity to impose on whatever forum or individual takes the decision a responsibility to observe and take seriously other vital ethical principles. It is not merely the initial question of whether or not we should endorse this practice which is relevant, but also how and in accordance with which principles (McLean, 1993).

The House of Lords Select Committee on Medical Ethics, reporting in 1994, was charged with the responsibility of addressing these, among other, questions about end of life decisions. Although many had hoped that the report would provide clarity in terms of principle and perhaps even a proposal for legislative intervention, they were to be disappointed. The simple way of describing their conclusion on persistent vegetative state is that doctors should think harder about initiating treatment and that – if this happened – there would be fewer cases raising this problem. With all respect, I find this conclusion puzzling and most unsatisfactory, for two main reasons. First, there is an underlying assumption that doctors do not currently think hard enough about initiating treatment, an assumption which is both incapable of proof and potentially insulting to the doctors concerned. Secondly, the failure to offer clarification might encourage doctors not to intervene in cases if they are not certain that treatment could subsequently be lawfully withdrawn. Surely, if this is the best that we can offer, there is a very real risk that some patients whose lives might have been saved would be denied that chance because doctors are reluctant to intervene, just in case.

Conclusions

'I must admit,' says Lord Mustill in the Bland case, 'to having felt profound misgivings about almost every aspect of this case' (at p.896). These misgivings are shared by many, even those who believe that the decision reached was the 'right' one – and there will be many of those. Opinion poll evidence suggests, for example, that 70 per cent of adults in the Netherlands do not wish even active killing to be a criminal offence' (*Lancet*, 1993, p.426). The *Bulletin of Medical Ethics* (1993) also notes that many adults in countries such as Denmark where the 'living will' has been given statutory backing are opting to choose for themselves what should and should not be done to them in situations in which they become incapacitated. In other words, there is a trend towards acceptance that life is not always preferable to death, a trend which might be sufficient to indicate to our legislators that the time is overdue for a reassessment of the relevant law.

If courts alone, without further guidance, are not the most appropriate fora for decision making, any alternative must nonetheless be properly established within a clear constitutional framework having regard to due process, formal justice and the consistent application of agreed tests. The Law Commission (England and Wales) expressed its concern about the possibility of inconsistency in decision making by courts, a possibility which legislation has the capacity to minimize if not eradicate (Law Commission, 1991).

In an important way, legislation can clarify the nature of the event. Decisions taken within a hospital do not become medical merely because of context. The application of the medical model, and the use of the Bolam Test, are to be firmly resisted in matters which go to the heart of the moral tone of the community. Equally, the liability of those charged with taking the steps which bring the decision to reality can be, and should be, clarified by legislative intervention.

It may well be true that 'The advances of medicine are amongst the most notable human achievements of the twentieth century' (Hastings Center, 1987, p.viii) but they have also posed non-clinical questions which it is the responsibility of the community, and not merely one part of it, to answer. The increasing number of cases in the USA, Canada and other jurisdictions suggests that this is a problem which will not decrease, indeed it may increase. Now is the time for us to address it firmly, honestly and openly, and for this we need the active response of our legislators. Let us not shirk this issue now. Rather than engaging in nitpicking, let it be conceded that the doctor who fails to continue life-sustaining treatment is *already* engaging in assisting death, and if we intend for this to continue, it is vital that it is carried out against a backdrop of respect for rights, and after full consideration of the values and consequences involved, rather than within the narrower confines of professional practice.

Notes

1 There may be between 1000 and 1500 persons in the UK suffering from PVS as well as others suffering from medical conditions of a similar nature (per Lord Lowry) in *Airedale NHS Trust* v. *Bland* [1993] 1 All ER 821, at p.878.
2 Thus reaffirming Butler-Sloss, LJ In *Re T* [1992] 3 Med. L.R.306, at p.314.
3 See, for example, *Re F (Mental Patient: Sterilisation)* [1990] 2 AC 1; *Re F* [1989] 1 MLR 58 (HL).
4 See comments in *Belchertown State School Superintendent* v. *Saikewicz* (1977) 370 NE 2d 417, at p.428: 'To presume that the incompetent person must always be subjected to what many rational and intelligent persons may decline is to downgrade the status of the incompetent person by placing a lesser value on his intrinsic human worth and vitality.'
5 Sidaway's case emphasizes that 'accepted medical practice' is never conclusive and that the court makes the ultimate determination.

References

Brazier, M. (1992), *Medicine, Patients and the Law*, London: Penguin Books.
Bulletin of Medical Ethics, November 1992.
Bulletin of Medical Ethics, February 1993.
Giesen, D. (1990), 'Law and Ethical Dilemmas at Life's End', *Law and Moral Dilemmas Affecting Life and Death*, Council of Europe, 1992, Proceedings of the XXth Annual Colloquy on European Law, pp.82–3.
Hastings Center Report, (1987), Guidelines on the Termination of Life-Sustaining Treatment and the Care of the Dying, Hastings Center.
Report of the House of Lords Select Committee on Medical Ethics, HL Paper 21–1, London, HMSO, 1994.
Illich I. (1985), *Limits to Medicine, Medical Nemesis: The Expropriation of Health*, Harmondsworth: Penguin Books.
Kennedy, I. (1981), *The Unmasking of Medicine*, London: Allen & Unwin.
McKeown, T. (1976), *The Role of Medicine*, London: Nuffield Provincial Hospitals Trust.
McLean, S.A.M. (1989), *A Patient's Right to Know: Information Disclosure, the Doctor and the Law*, Aldershot: Dartmouth.
McLean, S.A.M. (1993), *Minutes of Evidence Taken Before the Select Committee on Medical Ethics*, HL Paper 91-vi, London: HMSO.
Mason, J.K. and R.A. McCall Smith (1994), *Law and Medical Ethics*, London: Butterworths.
The Lancet, 1993, 426.
The Law Commission (1991), *Mentally Incapacitated Adults and Decision-Making: An Overview*, Consultation Paper No. 119, London: HMSO.

Cases

Airedale NHS Trust v. *Bland* [1993] 1 All ER 821.
Barber v. *Superior Court of Los Angeles County* (1983) 147 Cal App 3d 1006.
Belchertown State School Superintendent v. *Saikewicz* (1977) 370 NE 2d 417.
Bolam v. *Friern Hospital Management Committee* [1957] 1 WLR 582.
In the Matter of a Ward of Court (1995) 2 ILRM 401.
In Re T [1992] 3 Med. L.R. 306.
Law Hospital NHS Trust v. *The Lord Advocate and Others* (transcript), 22 March 1996.
Malette v. *Shulman* (1990) 67 DLR (4th) 321.
Re Eve (1987) 31 DLR (4th) 1.
Re F (Mental Patient: Sterilisation) [1990] 2 AC 1; *Re F* [1989] 1 MLR 58 (HL)
Rogers v. *Whitaker* (1992) 109 AL 625; (1992) 175 CLR 479.
Sidaway v. *Bethlem Royal Hospital Governors and Others* [1984] All ER 1018 (CA); [1985] All ER 643 (HL).

9 Gender and Equity: Emerging Issues in Australian Clinical Drug Trial Regulatory Policies

LEANNA DARVALL[1]

Introduction

Australian and American human subject research regulatory policies were shaped by human rights and safety concerns prompted by Nazi experimentation, unethical American research practices during the 1960s and publicity concerning the thalidomide disaster. Although initial regulatory policies in both countries were designed partly with a view to ensuring that research participants were treated as autonomous individuals, their main objectives were avoidance of harm to and exploitation of research populations. Against this background, the predominantly protectionist role of regulatory agencies found widespread public acceptance. However, by the mid-1980s, largely as a result of the HIV/AIDS crisis, regulatory systems in both America and Australia came under increasing pressure from gay rights activists and people with AIDS (PWAs) to broaden access to unapproved drugs. The willingness of many of these individuals to accept the possibility of risk of injury from unapproved drugs raised issues concerning the limits of patient autonomy vis-à-vis government as protector of public health and safety. Acknowledging the importance of autonomy and rights-based arguments, regulatory agencies in Australia and the USA developed mechanisms to 'fast track' drugs. Nevertheless, regulatory policies developed by the relevant agencies ensured that safety standards would not be compromised.

In America, the HIV/AIDS crisis highlighted a number of important issues, including the exclusion of women and ethnic minorities from clinical drug trial populations. The initial identification of HIV/AIDS as a disease affecting the male homosexual community has had important repercussions for women. This initial characterization impeded the development of suitable educational and health care programmes for women, including access to clinical trials of promising new drugs. As a consequence, despite the prevalence of AIDS-infected women and the possibility that they may need different treatment, drug trials have involved mostly men (Levine, 1991, p.18).

Exclusion of women is not limited to trials involving HIV/AIDS treatments (Minkoff *et al.*, 1992, p.137). In 1990, the US General Accounting Office noted that, despite a 1986 federal policy to the contrary, women continued to be insufficiently represented in research populations. According to the National Institutes of Health (NIH), this state of affairs has created significant gaps in knowledge about diseases affecting both men and women (Dresser, 1992, p.24). A recent editorial in the *New England Journal of Medicine* suggests that too many research studies of prevention, diagnostic methods and intervention for coronary heart disease have involved only male subjects. It further states:

> Decades of sex-exclusive research have reinforced the myth that coronary artery disease is a uniquely male affliction and have generated data in which men are the normative standard. The extrapolation of these male-generated findings to women has led in some cases to biased standards of care and has prevented the full consideration of several important aspects of coronary disease in women. The importance of oestrogen in women as an antiatherogenic agent and its role in both the primary and secondary prevention of coronary disease in women are examples. With an 'androgenic' research focus, oestrogen would be unlikely to be tested as a treatment for coronary disease. We must be challenged by the example of coronary artery disease to examine critically the extent to which the Yentl syndrome pervades medicine and medical research and to respond promptly whenever its influence is evident. (Healy, 1991, p.275)

This issue has received recent attention at an international level. Guidelines published in 1993 by the Council for International Organizations of Medical Sciences in collaboration with the World Health Organization state that the exclusion of women of reproductive age from clinical trials is unjust as it deprives women as a class from the benefits of research and because it is an affront to their right of self-determination. Accordingly, exclusion of such women can be justified only where there is evidence, or suspicion, that a particular drug or vaccine is mutagenic or teratogenic (Guidelines, 1993, p.34).

Despite publication of international guidelines and lively debate in the USA, scant attention has been paid to this issue by government, academics or public interest groups in Australia. Some recent signs of an emerging interest are evidenced by Australian Health Ethics Committee activity which includes a discussion paper and the establishment of a working party to draft appropriate guidelines in this area. This chapter outlines various perspectives which have shaped American discourse, together with government initiatives in the form of policies, regulations and guidelines. Against this background, a number of key issues are identified which must be addressed in the formulation of Australian policy and guidelines.

Arguments Concerning the Exclusion or Inclusion of Women in Clinical Drug Trials

A frequent justification for excluding women from clinical drug trials is that the inclusion of female participants of reproductive capacity would result in an unacceptable increase in development costs, especially in phase one or early phase two studies. Phase one studies usually involve less than a hundred healthy subjects and are designed to detect gross safety problems and to establish appropriate dosages for testing purposes. Phase two studies involve approximately 200 participants and are undertaken with a view to establishing efficacy and identifying adverse effects. Phase three studies may involve thousands of participants and are designed to elaborate on therapeutic value and adverse effects. It is argued that the inclusion of women in early phase studies would mean that preclinical studies would have to be commenced approximately one year prior to filing an Investigational New Drug Application, that is before it was established that the drug would be involved in human subject testing. This would increase both the time and costs involved in drug development. These justifications are also used in relation to the exclusion of women from phase three studies. Because young women are not studied to any great extent in the early phases of trials, information about gender differences in relation to absorption and metabolism of a drug and effects of the menstrual cycle remain unanswered. If there is concern that gender differences exist in relation to a particular drug, these differences can contribute confounding variables, thereby increasing the difficulty of obtaining clean data, so that larger studies to demonstrate efficacy will need to be undertaken. To attempt to address these specific problems during phase three studies would be significantly to delay the completion of such studies (Goldman, 1993, pp.171–2).

Critics of an economic approach to the inclusion of women in clinical drug trials argue that it is too narrowly conceived and that economic considerations must be balanced against competing ethical criteria. Following the implementation of the NIH Revitalization Act (1993), economy-based arguments are no longer acceptable in an American context. The legislation specifically provides that arguments based on costs are not permissible grounds for excluding women from clinical trials. In response to arguments based on the need for homogenous trial populations and clean data, Dresser contends that focusing on one type of human physiology reduces the generalizability of the data (Dresser, 1992, p.25). Further, as knowledge concerning disease processes in women emerges, increasing doubt is cast on the assumption that 'biological effects in women can be discerned from the experience of male subjects' (Minkoff *et al.*, 1992, p.137).

A major argument for excluding women of childbearing age from clinical trials is based on the prospect of common law liability for foetal injury. Following the thalidomide drug tragedy, women of childbearing age were excluded from clinical trials. The reason for the exclusion of this group is that drug-related foetal injuries *in utero* stem more easily from maternal exposure during pregnancy, as opposed to paternal or maternal exposure prior to pregnancy where a drug may damage the gametes. However, Charo argues that, if female subjects were adequately informed of possible risks of impairment of fertility and fetal injury and adequate precautions were taken against pregnancy during the course of the trial, it would be unlikely that a manufacturer would be found negligent, unless basic animal studies on teratogenicity had been ignored (Charo, 1993, p.146). Because common law liability may arise from omissions, as well as from positive acts, Merton contends that any consideration of drug manufacturers' legal liability should take into account the possible consequences of conducting trials excluding women. According to this line of reasoning, failure to undertake adequate clinical testing in terms of equal gender representation may constitute a breach of a manufacturer's duty of care to consumers to ensure the safety of its products (Merton, 1993, pp.416–22). It could also be argued, in an Australian context, that excluding women from clinical drug trials constitutes a breach of state equal opportunity legislation which prohibits a refusal to provide goods and services on the basis of gender. Another justification for excluding women from clinical trials is that their recruitment is difficult because of family responsibilities and lack of suitable child care facilities. Carol Levine suggests that research programmes must be devised which take into account the special needs of this group with regard to child care, employment, transport and family responsibilities (Levine, 1991, p.22).

The issue of whether pregnant women should be enrolled in clinical drug trials requires careful consideration of the interests of both women and fetuses. In discussing this issue, it is important to distinguish between the following situations: (a) inclusion of women in trials concerning pregnancy-specific indications, (b) inclusion of women in trials concerning medical conditions which are common in women of childbearing potential, and (c) inclusion of women in trials associated with potential cures for life-threatening conditions, such as HIV/AIDS. The above-mentioned *International Ethical Guidelines for Biomedical Research Involving Human Subjects* provide as follows:

> Pregnant or nursing women should in no circumstances be the subjects of non-clinical research unless the research carries no more than minimal risk to the fetus or nursing infant and the object of the research is to obtain new knowledge about pregnancy or lactation. As a general rule, pregnant or nursing women should not be subjects of any clinical trials except such trials as are designed to protect or advance the health of pregnant or nursing women or fetuses or nursing infants, and for which women who are not pregnant or nursing would not be suitable subjects. (*Guidelines*, 1993, p.33)

In an effort to avoid possible tensions between competing principles of beneficence, prevention of harm and justice, Levine *et al.* adopt a 'principle of proportionality' approach. In seeking to strike an appropriate balance, the authors argue that pregnant women should not be excluded categorically from phase two and three protocols, or from access under Treatment INDs. (Federal Food and Drug Administration (FDA) regulations for Treatment Investigational New Drugs (INDs) issued in 1987 permit drugs to be made available prior to marketing approval in certain circumstances to persons who might benefit.) However, women need not be included in phase one studies, as no benefit is likely to accrue to them. In the case of a potentially life-saving drug, and where no other treatment exists, they suggest that a pregnant woman must be permitted access to either a phase two or a phase three trial, or to a Treatment IND. The authors contend that the presumption that pregnant women are eligible for selection as research subjects can only be rebutted by showing that a serious risk to the future child exists and either that a potentially equally effective treatment is available or that little benefit to the woman from the particular protocol is expected (Levine *et al.*, 1991, p.16).

Carol Levine considers that this approach provides an appropriate guide for decision making in this area in relation to women of reproductive age, including pregnant women. For Levine, the major ethical issue to be addressed is as follows:

> How can the interests of society in developing safe and effective drugs for conditions that affect women, and the interests of individual women

> in obtaining access to experimental drugs that may prove of benefit to them, be balanced against the obligation to prevent harm, particularly to unconsenting future children that will be born? (Levine, 1991, p.20)

In the context of HIV/AIDS clinical drug trials, Levine identifies categories of risks to be considered in the formulation of exclusion criteria. In relation to most HIV/AIDS studies which do not present any known or foreseeable teratogenic risks, she argues that there is no reason to exclude women who are not pregnant, or who do not intend to become pregnant. She also argues that, where there are no acceptable alternative therapies, women should be permitted to participate in studies involving minimal to moderate risks to future children but which also offer the possibility of great benefit to the woman. In both these situations she believes that women, if adequately informed, should be permitted to decide for themselves whether to participate. However, she believes that exclusion of sexually active, fertile women would be justified where a research protocol presents a known high risk to future children and no known, or minimal, benefit to women. Levine justifies exclusion in these circumstances on the grounds that, as no form of contraception is absolutely reliable, foetal injury may occur at a time when a woman does not realize that she is pregnant. Further, she notes the difficulties in obtaining an informed consent, including those arising from a common misapprehension that the purpose of research is to benefit trial participants, rather than to acquire generalizable knowledge. Added to these difficulties is the likelihood that a subject's appreciation and concern regarding risks will decline over time. For these reasons, Levine contends that risks may not be fully appreciated, or remembered, by a woman who becomes pregnant during a clinical trial (Levine, 1991, pp.21–2).

Minkoff *et al.* argue that treating women and men differently in relation to reproductive potential and participation in clinical trials cannot be justified, given that teratogenic effects have been linked in some instances to changes in the male gamete (Minkoff *et al.*, 1992, p.138). The Community Research Initiative (CRI) which was established in New York in 1986 by the research arm of the People with AIDS Coalition endorses such an approach. CRI research protocols are accessible to everyone, including traditionally underrepresented groups such as IV drug users, Blacks, Hispanics, prisoners and women. In contrast to mainstream research, CRI policy does not treat women and men of reproductive age differently, unless there is a solid scientific basis for doing so. In assessing exclusion criteria concerning reproductive potential, including pregnancy, a higher value will not necessarily be placed on the potential risk to offspring than on the potential benefit to a trial participant. The availability of alternatives which pose a lesser risk to potential offspring will be taken into account in reaching a decision. CRI policy requires that trial participants receive adequate information about potential adverse reproductive outcomes (Merton, 1990, p.512).

The exclusion of women from clinical trials has important implications in terms of shifting risk from specific trial populations to drug users as a class. According to Professor Mirkin, an American professor of paediatrics and pharmacology,

> Society may choose to forbid drug evaluation in pregnant women and children. This choice would certainly reduce the risk of damaging individuals through research. However, this would maximise the possibility of random disaster resulting from use of inadequately investigated drugs. In the final analysis it seems safe to predict that more individuals would be damaged: however, the damage would be distributed randomly rather than imposed upon preselected individuals. (Mirkin, 1975, pp.110–11)

Because of this risk-shifting factor, Rebecca Dresser, amongst others, suggests that womens' exclusion from clinical trials should not be characterized solely in terms of protecting them from risks associated with unapproved substances. Instead, she believes that scientists and policy makers must recognize that choice is between exposing some consenting women to risks in a monitored clinical trial, or exposing larger numbers to risks in a clinical situation where the same safeguards are not imposed (Dresser, 1992, p.24). Certain practical ramifications of this risk-shifting process have been identified by Minkoff *et al.*, including reluctance on the part of doctors to prescribe approved drugs for women patients when these substances have not been used in trials with female populations. In addition, they suggest that sometimes physicians freely prescribe drugs which occasion adverse effects in far greater numbers than would have occurred within a trial setting (Minkoff *et al.*, 1992, pp.137–8).

Finally, it should be noted that those who argue for the inclusion of women in clinical trials are concerned to ensure that research participants' welfare and safety are not compromised. For this reason, Susan Sherwin, amongst others, stresses that, where it is proposed to recruit women as participants in clinical trials, researchers should be required to demonstrate that the results will be of specific benefit to the individuals in question. (Sherwin, 1992, pp.159–65)

American Developments Concerning the Inclusion of Women in Clinical Trials

Federal Food and Drug Administration (FDA) initiatives (1977–93)

In 1993, the FDA published a 'Guideline for the Study and Evaluation of Gender Differences in the Clinical Evaluation of Drugs' (*Federal Register*, vol.58, 22 July). This revised guideline replaces the previous guideline issued in 1977. Prior to outlining the new guideline below, a summary of the 1977 guideline, together with a statement of reasons for revision, are provided by way of background information.

1977 guideline The 1977 guideline states that in general women of childbearing potential should be excluded from phase one and early phase two studies. The guideline contains a broad definition of women of childbearing potential which includes all pre-menopausal women who are not surgically sterilized. Where adequate information on safety and effectiveness has been amassed during these phases, women of childbearing potential can be included in later phase studies, providing animal teratogenicity and the female part of animal fertility studies have been completed. The policy does not address the manner in which early human evidence of safety and effectiveness and the results of animal reproduction studies should be used to make decisions about participation of women in later trials. Instead, it is intended that these considerations remain part of risk–benefit assessment to be undertaken by researchers, subjects, institutional review boards (IRBs) and by FDA evaluators in the course of subsequent agency review. However, women of childbearing potential can receive investigational drugs in the earliest phases of testing, even in the absence of adequate animal reproductive studies, in the case of drugs intended for life-saving or life-prolonging treatment.

Reasons for revising the 1977 guideline The FDA acknowledges that the general effect of the 1977 guideline has been to exclude women from phase one non-therapeutic studies and from the earliest controlled effectiveness studies (early phase two), except for studies of life-threatening illnesses such as AIDS. It further acknowledges that, although the 1977 guideline has not resulted in a failure to include numbers of women in the later phases of clinical trials, it has restricted the early accumulation of information concerning responses to drugs in women that could be used in designing phase two and three trials and perhaps also delayed appreciation of gender-related variation in drug effects. In addition, the FDA states that there is reason to believe that earlier participation of women in studies would increase the likelihood that gender-specific data might be used to make appropriate adjustments (for example, adjusted dosages) in larger clinical studies. The FDA also acknowledges that the inclusion of women in early phase studies is consistent with congressional intent regarding gender-based discrimination and with a recent US Supreme Court decision concerning a woman's right to participate in decisions involving fetal risk. In withdrawing the restriction on the participation of women of childbearing potential in early clinical trials, including clinical pharmacology studies and early therapeutic studies, the FDA states that it is expected that, in accordance with good medical practice, appropriate precautions will be taken by women against becoming pregnant during the course of the trial. Further, that they will receive adequate counselling about the importance of taking such precautions and, that efforts will be made to ensure that women are not pregnant at the time of entering a trial and that full information is provided about animal reproduction studies and any other information concerning the teratogenic potential of the drug. It should be noted that, while explicitly rejecting a regulatory basis for routinely requiring that women in general, or women of childbearing potential, be included in early phase trials, the agency stated that it expects careful characterization of drug effects by gender and that it seeks to remove unnecessary federal impediments to the inclusion of women in the earliest stages of drug development. The FDA suggested that in some cases, such as when the disease being studied is serious and affects women, there may be a basis for requiring participation of women in early studies.

1993 guideline By way of an underlying rationale for issuing the 1993 guideline, the FDA states that variations in responses to drugs, including gender-related differences, can arise from pharmacokinetic differences (that is, differences in the way a drug is absorbed, metabolized, distributed or excreted) or pharmacodynamic differences (that is, differences in response to a given concentration of a drug in blood or other tissue). The FDA further notes that, for both practical and theoretical reasons, evaluation of possible gender-related differences in responses should initially focus on the evaluation of potential pharmacokinetic differences. Once reliable assays are developed for a drug and its metabolites, techniques exist for readily assessing gender-related or other subgroup-related pharmacokinetic differences. Pharmacokinetic evaluation also enables relevant assessment of pharmacodynamic differences or relationships.

The guideline states that, for most drugs, representatives of both genders should be included in clinical trials in numbers adequate to allow detection of clinically significant gender-related differences in drug response. Inclusion of women in the earliest phases of clinical development is therefore encouraged so that information on gender differences may be used to refine the design of later trials. The 1993 guideline does not include the strict limitation on the participation of women of childbearing potential in phase one and early phase two trials which was imposed by the 1977 guideline. The new guideline further states that analyses to detect the influence of gender should be carried out both for individual studies and in the overall integrated analyses of effectiveness and safety.

The guideline provides that appropriate procedures should be taken in clinical studies against inadvertent exposure of fetuses to potentially toxic agents and to inform subjects and patients of potential risks and the need for precautions. Consent documents and investigator's brochures should include in all cases all available information regarding the potential risk of fetal toxicity. The results of animal reproductive studies, if completed, should be explained. If such studies have not been completed, other relevant information concerning drugs with related structures or pharmacologic effects should be given. If no relevant information is available, the potential for fetal risk must be included in the consent document.

The FDA expects that reproductive toxicity studies will be completed before there is large-scale exposure of women of childbearing potential, that is usually by the end of phase two and before any expanded access programme is implemented. Clinical protocols should also include measures that will minimize the possibility of fetal exposures to the investigational drug, except in the case of trials to study the effect of drugs during pregnancy. Where abnormalities of reproductive organs or their functions have been observed in experimental animals, the decision to include women of reproductive age should be based on a careful risk–benefit analysis. The clinical studies in these circumstances should include appropriate monitoring and/or laboratory studies to allow detection of these effects.

The Department of Health and Human Services (DHHS) Initiatives

The DHHS has issued regulations governing human subject research which are codified in Title 45 Part 46 of the Code of Federal Regulations, Protection of Human Subjects (45 CFR 46), which was last revised in 1991. These regulations apply to all research involving human participants conducted by the DHHS or supported, in whole or in part, by the DHHS. It should be noted that regulations issued by the FDA apply to all research involving products regulated by the FDA, including drugs and medical devices for human use. FDA regulations governing human subject research are codified in 21 CFR 50 (Protection of Human Subjects) and 21 CFR 56 (Institutional Review Boards). However, when research involving products regulated by the FDA is funded by the DHHS, both DHHS and FDA regulations apply.

Promulgated in the mid-1970s, Subpart B of Part 46 of Title 45 of the Code of Federal regulations contains provisions relating to research involving fetuses and pregnant women. This subpart prohibits research involving pregnant women unless appropriate studies on animals and non-pregnant individuals have been completed, the purpose of the research is to meet the health needs of the mother or the particular fetus, and risk to the fetus is minimal. The relevant provisions do not define key concepts such as 'appropriate studies' and 'minimal risk'.

National Institutes of Health (NIH) and Alcohol, Drug Abuse and Mental Health Administration (ADAMHA) Initiatives

The NIH and ADAMHA promulgated a 'Policy Concerning Inclusion of Women in Study Populations' (*NIH Guide*, vol.20, 8 February 1991). The policy requires evaluation of the gender composition of each study proposed for funding and a statement of reasons for excluding members of one gender, or for a disproportionate representation of one gender. Gender representation should be appropriate to the known incidence/prevalence of the disease/condition being studied, and reasons for exclusion must be well explained and justified. Such justification must be 'compelling' in terms of either a strong scientific rationale or a need to protect the health of the subjects.

NIH Revitalization Act 1993 The NIH Revitalization Act 1993 was implemented following publicity concerning a Government Accounting Office report on the limited success of the NIH in enforcing its own policy. The legislation provides that the director of NIH must ensure that women and racial and ethnic minority groups are included as subjects in early research projects conducted or supported by NIH and ADAMHA. The director of NIH must also ensure that trials are conducted so as to enable a valid analysis of whether the variables being studied affect women, or ethnic minorities, differently from other trial subjects. However, these provisions do not apply to clinical research if the inclusion of women is deemed 'inappropriate' with respect to (a) the health of subjects, (b) the purpose of the research, or (c) or if it is deemed to be so under such other circumstances as the director of NIH may designate in guidelines. Further, in the case of a clinical trial, guidelines may provide that inclusion in the trial is not required if substantial scientific data demonstrate no significant differences between (a) the effects that the variables to be studied have on women (or minorities) and (b) the effects that the variables have on individuals who would serve as subjects in the trial in the event that such inclusions were not required. As previously stated, the cost of including women in clinical trials is not a permissible consideration in determining whether such inclusion is inappropriate. The legislation requires Clinical Research Equity Subcommittees to be established within each of the national research institutes. These bodies must include members with expertise in women's health. Finally, the legislation provides that the director shall conduct or support outreach programmes for the recruitment of women and minority groups as clinical trial subjects.

NIH guidelines on the inclusion of women and minorities as subjects in clinical research (1994) These guidelines were implemented pursuant to the NIH Revitalization Act 1993 and supersede the NIH and ADAMHA policy outlined above. The guidelines were drafted with the aim of ensuring that women and minorities are included in all NIH-funded research, unless a clear and compelling justification for their exclusion can be established. Such justification cannot be based on the cost of conducting clinical research. The guidelines provide that women of childbearing potential should not be routinely excluded from participation in clinical research. In addition, they require that research be conducted in order to elicit information about male and female research subjects and ethnic minorities and, in the case of clinical trials, to examine different effects on such groups. To this end, increased attention is required to be given to gender and ethnicity in the earlier stages of research to enable informed decision making at phase three concerning trial design. A further requirement is that programmes and support for outreach efforts be developed to recruit these groups into clinical studies.

Australian Policy and Guidelines Concerning the Inclusion of Women in Clinical Trials

In contrast to American initiatives described above, Australian policy is still very much in its infancy. In 1991, the Therapeutic Goods Administration (TGA) issued guidelines which provide that researchers are responsible for ensuring the equitable selection of research subjects. However, the guidelines do not specify how this policy is to be interpreted with respect to women (TGA Guidelines, 1991, para. 2.1.6). There has been little debate in Australian professional literature of this issue. Public comment has largely emanated from AIDS' and womens' groups. The AIDS Council of New South Wales has recommended that there should not be a blanket exclusion of women from clinical trials for the treatment of HIV/AIDS and recommends that trial protocols be developed which encourage the participation of individuals from populations which have been historically excluded, including women. The Council also stated that consent documents should fully describe risks which may be occasioned to women, fetuses and breast-fed infants and that counselling should be available to explain the risk–benefit ratio so that an appropriate choice can be made regarding participation (AIDS Council of NSW, 1990). The National Health and Medical Research Council (NHMRC) Womens' Health Strategy and Implementation Plan 1993 recommended that the Australian Health Ethics Committee (AHEC) develop a discussion paper concerning the involvement of women of reproductive age in clinical trials, taking into account cultural and linguistic differences. In 1995, a discussion paper was prepared by AHEC and a subcommittee was established to consider policy and guidelines in this area.

The NHMRC has recently addressed the issue of representation of women in research populations. Since 1993, project grant applications forms for the Medical Research Committee (MRC) and the Public Health Research and Development Committee (PHRDC) request details regarding the proportion of male and female subjects. Applicants for MRC funding are required to state whether the research project will include equal representation of male and female subjects. A brief explanation must be provided if equal numbers of both sexes are not to be included in a research project.

Conclusion

Public discourse concerning the inclusion of women of reproductive age in clinical drug trials has taken place almost exclusively in an American context. A notable feature of this debate is the emphasis placed on principles of equitable access and research participant autonomy. A conceptual framework adopting this approach leaves little room for regulatory paternalism, a philosophy embraced by Australian and American regulatory agencies during the 1960s and 1970s. Largely as a result of the HIV/AIDS crisis in America, gay rights activists, people with HIV/AIDS and ethnic minority groups joined forces with feminists and womens' groups in demanding regulatory policies which placed greater emphasis on research participant autonomy. Feminists, amongst others, argued that the principle of equitable access requires that individuals, regardless of gender, should be free to choose whether or not to participate in clinical drug trials. A follow-on effect from the efforts of these groups in securing changes in FDA and NIH regulatory policies and from the formulation of international guidelines, has been a growing local awareness of a need to include women of reproductive age in clinical drug trials. The challenge for Australian policy makers and all interested parties involved as a result of community consultation processes will be to develop policies and guidelines premissed on principles of autonomy and equitable access which do not compromise safety standards. In framing an Australian policy, it should be noted that, in the USA, in the absence of a national health scheme, clinical trials are perceived as a means of gaining access to potential cures or treatment by terminally ill individuals, including people with HIV/AIDS. In Australia, given universal access to health care via the Medicare scheme, participation in clinical trials is unlikely to assume such critical importance. This difference must be taken into account when balancing competing interests and ethical principles in the formulation of regulatory policy.

The various perspectives summarized above, together with FDA and NIH policy and regulatory responses, compel those involved in the formulation of Australian guidelines to address a number of key issues. Clearly, it will be necessary to determine in what, if any, circumstances pregnant women will be permitted to participate in clinical trials. This in turn will necessitate an appropriate balance to be struck between the interests of the fetus in avoiding infliction of injury and principles of autonomy and equitable access in relation to women research participants. It will also be necessary to consider whether there are any circumstances in which sponsors and researchers may be justified in excluding women of reproductive age from clinical trials and what standard of proof should be required in support of such exemptions.

Women are not and should not be treated as a homogeneous group. It is therefore imperative that policies and guidelines acknowledge women's differences. Issues including those of competency and ethnicity are of crucial importance in developing guidelines in this area. A fundamental issue is whether women who are not legally competent to decide for themselves should nevertheless be permitted to participate in clinical trials. This question is rendered all the more complex because relevant Australian state legislation differs as to whether guardian consent alone is adequate in these circumstances. Where consent from a statutory body such as a guardianship board is not an additional requirement, responsibility will fall to institutional ethics committees (IEC) to ensure that the interests of incompetent research participants are adequately protected. In these circumstances, it is vital that guidelines require that at least one IEC member be given responsibility for continuing review of the relevant trial to safeguard incompetent participants' welfare. It is equally important that IEC members receive educational training in relation to competency and other complex issues arising out of interpretation and application of the guidelines.

Taking account of ethnic and cultural diversity is essential in framing regulatory policies in this area. Differences between women research participants assume the utmost importance in relation to communication between researchers and participants for the purposes of recruitment and obtaining consent. Acknowledging cultural differences may require, for example, that indigenous women representatives be included on IECs when indigenous women participate in clinical trials. The framing of Australian policy and guidelines in relation to free and informed decision making by women of reproductive age as to whether or not to participate in clinical trials provides an important challenge for regulators and interested community members. In undertaking this task, American policy and regulations will undoubtedly serve as useful precedents. However, the existence of an Australian national health scheme and an awareness of and sensitivity to the needs of various communities are factors which must necessarily inform and shape this undertaking.

Note

1 The contents of this chapter, with the exception of the final section, are substantially the same as the contents of a discussion paper prepared for the Australian Health Ethics Committee (AHEC) by the author. The relevant material is reproduced here with the kind permission of AHEC.

Bibliography

AIDS Council of New South Wales (1990), *Trialing Approval and Marketing of Treatment for HIV/AIDS and Related Illnesses in Australia.*

Bell, N.K. (1992), 'Women and AIDS: Too Little, Too Late?', in H.B. Holmes and L.M. Purdy (eds), *Feminist Perspectives in Medical Ethics*, Bloomington and Indianapolis: Indiana University Press, p.49.

Charo, A. (1993), 'Protecting Us to Death: Women, Pregnancy and Clinical Research Trials', *St. Louis University Law Journal*, **38**, 135.

Darvall, L. (1994), 'Autonomy and protectionism: striking a balance in human subject research policy and regulation', *Law in Context*, **11**, (2), 82.

Dresser, R. (1992), 'Wanted Single, White Male for Medical Research', *Hastings Center Report*, **221**, 24.

Gillespie, R. (1988), 'Research on Human Subjects: An Historical Overview', *Conference Proceedings – Can Ethics be Done by Committee?*, Monash University: Centre for Human Bioethics, **3**.

Goldman, B. (1993), 'A Drug Company Report: What is the Same and What is Changing with Respect to Inclusion/Exclusion of Women in Clinical Trials', *Food Drug and Cosmetic Law Journal*, **48**, 169.

Healy, B. (1991), 'The Yentl Syndrome', *New England Journal of Medicine*, **325**, 275.

International Ethical Guidelines for Biomedical Research Involving Human Subjects (1993), Geneva: Council for International Organizations of Medical Sciences in collaboration with the World Health Organization.
Levine, C. (1991), 'Women and HIV/AIDS Research: The Barriers to Equity', *IRB: A Review of Human Subjects Research*, **13**, 18.
Levine C., N. Dubler Neveloff and R. Levine (1991), 'Building a New Consensus: Ethical Principles and Policies for Clinical Research on HIV/AIDS ', *IRB: A Review of Human Subjects Research*, **13**, 1.
Levine, R. (1986), *Ethics and Regulation of Clinical Research*, Baltimore: Urban and Schwarzenberg.
Merton, V. (1990), 'Community-Based AIDS Research', *Evaluation Review*, **14**, 502.
Merton, V. (1993), 'The Exclusion of Pregnant, Pregnable and Once-Pregnable People (A.K.A.) From Biomedical Research', *American Journal of Law and Medicine*, **14**, 369.
Minkoff, H., J.D. Moreno and K.R. Powderly (1992), 'Fetal Protection and Access to Clinical Trials', *Journal of Women's Health*, **1**, 137.
Mirkin, B.L. (1975), 'Drug Therapy and the Developing Human: Who cares?', *Clinical Research*, **23**, 110.
Sherwin, S. (1992), *No Longer Patient: Feminist Ethics and Health Care*, Philadelphia: Temple University Press.
Therapeutic Goods Administration Guidelines for Good Clinical Practice in Australia, 1991.

10 The Science of Biotechnology: Present, Past and Future Quagmires

PHILIPPA GANNON

Introduction

During this century we have witnessed unprecedented breakthroughs in the biological sciences. Sophisticated advances in biological techniques, for example gene splicing, have facilitated the manipulation of cellular life. The words 'biotechnology' and 'genetics' are now common to our vocabulary. Yet defining these terms is difficult. For example, Gorstein has discovered that, 'In a recent study on genetic engineering in Europe, it was found that there were 41 different definitions of Biotechnology in the European Union documents' (Gorstein, 1996, p.169). For the lay person, the difference between biotechnology and genetics is minimal; both terms basically represent the human interference with biological material. For the purposes of this chapter, a loose definition and understanding of the nature of these sciences will suffice. Biotechnology is the use and manipulation of living microorganisms, for example bacteria, to perform chemical functions or produce other materials. Genetic engineering is the alteration of the DNA of a cell for the purposes of research. This research may encompass the manufacture of artificial proteins, correcting genetic defects or making improvements in the genetic structure of humans, plants and animals. Both 'biotechnology' and 'genetics' therefore encompass practical experimentation with cellular life.

To date the innocuous application of biological advances has introduced to the world transgenic animals such as cancerous and hairless mice, geeps (a cross between a goat and a sheep) and new food technology. In medical treatment biological advances are increasingly augmenting the capacity to screen for genetic diseases and to manufacture cures. However, despite such philanthropic successes, a general malaise surrounds the new biology. Experiments with living cells continue to be surrounded by controversy. From Brave New World to Nazi Germany, the future misapplication and possibilities of biology are frequently invoked. Caplan encapsulates the common images: 'Horrifying futuristic time worms in which hordes of clones derived from the embryos of businessmen, sports stars and politicians (no attempt is made to mitigate the horror) descend on an unsuspecting and defenceless world' (Caplan, 1992, p.137). This imaginative speculation is not without a purpose however, as invoking such possibilities while they are not scientifically feasible may prevent their occurrence at a later date. That is, an awareness of what may be possible may prevent horrors descending upon an unprepared world: to be aware is to be forewarned. This approach is to be welcomed as the boundaries of biological feasibility are increasingly eroded. Moreover, the whole community is encouraged to be involved in debate and the decision-making process surrounding the social desirability of the new life sciences. This strategy ensures that the values of one group or sector of society do not monopolize genetic decision making. This attention is both merited and necessary. Yet, by concentrating upon the prevention of future horrors, one imminent horror has gone largely unnoticed: the commercialization of science.

Increasingly, science is a highly lucrative industry. Lucrative returns are especially feasible in relation to biotechnology, as revealed by the following data:

> Biotechnology is at its economic take off stage. World markets are estimated to grow by some 30% per annum for the rest of the decade, reaching over £60 billion by the year 2000. Within the European Union, industry sectors using biotechnology account for 17% of all employment, 9% of gross asset value and over 20% of European industrial production (Department of Trade and Industry, 1996, p.1)

Throughout the world the potential of the biological sciences is increasingly realized,[1] yet, amid such success and excitement, it is easy to overlook the fact that controversy surrounds the new biology. The manipulation of life by artificial methods is not problem-free. First, the environmental risks posed by biotechnology are not insignificant; catastrophic ecological problems may occur if genetically modified organisms escape (deliberately or accidentally) into the environment. Secondly, many individuals hold moral objections to the manipulation of life for commercial profit. However, the constant emphasis on the new biology as the panacea for some of the most debilitating conditions affecting humans tends to block discussion of these issues.

Undoubtedly, the ubiquitous application of the biological sciences is integral to unprecedented commercial application and success. In health care both biotechnology and genetics offer miraculous treatments for genetic conditions and the manufacture of novel drugs and compounds. For the entrepreneur and investor, the revenue expected from such substances is huge. For the scientist, the opportunity to be immortalized by developing treatments for many genetically based human conditions is tantalizing. At present, the investor, the scientist and the entrepreneur may be the same individual. It is this capacity of the new biology simultaneously to offer financial, professional and academic rewards which is problematic. This is because it is necessary to determine the manner in which such multiple interests share the rewards and prestige associated with work in this domain. This chapter will detail the difficulties of achieving this goal. Problems have arisen because the application of developments emanating from biology laboratories has invoked major conflicts of interests. This is due to the fact that the biotechnology industry has expanded simultaneously with the actual embryonic development of biotechnology as a science. Moreover, as the body of scientific knowledge about biotechnology increases, the immediate application and financial return from such developments are simultaneously acknowledged and exploited. Scientific research is therefore increasingly concerned by a commercial agenda. However, current legal mechanisms fail to protect, reward and acknowledge the numerous interests that are involved in research in the biological sciences.

At present, biotechnology research is conducted under the auspices of numerous organizations which straddle both the public and the private sector. As a society we are accustomed to the public support and promotion of scientific activities, but biotechnology research is increasingly characterized as a commercial enterprise. This privatization is problematic to legal regulation. Frequently, legal mechanisms are advocated which will reward those who invest and conduct this philanthropic research. However, it is necessary to develop such mechanisms simultaneously with the protection of the public interest considerations and implications inherent in this research. Moreover, the requirement of legal systems to protect the public interest is as important as the ability to offer private rewards and inducements. Consequently, biotechnological research poses several challenges for legal control and regulation.

Research and developments in the biological science laboratories are undoubtedly causing public concern, but this is not the first occasion that scientific advances have created controversy: Consider, for example, the nuclear industry, at which environmental and moral objections continue to be voiced. What renders the biotechnology industry unique (and integral to its controversial status) is the ability to obtain intellectual property rights, in particular patents, for the fruits of its research. Many objections exist to the grant of such intellectual property rights. The premises of objection are numerous, so representing the many interests affected or affronted by biotechnology research. Arguments can be distinguished, however, depending upon whether the subject matter of the patent is in relation to human or non-human material. This chapter will focus upon the grant and practice of patents over human cells. While the technical interpretation of patent legislation is fascinating (for example, is a gene a discovery or an invention?) this will not be the focus of this chapter. Instead, the ethos and scientific implications of seeking and granting patents over biological products and processes will be questioned. In particular, the implications of granting intellectual property rights to current scientific undertakings will be investigated. To illustrate this point, the Human Genome Project, the most important biological project ever undertaken, will be used to illustrate that scientific policy may not be in accord with the pragmatic realities of the current scientific funding climate.

Throughout the world, legal systems have failed to acknowledge the lucrative nature of biotechnology. This has resulted in a paucity of legal regulation of science. In addition, such an approach has not facilitated the commercialization of laboratory developments and has also failed to indicate the acceptable boundaries of research. Integral to this state of affairs is the prevalent belief that science is a benign quest for knowledge.

What is Science?

Science is one of the last bastions of knowledge. While other disciplines have experienced public scrutiny and expectations of accountability, science remains sacrosanct. Society trusts science with its clandestine operations and strives to protect its independence; the neutral motives of the scientist are assumed and seldom questioned. The scientist is traditionally portrayed as the eccentric academic whose life is devoted to test-tubes and protracted experiments. The business suit in this world is an anachronism. Occasionally, the work of one such eccentric will effect an upheaval in the work and direction of the scientific community, usually referred to as a paradigm shift. For this achievement the scientist will be assured of a place in the history of popular science.

Scientific knowledge is objective, true and neutral. It is only when scientific knowledge is applied and utilized by society that it loses its neutrality and causes concern. This point can be illustrated by considering the work of one of the greatest scientists, Albert Einstein. Einstein's pioneering work in theoretical physics fundamentally changed the scientific perception of the world. Einstein worked on a theoretical level, but his work had a subsequent practical application. White and Gribben illustrate the importance of his contribution:

> Like his thesis, Einstein's 'quantum theory of radiation' paper is one that has been extensively cited in recent decades, as lasers have come into their own. The uses of lasers are now legion, but it is perhaps worth reminding you that every compact-disc player uses a laser beam to scan the CD itself. The science behind the CD player stems directly from one of Einstein's lesser-known insights – something he came up with within months of the completion of the general theory of relativity. (White and Gribben, 1994, p.173)

This example illustrates the cumulative and progressive nature of developments in scientific knowledge. Yet not all scientific advances offer positive benefits to modern society. For example, a logical application of Einstein's theoretical work was the possibility of atomic energy culminating in development of the nuclear bomb. However, Einstein was not directly involved in the development of nuclear power: in fact, quite the contrary. White and Gribben explain the situation:

> Einstein was later perceived by many as the father of the atomic bomb. This is entirely wrong. Einstein made two contributions to the production of the bomb. His first was the formulation of the equation $E = mc^2$; the second, his effort to alert the US president to the danger that the secrets of nuclear fission might fall into enemy hands. Contrary to popular myth, Einstein had absolutely nothing to do with the Manhattan project to build the bombs dropped on Hiroshima and Nagasaki. He was not present at any nuclear test.
>
> Nonetheless, his association with the horrors of the atomic bomb was, in later years, a source of great sadness for Einstein, and he felt that his role in the process had been completely misinterpreted and exaggerated. (White and Gribben, 1994, p.239)

So, while Einstein was not actively involved in the development of the atomic bomb, his theoretical work had made this weapon a feasibility. However, his efforts to halt the development of the bomb were futile in the face of increasing societal and government desires to develop nuclear weapons. Einstein's vain pleas illustrate that in reality it is the cumulative force of society which dictates the application of scientific knowledge, as opposed to the wishes of the individual scientist.

'Science' is utilized in our vocabulary in numerous contexts. Zinman, in stressing the importance of acknowledging the breadth of activities which constitute science, categorizes the nature of science as follows:

> the product of research; it does employ characteristic methods; it is a body of organised knowledge; it is a means of solving problems. It is a social institution; it needs material facilities; it is an educational theme; it is a cultural resource; it requires to be managed; it is a major factor in human affairs. (Zinman, 1984, p.2)

The nature of science is encapsulated in the activities which are deemed scientific, that is, the search for understanding characterized by statements of general laws or principles which can be tested experimentally. This comprehensive definition of science can be further divided. An important distinction can be made between pure and applied science. In general terms, pure science is concerned with abstract concepts, whilst applied science is the use of pure science for a practical purpose. This distinction needs further elaboration. Feibleman's explanation is helpful:

> Pure science has as its aim the understanding of nature; it seeks explanation. Applied science has as its aim the control of nature; it has the task of employing the findings of science to get practical tasks done. Pure science has as a result the furnishing of laws for application in applied science. (Feibleman, 1983, p.33)

Distinguishing science as pure and applied is only one manner of classifying science. Other categories of science distinguish between engineering and technology. Again, Feibleman explains the nature of technology:

> The applied scientist as such is concerned with the task of discovering applications for pure theory. The technologist has a problem which lies a little nearer to practice. Both applied scientist and technologist employ experiment; but in the former case guided by hypotheses deduced from theory, while in the latter case employing trial and error or skilled approaches derived from concrete experience. (Ibid., p.36)

Finally, he explains the nature of engineering:

> engineering is the most down-to-earth of all scientific work that can justify the name of science at all. In engineering the solutions of the technologists are applied to particular cases. The building of bridges, the medical treatment of patients, the designing of instruments, all improvements in model constructions of already existing tools – these are the work of the engineer. But the theories upon which such work rests, such as studies in the flow or 'creep' of metals, the physics of

lubrication, the characteristics of surface tensions of liquids – these belong to the applied scientist. (Ibid., p.37)

It is therefore apparent that science is conducted in many guises, with numerous objectives in mind. Moreover, we tend to assume that there is a logical progression from pure scientific research to its application either in technology or in engineering. This point will be returned to later. It is important to bear in mind that all these scientific endeavours are integral and essential to the perusal of scientific research and, moreover, ensure the cumulative progress of society.

The classification of science as pure and applied has traditionally been reflected in the personnel and locations where 'science' takes place. The universities are perceived as the domain of pure scientific research, whilst the development and application of research is the preserve of large companies.[2] However, in the science of biotechnology, there is not such a clear distinction to be made. This is because the distinctions between applied, pure and technology are not particularly defined in biotechnology research. Sherman explains the situation: 'research, especially in such fields as biotechnology and information technology, is no longer as far removed from commercial application as it once was. ... What has occurred, in effect, is a shift in the boundary that distinguishes pure from applied research' (Sherman, 1994, p.520).

So why is it difficult to make distinctions in biotechnology between pure science, applied science and technology? This is mainly because of the nature of biotechnology research. Basic biotechnology research revolves around the elucidation of genetic sequences. This is both a laborious and a costly endeavour. This research leads to an understanding of the operation of genetic sequences. Genetic research is increasingly akin to discovering a code. Once the code for a particular genetic structure has been discovered it is then possible to manufacture artificially products and processes which are based upon this structure. This is useful as many genetic conditions are caused by a deficiency of a particular substance or a 'defective' version of genetic material:

Considering how many letters there are in the human genome, nature is an excellent proofreader. But sometimes there are mistakes. An error in a single 'word' – a gene – can give rise to the crippling disease of cystic fibrosis, the commonest genetic disorder among Caucasians. Errors in the genetic recipe for haemoglobin, the protein that gives blood its characteristic red colour and which carries oxygen from the lungs to the rest of the body, give rise to the most common single-gene disorder in the world: thalassaemia. A different error in the same gene – a mistake in just one letter among those 3 billion or so – is responsible for another of the most widespread inherited diseases, sickle-cell anaemia. (Wilkie, 1993, p.2)

Commercial genetic products are premissed upon the functioning of a normal gene. For example, a genetic test will detect the presence or absence of a genetic structure and genetic medicines will attempt to administer an artificial version of a 'healthy' gene to an individual. However, both approaches require an initial understanding of the particular sensibilities and manifestation of the particular gene. Obtaining this information is the most time-consuming aspect of research. Once the 'code' has been cracked, the development of its artificial application is less daunting. Pure research is therefore vital to applied research i.e. the development of genetic tests and cures. This associating link is unproblematic. However, what is at issue is that the aims and justifications for initially embarking on pure research differ from those which relate to applied research, engineering and technology. That is, pure research is seeking to understand, whilst applied research is seeking to develop. However, to what extent has vital research upon pure science been jeopardized by the concentration upon the *application* of pure science and the development of products? Are we failing to appreciate that pure research is a precursor to applied research? Moreover, increasingly it appears that not all biotechnology research is directed towards gathering neutral information. This is because a research team may be gene seeking (that is elucidating a particular gene) with the specific aim of using the gene to manufacture a particular product with commercial expectations.

Scientific Progress

Science is a progressive body of knowledge. Advancements arise via a willingness on the part of members of the scientific community to cooperate and to share the outcome of research. Occasionally, an event will occur in the scientific community which fundamentally alters the manner in which the particular subject matter has been approached.[3] One such revolution occurred in biotechnology. In 1953, Crick and Watson published their explanation of the spiral structure and copying nature of DNA.[4] Once this structure was explained, the complex interrelation of genes was apparent. Numerous unprecedented biological techniques followed from this momentous breakthrough. It must be emphasized, however, that none would have occurred without the work of Crick and Watson, whose breakthrough marked the commencement of the phenomenal growth of the biological sciences. As Hood states,

> During the past twenty years, brilliant advances in technology and fundamental new insights have led to a striking revolution in biology, which is slowly beginning to change medicine. This revolution will be accelerated as we move into the twenty-first century by even more far-reaching developments, especially the deciphering of the human genome, our blueprint for life. (Hood, 1992, p.136)

During the 1970s, the genetic basis of the most debilitating of genetic conditions (including various cancers) were increasingly acknowledged. It was therefore vital to obtain information regarding the manner in which human cells operate. Ironically, it appeared that, as more information about genetics became available, more explanations were necessary. The possibility of organizing a project dedicated to genome research was originally discussed in 1985 by scientists gathered at a meeting at the University of California at Santa Cruz.[5] A concerted cost-effective attempt to gather this information was welcomed. Further, as collaboration was integral to the scientific community, this was not generally perceived as being a problem. The envisaged strategy was a systematic trawl through the letters (a gene is a collection of letters) which constitute the human genome. After all the letters were collated, it would then be possible to 'read' the patterns of the letters, and as this was done the codes for specific genes would appear. It is important to stress that this visionary idea was based on the premise that genetic information is meaningless, and that a systematic trawl through the genome would be the preliminary to the analysis and application of this information. The American initiative was rewarded with considerable federal funding for the endeavour and gradually the project was embraced by scientists internationally.[6] The Human Genome Project, as the initiative is named, is constantly hailed as the most important and impressive biological, if not scientific, undertaking ever attempted. As Annas and Elias state, 'The Human Genome Project has frequently been compared to both the Manhattan Project and the Apollo Moon Program. These comparisons generally have to do with the magnitude of the project, and big "biology" is clearly happy to have its own megaproject' (Annas and Elias, 1992, p.4).

Most countries are now committed to genome research. An element of harmonization is supplied by the Human Genome Organisation (HUGO), which attempts to coordinate research amid disparate research teams working towards a common goal. The year 2001 is frequently given as a date by which human genome project research will be completed. However, this completion date is likely to be a relatively low-key event, because it will still be necessary to analyse and apply to a specific context the data that have been generated.

The Human Genome Project

While much has been written about the future application and awareness of the information that the Human Genome Project will uncover, little discussion has addressed the imminent administrative and structural problems of the Human Genome Project. These problems are generally overlooked in the panic to address the issues which will result from increased scientific understanding of human DNA. The Human Genome Project also illustrates the problems inherent in the structure of science. Despite its admirable and ambitious philanthropic motives, the Human Genome Project is beleaguered by problems. The grandiose title, 'The Human Genome Project' is deceptive. The title conveys the image of a huge headquarters where research is directed with a military-like precision. However, the Human Genome Project is more of a sprawling network of scientific undertakings, united through a common goal. The problems of coordinating and conducting research on such an immense scale have always been considerable. First, the Human Genome Project is characterized by ad hoc teams of research scientists who, despite working towards a common goal, work upon their own agendas. Secondly, there is a distinct absence of concerted finance for the project; instead, finance has been collated from numerous sources. Thirdly, it was initially not appreciated that an incentive to embark upon human genome research would be the lucrative financial rewards it promised. Consequently, the human genome project is a philanthropic quest for knowledge, in a world where the financial implications of genetic research and biotechnology are high.

In conjunction with Human Genome Project research, work is being undertaken on biotechnology and genetic techniques by scientists elsewhere. This means that it is possible for access to the research of genome researchers to be gained by individuals who do not possess similar philanthropic aims. Methods of blocking unauthorized access to genome data are sought, yet results can enter into the public domain directly or indirectly. This state of affairs creates administrative problems, for example the unauthorized access to the numerous databases which hold genome data. Such databases are integral to genome research: research scientists place their research results in these bases so they may be accessed by others. However, enabling the easy access of these bases while simultaneously preventing unauthorized access has proved difficult.

The Human Genome Project is financed by both private and public funding. At the outset of the project, the participation of private investment in genome research was deemed vital to the progress of the project. Private biotechnology research companies have filled the void which used to exist between fundamental university research and the pharmaceutical companies that manufactured drugs. In addition, increasingly, academic research is sponsored by private enterprise, affiliations and arrangements lured by the lucrative nature of genetic research. Nelkin provides an insight into the situation in the USA where commercially sponsored scientific research is rife:

> Today, virtually every major biotechnology and genetics research group has some association with a company, and most biotechnology companies are collaborating with university research teams. The arrangements vary: they include direct corporate sponsorship of academic research, special licensing agreements, biotechnology institutes, individual consulting contracts, and various types of consortia. (Nelkin, 1992, p.30)

In retrospect, was the encouragement of commercial companies in Human Genome Research shortsighted? That is, did this encouragement instigate the commercialization of the results of research in order to recoup the heavy investment costs? Perhaps, at the inception of the Human Genome Project, the ease with which biotechnology products and processes could be incorporated into the patent system was not realized. Further, the time span between the elucidation of genetic material and its patentability has been seen to be short. Vociferous criticism is frequently levelled at those who attempt to commercialize the results of biotechnology research via the patent system. However, was it not naive to fail to predict that patenting would be a potential outcome of the encouragement of commercial companies to participate in biotechnology research?

Why Patent?

The goal of patents[7] is to encourage inventive activity; that is, the existence of a patent is perceived as an incentive to invent. As the UK Patent Office acknowledge, patents are associated with commercialization:

> The annual number of patent applications acts as a barometer to the health of the economy. And the subject matter of patents mirrors developments in technology and the changing concerns of industry and commerce. The latest figures show a growing number of patents in the field of genetic engineering. (The Patent Office, 1989, p.7)

However, in contrast to other industries, biotechnology patents have not been perceived quite so positively. The reasons frequently adduced to explain such a hostile reception are as follows. First, the possibility of obtaining patents may mean that research is not disclosed to other scientists for fear of jeopardizing the grant of potential intellectual property rights. For example, in order to obtain a patent, an 'invention' has to be completely novel. Novelty is interpreted restrictedly: in the UK, for example, the disclosure of an invention to scientific peers has the potential to defeat a subsequent patent application. If research has the potential for industrial application, it has to be kept secret. This clandestine tactic is in direct contrast to the collegiality of science.[8] Secondly, patenting implies proprietorship and ownership, a state of affairs which is counter to the whole ethos of genetic research and collaboration. Consider, for example, the following assertion: 'For all their personal rivalries, and occasional secretiveness in the race for priority, academic scientists are unanimous on the importance of publishing new data and theories as soon as they can be presented as sound and convincing' (National Academics Policy Advisory Group, 1995, p.5).

Patenting has particular implications for the Human Genome Project. First, the actual existence of patents makes conducting genome research difficult, in that it may make research more expensive and bureaucratic if patented material is being researched or developed. To date, most patent systems include research exemptions. However, as the boundaries between research and development in biotechnology become increasingly blurred, this may prove difficult to continue to apply. Secondly, the interrelation of genes is complex. If one individual has an existing monopoly over a genetic structure, will this deter others from working in the same field? Finally, the possibility of obtaining patents may instigate research which is specifically directed to elucidate a particular gene. This threatens the non-specific trawl for knowledge which has been so celebrated. However, there are numerous positive aspects of patenting: patenting encourages the dissemination of research results; it provides an incentive to conduct research in this field; it rewards those who have invested valuable time and money in embarking on this research.

So patenting has positive and negative repercussions. However, the positive aspects of patenting are frequently overlooked in the controversy surrounding the grant of patents over the products and processes of the biological sciences. These considerations are not merely academic. In 1991, the USA National Institutes of Health (NIH) applied for individual patents over more than a thousand fragments of human genes.[9] The NIH is one of the main protagonists of genome research in the USA. It was apparent that the complete genetic sequences were important to the functioning of the brain, though their specific purpose had yet to be ascertained. The main opposition contained in the objections to these patent applications was the fact that, as the exact function of the gene fragments had not been ascertained, this application was premature. Moreover, if the patent were granted, other research scientists might be deterred from conducting research upon this patented material. However, despite condemning this action, research teams in other jurisdictions made corresponding moves to protect potential intellectual property rights emanating from genetic material.[10] The NIH defended their application on the grounds that patenting enabled the NIH to bring the patents into the public domain and was an attempt to commercialize funded research.[11] The filing of the patent applications would also provide a mechanism whereby the exact stage of scientific progress could be ascertained by other scientists. The situation illustrated the fact that seeking and granting patents may have dire consequences for scientific research.

The Scientific Climate

The practice of patenting ought not to be extrapolated from the current scientific research climate. This climate is characterized by frugal public funding, financial competitiveness and revolutionary time-saving technology. As one commentator has stated, 'The private sector is filling a vacuum created by the uncertain, fluky currents of public support for biological and other forms of basic inquiry' (Beardsley, 1994, p.73). Those who have sought to patent have done so within an international framework which actively encourages the commercialization of science. To illustrate this point, two countries actively involved in biotechnology research will be examined: the USA and the UK.

The USA Congress has passed several statutes, such as the Technology Transfer Act 1986, to encourage and instigate the development of science. As the Congress of the USA, Office of Technology Assessment emphasizes,

> Congress appropriates funds to support scientific research for several reasons, the principal one for biomedical research being to improve health. Increasingly, however, biomedical research is being regarded as a national investment, and policies to facilitate economically fruitful applications of new knowledge are receiving attention in Congress. (Congress of the United States, Office of Technology Assessment, [1988] p.15)

Moreover, in both public and private research ventures, the commercial development of biotechnology products and processes has been paramount. According to Eisenberg, 'U.S. policy since 1980 has reflected an increasingly confident presumption that patenting discoveries made in the course of government-sponsored research is the most effective way to promote technology transfer and commercial development of those discoveries in the private sector' (Eisenberg 1994, p.635).

So, in the USA, the scientific community is aware of the potential of patents and their importance. In the UK the domain of pure research has traditionally been perceived as the publicly funded universities. However, these numerous institutions are increasingly experiencing drastic funding cuts, so it is now enticing to conduct research which offers recuperation of research costs. Indeed, this may be the only feasible way of conducting research. The result has been the awareness of obtaining intellectual property rights over research. Indeed, in such a climate, research bodies will be vigilant to ensure that they are not excluded from any financial potential. In consequence, intellectual property clauses are becoming standard clauses in research proposals and funding applications. The academic and commercial output of UK universities is constantly under scrutiny and, as public bodies their accountability is expected. In 1992, the National Academies Policy Advisory Group (NAPAG) was formed in the UK to be a forum to address the role of universities in the UK. In 1993, NAPAG formed a working party comprising ethicists, scientists and commercial and legal experts and issued the report, *Intellectual Property and the Academic Community*. The report makes numerous recommendations in relation to the role and use of intellectual property in academic science. For example, the group perceives that 'Pressures on research funding are such that no institution can now adopt an attitude which neglects any potential for commercial development, where that exists. Moreover, Intellectual Property Rights are essential building blocks in that progress' (NAPAG, 1995, p.34).

The overall tone of NAPAG's findings is to highlight the increasing commercialization of UK academic research. The findings of the report are supported by other government publications. For example, according to the UK Department of Trade and Industry, there exist

> a number of schemes to promote collaboration between academics and industry. Thus a number of Councils operate schemes in which research undertaken in academic institutions in the UK in partnership with a company may be funded jointly by the Council and the company. (Department of Trade and Industry, 1996, p.42)

This report looks to the USA as a role model for a scientific community, as the USA scientific community appears to be more accommodating to the exploitation of research results via patents. For example, the UK Office of Science and Technology reported in 1994:

> With certain exceptions the UK has been slow to pick up on commercial opportunities in biotechnology and there is still much technology languishing in academic laboratories that has not been adequately exploited. This is largely an infrastructural problem. The USA model of technology transfer (and wealth creation) is based on the formation of small 'start-up' companies around academic laboratories (or several related investigators) generally funded by venture capital.

They continue,

> in this country we have a small and slightly risk-averse venture capital community in a financial climate which is not sympathetic to small companies with reasonably long time frames (five to ten years) before products and profitability. With the new opportunities arising from the human genome project, this has to change. (The Office of Science and Technology, 1994, p43)

So the promotion of intellectual property rights is now expected from academic institutions in the UK and the USA. This trend has also been witnessed in other jurisdictions. Sherman's statement is illustrative: 'as public resources, universities and public sector research laboratories need to justify the financial contributions that are made to them. That is, money spent on research is increasingly seen as a form of "investment" which is expected to yield a return' (Sherman, 1994, p.515).

While other manufacturing sectors have declined, science has been embraced as a manufacturing industry. However, in protecting the immediate fruits of biotechnology research, are we in danger of failing to protect the traditional role of universities and academic institutions in scientific research? The direct implication is that basic biotechnology research is under threat. Loughlan illustrates the problems which can emanate from this situation:

> A university which is increasingly patent-orientated and increasingly dependent on the income generated by patent licensing is unlikely to continue to perceive its primary mission as one of basic rather than applied research when basic research does not yield discoveries of a patentable nature. (Loughlan, 1996, p.347)

Legal Response

It is trite to state that the future legal, social and moral quagmires to be created by the new biology will be acute. Yet, the present problems posed by the commercialization of this science cannot be avoided. We have seen that the participators are increasingly aware of and motivated by the commercial potential of biotechnology research. As a result, the commercial implications of research are high on the scientific agenda. This is not to suggest that research is in any way tainted by this commercialization, or in any way inferior to non-commercially directed research, but to stress that commercialisation is now an important factor on the scientific agenda. However, the current economics and entrepreneurial spirit of biotechnology research have not been fully grasped by legal systems. This has resulted in a paucity of legal protection or acknowledgement of the commercial implications of scientific research. Hesitation at legislative intervention and control of biotechnology is understandable. Rapid developments in biotechnology appear to render it unsuitable to cumbersome legal machinery. Moreover, a legal response has the potential to frustrate and hinder scientific progress. However, given the high interests at stake, it is necessary that an equitable commercial framework supported and guided by the law be formulated sooner rather than later.

It would be wrong to suggest that biotechnology and genetics have been ignored by the law. Internationally, legal responses which promote the biotechnology industry have been sought and adopted. However, if we consider the current picture of biotechnology research, it appears that no entity is satisfied with the current situation whereby laws attempt to regulate, control and promote. First, the biotechnology researchers bewail the prevailing legal uncertainty surrounding their work. Secondly, those who are removed from the commercialization of research question their reward (or lack of it) in the cumulative scientific process. Thirdly and finally, the layperson is left uncertain as to the current control and role of biotechnology. So, while attempting to engender flexibility in order to accommodate new developments, this legal response has also created confusion and uncertainty. This malaise could be detrimental to the delicate balance of scientific research. Yet, legal participation is problematic, given that the general public hold a warped perception of biotechnology. This ranges from general mistrust of scientists to vociferous hostility towards the patenting of life forms.

Legislators have therefore had to placate and take into account conflicting concerns. Consequently, attempts have been made to accommodate biotechnology and genetics within existing legislation, in the expectation that controversy will eventually abate. This is particularly apparent in relation to patents, where living cells have been interpreted according to the same legislative criteria as standard mechanical inventions. In addition, the control of biotechnology as an industry has been attempted simultaneously with its promotion and scientific validity. Such attempts have been admirable, yet it is apparent that the biological sciences are now creating problems which necessitate a multi-strategy legal response to resolve various issues.

Acknowledgment of the present complex structure of biotechnology research namely the many interests it encompasses has been sacrificed to speculation upon the future problems of biotechnology research. However, if the scientific agenda is controlled in a systematic way, would this not mean that we would not have to face the fantastical horrors emanating from the scientific laboratories of the future? At present, scientists have a prized independence to investigate, but the scientific agenda is not neutral, and is increasingly directed and influenced by commerce which may be encouraging research in a particular direction. There is obviously a commercial demand for specific genetic tests to be utilized in different areas of life. The utilization of such tests will be questioned increasingly in the future, but if there is an envisaged commercial market (however controversial) for such tests, there may actually be an incentive to develop them. Would legal intervention not be more opportune now, to oversee, or even prevent, the development of these tests? Indeed, would this not curtail future problems? This is not to imply that science should be treated with suspicion, or subject to overt accountability and bureaucracy, but to indicate that it ought to be recognized that commercial viability and application has the potential to guide research. Consider the following hypothetical example: 25 per cent of the population are afflicted by condition X. Company A sees a market for tests and therapies for condition X and therefore finances research on condition X. The gene for condition X is discovered and tests and screening kits are offered (developed by company A). Eventually, condition X is seen as a condition which ought to be avoided or treated; that is as the research and tests are now available, individuals feel that it is irresponsible not to use these tests. Moreover, those who suffer from condition X then face discrimination from employers and insurance companies who have begun to utilize the test as a selection procedure. However, those who suffer from condition Z, which affects 10 per cent of the population, do not experience similar problems, merely because the appropriate gene has not been researched as it is perceived as being of non-commercial viability. At present, we fail to acknowledge that the direction of science is increasingly pushed by commercial implications.

There are numerous legal responses which may validly accommodate the interests concerned in biotechnology research. However, the following would be integral to any developments. First, international participation is necessary. If the laws of one legal system are more accommodating to biotechnology, this may have the potential to instigate research and investment in this jurisdiction. Harmonization of international laws is a certain priority; an obvious starting point would be the encouragement of the harmonization of international patent law specific to biotechnology. Secondly, legislative response needs to acknowledge those who have an interest in genetic research. As we have seen above, there are numerous interests at stake. One legislative approach would be an international convention specifically addressing commercial science. The value of this approach would be that it would represent a concerted attempt to acknowledge and reconcile the numerous interests entwined in present biological research. It is envisaged that this would incorporate several issues. For example, it might incorporate tax reforms for private companies who participate in biotechnology research, *sui generis* intellectual property rights for biotechnology and ethical fora within the patent process.

Conclusion

Any proposed legal response to biotechnology developments ought to be comprehensive. That is, it ought to take account of all manifestations and interests which are currently at stake within this scientific climate. Moreover, legal systems have to address the extent to which the motivation to conduct scientific research may be commercially driven. The participation of legal systems is necessary in order to ensure that justice prevails in the rewards which emanate from successful research projects. In addition, there is a need to protect the dual public and private aspects of scientific research. Though controversial, an element of accountability ought also to be demanded from scientists. The role of law is therefore multiple.

The increasing commercialization of scientific products and processes illustrates the industrial potential and direction of scientific research. Consequently, public money may need to be invested wisely; private finance may expect a return. However, ultimately money is not donated gratuitously. While the potential of biotechnology to provide new medicine and treatments is welcomed, it is also inevitable that an outcome of this will be the commercial promotion of such developments. Patents are symptomatic of this commercialization of science, but patenting should be perceived as an integral aspect of the current scientific climate and not as the practice of a few unscrupulous entrepreneurs. Inevitably, it is necessary for a society to determine the manner in which those who invest in biotechnological research are to be rewarded, and to create the legal mechanisms to achieve this. Undoubtedly, new biological techniques will transform modern medicine in its creation of a new skeleton, physiology and pharmacology. However, if we do not encourage, instigate or protect these advances, potential benefits may be curtailed.

Notes

1 The position in the UK is as follows: 'The runaway success of British Biotech almost led it into the FT-SE 100 index, while the others have seen remarkable rates of growth in share values – the sector is now capitalised at £5 billion. Advances in science are revolutionising the production of new medicines, foods and chemicals, and the financial markets are seeing the potential for rich pickings' (Magee and Murden, 1996). The success of the biotechnology industry has been experienced elsewhere. Consider the following statement in relation to the USA: 'Biotechnology firms, which constitute one of the more volatile sectors of the stock markets, had a combined capitalization of $41 billion in 1994, according to Ernst and Young' (Beardsley, 1994, p.72).

2 In the UK, this distinction was recently reiterated: 'Traditionally the institutional separation of universities from government and industry has ensured that academics decide what scientific research they will do. This freedom has always been subject to the task of obtaining resources. ... Generally speaking, however, academics have set their own agenda, often with generous unfettered support for well-conceived projects from both the public and the private sectors' (National Academies Policy Advisory Group, 1995, p.4).

3 Goldstein and Goldstein describe this as follows, 'Scientific revolutions have occured and will occur again, with dramatic consequences for our previous conceptions of ourselves and of our universe, as happened with Darwin's statement that we are descended from animals, with Einstein's discovery that matter and energy are different manifestations of a single entity, with Freud's revelations of the sources of our deepest feelings' (Goldstein and Goldstein, 1984, p.388).

4 Moreover, the work of Crick and Watson also provided the explanation for the chemical basis of the operation of genes: that is, a gene contains a coded message. This code is within a sequence of letters. The code specifies the 'recipe' for the manner in which a protein is made. This explanation is the central basis of the life sciences and is now referred to as the 'central dogma' of molecular biology.

5 For further information on this point, see J. Watson and R. Cook-Deegan, 'Origins of the human genome project', *The FASEB Journal*, **5**, January 1991, 8–11.

6 This may be interpreted as an attempt to be involved in genome research, and also to prevent one country from monopolizing these data.

7 A patent is a contract between society and an individual. On disclosing a new invention to the rest of society, the inventor is rewarded with a time-limited monopoly. During this specified period the inventor is able to exploit the invention to the exclusion of all others.

8 As the National Academies Policy Advisory Group state, 'the patent system's requirement of initial secrecy operates in direct conflict with the academic norm of full and prompt publication' (1995, p.5). In the USA, the problem of publication is less acute. This is because American Patent Law allows for a 'grace period'. This means that, if a patent application is filed within a year of the initial disclosure, such disclosure will not be detrimental to the patent.

9 For further information, see R. Eisenberg, 'Genes, patents, and Product Development', *Science*, **257**, 1992, 903; S. Maebius, 'Novel DNA Sequences and the Utility Requirement: The Human Genome Initiative', *Journal of the Patent and Trade Mark Office Society*, **651**, 1992.

10 In the UK, the Medical Research Council (MRC) declared that Venter's actions made the MRC seek to protect its own intellectual property rights.

11 For further information, see B. Healy, 'Special Report on Gene Patenting', *The New England Journal of Medicine*, **327**, (9), 1992, 664–8; A. Coghlan, 'Moves to defuse row over genome patents', *New Scientist*, **21**, 1992, 3.

References

Annas, George, J. and Sherman Elias (1992), 'The major social policy issues raised by the human genome project', in G.J. Annas and S. Elias (eds), *Gene Mapping, Using Law and Ethics As Guides*, Oxford: Oxford University Press, pp.3–17.

Beardsley, Tim (1994), 'Big-Time Biology', *Scientific America*, November, 72–9.

Caplan, Arthur, L. (1992), 'If Gene Therapy Is the Cure, What is the Disease?', in G.J. Annas and S. Elias (eds), *Gene Mapping, Using Law and Ethics as Guides*, Oxford: Oxford University Press, pp.128–41.

Congress of the United States, Office of Technology Assessment (1988), *Mapping Our Genes Genome Projects: How Big, How Fast?*, Washington, DC: Harper Row Publishers.

Department of Trade and Industry, (1996), *Bioguide, Regulations, Information and Support for Biotechnology in the UK*, HMSO, London.

Eisenberg, Rebecca, S. (1994), 'A Technology Perspective on the NIH Gene Patenting Controversy', *University of Pittsburgh Law Review*, **55**, (3), spring, 633–52.

Feibleman, James, K. (1961), 'Pure Science, Applied Science and Technology: An Attempt at Definitions', reproduced in C. Mitcham and R. Mackey (eds), *Philosophy and Technology Readings in the Philosophical Problems of Technology*, London: The Free Press, 1983, pp.33–41.

Goldstein, M. and I. Goldstein (1984), *The Experience of Science, An Interdisciplinary Approach*, New York: Plenum Press.

Gorstein, Hartley (1996), 'The Regulation of Biotechnology in Canada: Social and Moral Issues', *Medical Law International*, **2**, 169–82.

Hood, Leroy (1992), 'Biology and Medicine in the Twenty-First Century', in D.J. Kelves and L. Hood (eds), *The Code of Codes*, London: Harvard University Press, pp.136–45.

Loughlan, A. (1996), 'Intellectual Property, Research Workers and Universities', *European Intellectual Property Law Review*, 345–51.

Magee, Bill and Terry Murden (1996), 'A bullish market for Tracy the super sheep', *The Sunday Times*, 9 June, 11.

National Academics Policy Advisory Group (1995), *Intellectual Property and the Academic Community*, London: The Royal Society.

Nelkin, Dorothy (1992), 'Prospecting for genes', *The Times Higher Education Supplement*, 9 October, 30.

Sherman, Brad (1994), 'Governing Science: Patents and Public Sector Research', *Science in Context*, **7**, (3), 515–37.

The Office of Science and Technology (1994), *The Human Genome Project in the UK: Priorities and Opportunities in Genome Research*, London: HMSO.

The Patent Office (1989), *An Introduction to the Services of the Patents Office and Trade Marks and Designs Registries*, London: Central Office of Information.

White, M. and J. Gribben (1994), *Einstein: a Life in Science*, London: Simon & Schuster.

Wilkie, T. (1993), *Perilous Knowledge: The Human Genome Projet and its Implications*, London: Faber & Faber.

Zinman, J. (1984), *An Introduction to Science Studies: The Philosophical and Social Aspects of Science and Technology*, Cambridge: Cambridge University Press.

11 Dissecting Medical Power

KERRY PETERSEN

Introduction

It is well recognized that the medical profession is one of the most powerful social institutions, displacing religion and competing with law for social control. As part of the western culture, the role of the doctor has expanded over time and many facets of human living have come under the province of medical jurisdiction. In the broad societal sense, as well as in specific contexts, the state has delegated increasing power to the medical profession, buttressing this authority with professional autonomy over its distinctive work and self-regulation over membership. In addition, by the abdication of the power to define health and illness and decision-making power to medicine, the contribution of the general community to participating in this process is seriously diminished and the potential to challenge medical authority is severely restricted. As a civilization we are fast reaching the point of being seduced by scientific and medical advances into higher and higher expectations of medicine's capacity to alleviate and cure all the ills of humankind. Medicine's role extends beyond the prevention of sickness and the maintenance of health to the two poles of human existence: the beginning and end of life. This expansion of medical power, aided by technology, is altering societal perceptions of the manner of procreation as well as of dying and death. Technology is not necessarily a negative product of modern living because in some circumstances it frees us from the determinism of nature's roulette; however, as we recognize medicine's achievements of the twentieth century, it is also imperative to ask what human values are at stake.

Western society confers many privileges and benefits on the medical profession and in return it promotes societal goals and preserves dominant cultural values. Moreover, the broad spectrum of 'medicalization' has permitted the medical profession to shape and influence legislative frameworks, judicial adjudication and administrative processes. Under the mantle of a refined Hippocratic Oath, the therapeutic privilege, 'in-house' ethical codes of practice and clinical autonomy, medical practitioners have been given the right to determine what constitutes medical practice; and legal and administrative institutions have reinforced professional control by acknowledging medical practice as a yardstick for legal and ethical criteria (Britton, Chapter 1 of the present volume; McLean, Chapter 8 of the present volume). Correlatively, clinical autonomy is juxtaposed with patient autonomy, which stems from the right to self-determination. This autonomy right should enable patients to control and determine, as far as possible, the circumstances of their living and dying and protect them from non-consensual interventions.

As part of the struggle for universal self-determination, we seek the right to control our bodies. The denial of self-determination is particularly evident in medical decisions affecting human reproduction as well as dying and death. Moreover, rapid advances in technology exacerbate the issue by introducing further layers of complexity and obfuscating the sources of control and the way control is exercised. Laws governing informed consent to and informed refusal of medical interventions form the legal foundation of the patient–doctor relationship. However, analysis only of this formal legal framework fails to get to the kernel of the matter because it does not recognize the intersection between the technical and non-technical aspects of medical decisions. As Freidson says, 'Only part of any kind of work is technical, based on truly esoteric knowledge and skill; only part of what enters into discretionary action is technical rather than social and moral' (Freidson, 1994, p.166). It is also necessary to attach importance to the process of decision making as well as the consequences.

Links need to be made between medical power and illness because, although 'illness' is a vague term, it is a central concept of medicine. As Kennedy argues, illness is 'a term used to describe deviation from a notional norm' and the choice to call someone ill 'is a matter of social and political judgement'. He also argues that the normal state 'is not some static, objectively identifiable fact' and 'deviation from the norm ... will also vary and change in its meaning' (Kennedy, 1981, p.7). Illness in these terms is therefore a mutable label because normality is a product of cultural values. It can also be added that redefining social deviance as illness, in other words 'medicalizing' deviance, gives doctors power to promote conformity to cultural values. Moreover, giving medical practitioners the power to judge deviation from a so-called 'normal' state as illness prioritizes medical outcomes over other considerations and reinforces the claim to immunity from external accountability. After assessing a set of circumstances as abnormal, a judgement has to be made and the power to judge illness is not insignificant. Kennedy points to the obvious implications of illness being a product of social, political and moral values and argues that, 'if illness is a judgement, the practice of medicine can be understood in terms of power'; and he adds, 'he who makes the judgement wields the power' (ibid.). These are some of the preliminary issues which underlie public interest questions and the distribution of power between the patient and the doctor.

As a society we are philosophically committed to the value of personal autonomy and respect for private morality. The law may not be invoked in order to impose the particular moral views of one segment of society on another (Charlesworth, 1993, p.19). The medical profession, however, has been accorded this privilege by the courts, legislatures and even by the absence of regulation. The professional autonomy of medicine has permitted medical opinion and professional practice to determine what is legally permissible. In this chapter I address the way power is delegated to the medical profession over circumstances it and others define and accept as medical work and which is exempt from evaluation and control by those outside the profession. These questions are not new. The breadth and depth of scholarship reveals common links and patterns. In the following discussion I examine these issues and argue for legal and societal recognition of the broader non-technical dimensions of medical decision making. I am using legal developments and the law mainly for illustrative purposes and this is not intended to be a discussion of all legal aspects in each of the areas, or a comprehensive analysis of legal doctrines and principles.

Medicalization

The term 'medicalization' refers to the process whereby the medical profession has assumed and been given authority over numerous spheres of human activity, including life and death, as well as many areas between these points. Medicalization also refers to the increased incidence of medical interventions by doctors who are highly trained to understand the mechanisms of the human body. As Mitchinson says, in Chapter 2 of the present volume, it is becoming increasingly difficult to find many aspects of our lives that are not medicalized or at least not subject to the influences of the medical profession. Nevertheless, the importance of medicalization cannot be gauged in quantitative terms. Its true significance lies in the power and social control the state vests in the medical profession over medical work.

Human Reproduction

Women have been especially affected by the extensive net of medicalization. Although women have always sought the means to control fertility, this goal has been most effectively realized throughout the twentieth century. Reproductive autonomy extends beyond maternal and fetal concerns; it is also a social issue which influences the capacity of women to be involved in, and contribute equally at, all levels of society.

Important aspects of women's reproductive lives, which were traditionally undertaken by informal medical practitioners, converted natural phases into medical events warranting medical surveillance and intervention. Medical practitioners took steps to eliminate competition and, through the assertion of medical dominance, they professionalized human reproduction by subsuming 'informal' health practitioners such as female midwives and other women healers into and under the control of the medical hierarchy. Other competitors were labelled as 'quacks' or 'irregulars' and the medical speciality, obstetrics and gynaecology, gained a secure footing over reproductive medicine in the early decades of this century. As medical practitioners became the recognized experts in reproductive medicine, they gained control over and promoted the further medicalization of fertility, infertility, pregnancy and giving birth. Women were valued because of their childbearing capacities, but were denied the power to make decisions over their own lives.

Sherwin observes:

> Medical experts have claimed the authority to determine the range of the concepts of health and illness. They have used this authority to declare that many conditions that constitute normalcy for women are unhealthy and therefore, suitable subjects for medical management. ... Classifying the ordinary events of women's lives as illness, licenses wide-scale medical management of women under the claim of beneficence. Feminists are understandably critical of the wholesale classification of ordinary female experience as illness. (Sherwin, 1992, pp.179–80)

Medical practitioners also paid a lot of attention to women's bodies and defined them as deviant because they differed from 'normal' male bodies. As a result, doctors have medicalized and problematized women's bodies and played a significant role in socializing processes (see Chapter 2 of the present volume). Medicalizing a normal bodily function such as menstruation enabled medicine to collude with the state to exercise social control over women in nineteenth-century North America. By defining menstruation as a disability, medical practitioners assisted the state in excluding women from involvement in public affairs. Sherwin says that, by the end of the nineteenth century, 'physicians were in the forefront of the campaign to drive women out of the universities and to restrict their participation in the suffrage campaign that increasingly brought women into the political sphere'. However, when economic needs altered and women were needed in the workforce, 'medical authorities revised their views on menstruation and encouraged continuous activity throughout menstruation' (Sherwin, 1992, p.183).

As cultural attitudes towards sexual mores became more relaxed, and effective birth control such as the contraceptive pill, as well as legal abortions, became available, the question of whether a child under 16 years could give consent to contraceptive advice and treatment became a legal issue in the 1980s. Traditionally, parents, and particularly fathers, have had the right to make guardianship decisions concerning the welfare of their minor children. Generally, medical decisions come within this province. However, in *Gillick* v. *West Norfolk and Wisbech Area Health Authority*, the House of Lords decided that the capacity of a child to consent to medical treatment is dependent on the understanding and maturity of the child. This ruling permits a doctor to decide if the minor is 'Gillick competent' and has the capacity to give consent. Gillick's case is commonly regarded as a landmark in the development of children's rights and the diminution of parental rights. Alternatively, and importantly for the purpose of this discussion, it must also be recognized that the test of Gillick competence extends the medical authority of doctors over parents by permitting doctors to advise and treat 'mature' minors without parental knowledge or consent (see Chapter 3, above).

Disability is a condition which has not always been regarded as medical. However, the medicalization of disability shows the way in which medical authority has concealed human rights issues and also the way in which the label 'medical' was extended to include non-clinical issues. The involuntary sterilization of a disabled woman was, until recently, assumed to be primarily a medical intervention and criteria for decision making were determined in a medical framework (see Chapter 3). Involuntary sterilizations have been commonly performed for contraceptive reasons as well as menstrual management. Over the last two decades, however, this has become a controversial issue. In Australia, this question of consent was finally resolved in the *Secretary, Department of Health and Community Services* v. *JWB and SMB*. In this case, the High Court of Australia found that sterilization in these circumstances breached a common law right to personal inviolability and held that parents as joint guardians of an incompetent child could not authorize the operation without a court order. It was further held that the Family Court of Australia had the jurisdiction to carry out such a procedure on the basis of a 'best interests' test and that the best interests test in these cases is subject to sterilization being a step of last resort. The court recognized that the question had been medicalized to a great degree and emphasized that sterilization is not merely a medical issue:

> The decision to sterilise, at least where it is to be carried out for contraceptive purposes, and especially now when technology and expertise make the procedure relatively safe, is not merely a *medical* issue. This is also reflected in the concern raised in several of the cases reviewed, that the consequences of sterilisation are not merely biological but also social and psychological. (At pp.79,181)

As I have noted, menstrual management is also regarded as a justification for sterilizing disabled women without their consent. However, the Australian Family Court decision *P and P* (1994), which was reversed on appeal by the Full Court of the Family Court in 1995, reflects differing judicial attitudes to the question of menstrual management. The broad grounds for seeking the court ordered hysterectomy of an intellectually disabled young woman were the prevention of menstruation and the removal of the risk of pregnancy. The trial judge, Moore J, dismissed the application after hearing evidence from a range of medical and non-medical witnesses. She found that the problems associated with menstruation were not a justification for sterilization and further ways of dealing with the problem should be sought. Implicitly, she recognized that, if menstrual management is viewed in broad terms, rather than purely medical ones, there is more scope for considering outcomes that are not based solely on medical considerations and more opportunity to explore other options which do not infringe human rights. The Full Court, however, allowed the appeal and a hysterectomy was permitted. The Full Court decided that menstruation alone would not justify sterilization; however, in these circumstances, the court viewed menstrual training as an end in itself which appeared to have little value, given that a pregnancy would have been detrimental to the young woman.

Infertility is another condition which has not always been labelled a medical matter (see Chapter 5 of the present volume). Infertility constitutes a form of deviance from parenthood and family norms and, with the assistance of modern technology, more and more people can be relieved of the consequence of infertility – involuntary childlessness. As a means of promoting normative standards, legislation in some jurisdictions regulates reproductive technology by requiring candidates to be screened for treatment and imposing conditions which mimic traditional family structures (see Chapters 5 and 6, above). The combination of technological and scientific developments in reproductive medicine has introduced a new dimension to the means of controlling women's bodies through medical surveillance and intervention. Reproductive technologies may appear to expand reproductive choice, but they also narrow the ambit of choice by subjecting women to greater social and medical control and by further pathologizing women's bodies (see Chapters 4–6 of the present volume). As Sherwin correctly says, 'Because effective forms of technology increase the possibilities for human intervention in reproduction, they create the opportunities for greater power in the hands of whoever controls the technology' (Sherwin, 1992, p.119). Even procreation itself has become a medical event.

In another sense, a woman seeking an abortion is regarded by some as deviant because she is not conforming to motherhood norms. This perceived form of deviance was classified as a criminal act by nineteenth-century statutes and was later medicalized as doctors gained control over therapeutic abortion (Petersen, 1993, pp.49–70). Canada is the only western jurisdiction which has repealed criminal abortion statutes, but even in Canada, as in all other western jurisdictions, social and structural limitations are placed on women's choice to terminate a pregnancy and the medical profession is the moral 'gatekeeper' to abortion (Chapters 4 and 4 of the present volume; Sherwin, 1992, p.114).

The practice of referring to the fetus as a separate patient has crept into obstetric medicine in response to advances in reproductive and fetal technology. The medical model of pregnancy encourages the physician to regard the pregnant woman and the fetus as two entities and this model of pregnancy has contributed to the development of the so-called 'maternal/fetal conflict' (McLean and Petersen, 1996). In addition, it is becoming difficult to regard the embryo or fetus as an inert non-being as preconception tests, prenatal tests and fetal monitoring emphasize the individuality, current well-being, future well-being and gender of the potential being.[1] Although the law consistently holds that a fetus does not become a legal person with enforceable rights until live birth, medical interventions and technology have led to the increasing personification of the fetus and present grave dangers to women's reproductive autonomy. Court decisions concerning the status of the fetus reinforce changing perceptions of the relationship between the pregnant woman and her fetus, highlighting 'the potential for conflict between the autonomy of the pregnant woman and the development of the fetus' (Mair, 1996, p.87). As well, courts have ordered Caesarian operations in the UK and the USA without the consent of the pregnant woman (*Re S (Adult: Refusal of medical treatment)*; *Re A C*). The conflictual and urgent nature of these decisions has been used to justify the judicial deprivation of the woman's right to personal inviolability and undue reliance being placed on medical opinion.

Advances in genetics, preconception and postconception screening and fetal technology encourage the desire for 'designer' babies, even though this cannot be guaranteed by science. Increased medical intervention and screening techniques, on the surface, appear to give many women in western societies more choice over the kind of child they wish to mother than ever before. Obviously this has many benefits. Many women will choose not to give birth to a child who they believe will live a life of suffering and pain or have a significantly diminished quality of life. Furthermore, some women will choose not to assume the responsibility of caring for a sick or disabled child for personal or family reasons. However, the decision to terminate a pregnancy will frequently be based on a realistic assessment that society is unwilling to meet the demands of 'special needs' families. Various forms of pressure may also be placed on a woman in these circumstances. McLean notes that in 'some areas no screening will be offered unless the prospective parents agree that they will not rule out a termination should the results of the test indicate genetic handicap' (McLean, 1994, p.1224). New technology offers more choices but it also presents dangers because of the potential for 'new structures and limitations on choice' (Katzman, 1994, p.14).

Before turning to dying and death, one further point can be made about women and the medical profession. In spite of the intensive medicalization of women's bodies, discriminatory exclusion practices have been identified in the area of human subject research. Historically, paternalistic practices have excluded women, or certain classes of women, from clinical trials and drug experiments, among other things because of hormonal changes, recruiting problems and fear of liability for fetal injury (see Chapter 9, above). Autonomy-based arguments opposing beneficence and moral obligations to potential lives continue to be the major focus of the debates. The issue is extremely complex and women can benefit greatly from the information to be gleaned from clinical trials. Recognition that competent women have the right to self-determination as well as full disclosure about the trials must be given the highest priority. Moreover, it is vital that women are included in the debate over future regulatory policies.

Dying and Death

Doctors define death and issue certificates pronouncing that a person has died. In many cases death is obvious. In other cases it is a matter of medical judgement and not necessarily an objective or scientific fact. If robbed of the capacity to make competent decisions, human beings are entitled to decisions about their bodies being based on a respect for human rights. Important practical, ethical and legal consequences follow when a clinical definition of death is necessary because of life-saving and life-preserving treatment or where there is a possibility of organ transplantation. Traditionally, the heart and lungs were the major focus and when vital functions such as breathing and blood circulation ceased the person was presumed to be dead. Using a botanical metaphor, Singer says: 'doctors knew that, if breathing and circulation ceased, then after a decent interval you could be sure that the patient was dead. In much the same way as gardeners know that if the sap has permanently ceased to flow and twigs are stiff and dry the tree is dead' (Singer, 1994, p.21). It could also be added that a similarly competent assessment could be made by persons other than doctors. Singer also reminds us of the Norwegian Blue Parrot sketch in the *Monty Python's Flying Circus* series, where John Cleese disputes the shopkeeper's suggestion that the bird kept very still because it was pining for the fjords! Cleese loudly exclaims that the bird is 'stone dead ... definitely deceased ... bleeding demised ... ceased to be ... a stiff' (ibid.).

Improvements in resuscitation and other life-saving support measures can render the traditional cardiorespiratory tests obsolete in some circumstances. This has led to the development of terms such as 'brain death' or 'brain stem death' which apply when there has been an irreversible cessation of brain function. When a patient's brain is severely damaged but the brain stem has not been destroyed, the patient is a comatose but live person – and there may be no prospect of recovery. The anomalous condition, known as persistent vegetative state (PVS), occurs when an individual has suffered permanent loss to the cortical function of the brain, the part of the brain which is responsible for human intellectual function, but the brain stem has survived. These people rarely have any prospect of recovery but, because they are legally alive, withdrawing life-sustaining treatment is potentially a criminal act (*Airedale National Health Service Trust* v. *Bland; Law Hospital NHS Trust* v. *The Lord Advocate and Others* (transcript), 22 March 1996). McLean goes to the core of the question when she points out that these are medical decisions which result in death. She argues that, 'if we intend for this to continue, it is vital that it is carried out against a backdrop of respect for rights rather than the narrower confines of professional practice' (Chapter 8 of the present volume).

In the UK there is no statutory definition of death and this encourages courts to rely on a clinical definition. Legislation in other jurisdictions has attempted to solve the problem by designing dual criteria for death. For example, section 41 of the Human Tissue Act (Vic.) defines death as occurring when blood circulation and all brain functions have irreversibly ceased. This statutory approach still requires a clinical definition of death and, in an era of galloping technology, it is difficult for the law to keep up with medical science. Mason and McCall Smith argue that legislative measures of this kind merely but appropriately 'spell out good medical practice within a legal framework' (Mason and McCall Smith, 1994, p.290) However, this approach continues to perpetuate circularity by reinforcing medical opinion as the determinant of ethical and legal practice.

The relatively new medical practice of maintaining brain dead pregnant women with life support measures for the sole purpose of maximizing the chances of fetal survival is a dual dilemma because it poses questions about reproductive autonomy as well as the clinical definition of death (see Chapter 7 of the present volume). When a decision to maintain a dead pregnant woman's body is made purely within the confines and according to the dictates of medical practice, issues about the dead woman's right to control over her body are endangered because her right to personal autonomy is transferred to others without her consent or agreement.

The medicalization of death has transformed death and dying from a human and religious experience to 'a problem of bodily function' (Charlesworth, 1993, p.57).[2] Advances in technology have altered the way we view dying and death, increasing our expectations of and dependence on the medical profession. In addition, social and cultural attitudes have been influenced by the hospitalization of dying and death: 'The hospital is now in our society the principal context ... within which death takes place' (ibid., p.58). Fear of death is obviously not new, but as people become less used to being around dying people in the home the taboo and mystery of death intensifies.

The other side of increased confidence in sophisticated life-sustaining capacities is the fear of being forced to endure a protracted existence which by many standards may be judged as not worth living. Moreover, advances in genetics which provide new genetic knowledge, including information about late onset conditions, are forcing people to consider issues about their lives, health care and manner of dying more than ever before. As Dworkin argues, the 'increased power of new medical technology has plainly increased people's interest in the way of controlling the time and manner of one's death' (Dworkin, 1993, p.183). There is a growing demand for the recognition that personal autonomy should encompass the right to determine and control, as far as possible, the circumstances of dying and death. This is reflected in increased legislative and judicial support for a patient's right to refuse medical treatment (see Medical Treatment Act 1988 (Vic.); *Re T (Adult: refusal of medical treatment)*; *Re C (Adult refusal of medical treatment)*) as well as considerable debate and controversy about advanced directives, euthanasia and physician-assisted suicide. These developments underpin challenges to medical practices and, legal principles as well as the ethical values embodied in the Hippocratic Oath (see Chapter 1 of the present volume). Furthermore, as McLean observes:

> Knowledge of the manner of one's death, or the quality which can be expected of one's dying, may profoundly shift attitudes about the value and importance of autonomy in choosing the method and time of death, supervening the current, rather emotional, debate. This will clearly have an impact on doctors as well as on patients ... it may well be that a powerful force for legal change in this area has already been unleashed and can only gather momentum. (McLean, 1996, p.42)

Professionalism and Medical Work

The right to control over work and its outcome is the essence of professionalism. Furthermore, the label 'medical work' has evolved over time in response to changing notions of illness. As Freidson argues, medical work is not just *any* kind of work. He describes it as a special kind of work which stems from a body of knowledge which 'is esoteric, complex, and discretionary in character' and 'sufficiently complex and uncertain to require the exercise of discretion and judgment from case to case' (Freidson, 1994, p.164). He adds that the community regards this work as intrinsically special because it is perceived as providing benefits to individuals and to the community at large. Professional autonomy gives the medical practitioners the right to be arbiters over their own work and to exercise discretionary authority (ibid., p.166). Abortion, for example, is prima facie a criminal act. Nevertheless, the Abortion Act 1967 (UK) gives doctors the right to decide if an abortion is a lawful medical intervention when indicated for social as well as physical, life-threatening and eugenic reasons. Social indications for abortion have been medicalized and doctors rather than the woman concerned have been delegated with the authority to decide whether or not an act is criminal, let alone moral. Judicial attitudes to the role of the doctor in abortion decision making are captured in Baker P's oft-quoted statement in *Paton* v. *BPAS*, where he said: 'it would be a bold and brave judge ... who would seek to interfere with the discretion of doctors acting under the Abortion Act 1967' (at p.282). Freidson regards this discretionary power as *central* to the ideology of professional autonomy.

Professional autonomy is further justified on the grounds that professional supervision, evaluation and regulation can only be done by peers because no-one else is competent enough to make an evaluation (ibid., p.200). The claim to self-regulation is also justified on the grounds that the profession and its individual members are committed to ethical practices and to the maintenance of professional standards. The combination of medicalization and professional autonomy has secured for medical practitioners clinical freedom over medical work even though it is well established that 'only part of any kind of work is technical, based on truly esoteric knowledge and skill; only part of what enters into discretionary action is technical rather than social and moral' (ibid., p.166).

In some areas medical discretion or authority is becoming subject to more restriction. Legislation governing reproductive technologies has placed regulatory frameworks over medical practices in some jurisdictions for the purpose of achieving social goals and upholding cultural norms (see Chapters 5 and 6 of the present volume) and they also affirm the right of medical practitioners to exercise clinical authority. Legal affirmation of medical dominance is also part of the legislative frameworks. This is significant, given that many of the health professionals on these teams are not medical practitioners. The major focus of these statutes is to implement social screening, provide for access to non-identifying and/or identifying information and regulate research practices. Within this framework, clinical authority remains with medical practitioners. As has already been noted, claims to personal inviolability have led to some restriction of medical autonomy in the involuntary sterilization cases. The fusion of therapeutic and non-therapeutic reasons underlying decision making in theses cases has been addressed, with closer scrutiny being paid to the non-therapeutic reasons (*Re D (a minor) (wardship: sterilisation)*). In *Re Eve*, the Canadian justice, Forest J, went further and concluded that non-consensual sterilizations should never be authorized by Canadian courts. Nicholson CJ adopted another strategy, but on the same theme, in the early Australian sterilization case *Re Jane*. In his view, the principal or major aim of the procedure is the critical question (pp.77, 260). However, in *Re B (a minor) (wardship:sterilisation)* the House of Lords was not prepared to analyse therapeutic versus non-therapeutic reasons and their Lordships preferred to rely on the best interests test. Significantly, medical evidence played an important role in the reasoning process adopted by the court in that case (Petersen, 1996, p.66). However, these approaches to respecting the underlying right to personal inviolability demonstrate a limited understanding of the problem because they do not treat health or illness as a social construct. As Brazier asks, 'is childbirth, unattended by gross complications, therapeutic or non-therapeutic treatment?' (Brazier, 1992, p.87). Moreover, does it matter if the reasons for a medical procedure are non-therapeutic if a major violation of human rights is at issue?

Conclusions

Autonomy over medical decision making and the power of medicine to define medical practice has elevated medical opinion to the status of a legal test. Although the courts are now frequently involved in reviewing medical decision making where ethical and social questions are at issue, judicial deference to medical opinion is a common theme in these cases. The Bolam Test, which was established in *Bolam* v. *Friern Hospital Management Committee* and later upheld and modified in *Sidaway* v. *Board of Governors of the Bethlem Royal Hospital and Maudsley Hospital,* [3] illustrates the significance of medical opinion in legal proceedings. According to these cases, established and accepted medical practice is the test for medical negligence. Its application, however, has become more pervasive. In the non-consensual sterilization case *F* v. *West Berkshire HA*, the House of Lords ruled that, if a person is unable to give consent to a medical procedure because of mental incompetence, a doctor must provide treatment which he or she thinks is in the best interests of the patient according to the standard of care laid down in *Bolam* (Brazier, 1992, pp.390–2). Moreoever, in the criminal case *R* v. *Arthur*, Dr Arthur was charged with murder (later reduced to manslaughter) of a baby born with apparently uncomplicated Down's syndrome. During the criminal trial, the court accepted evidence of standard medical practice concerning the care of neonate babies even though this evidence had no technical relevance to the criminal charge. Dr Arthur was acquitted on the application of the civil test and the treatment of severely disabled babies continues to be shrouded with legal uncertainty. Using medical opinion as the measure of what is legally permissible conceals significant social and moral aspects of medical work and permits medical practitioners to be the arbiters of legal rights. It also imposes a great responsibility on the shoulders of medical practitioners – which they may not necessarily greet with enthusiasm.

It must be acknowledged that the medical profession offers important technical expertise, but, as Freidson points out, supervision is needed over 'those social and moral areas of work where technical peer review is overly narrow [and] evaluation and control by those outside the profession becomes essential' (Freidson, 1994, p.166). The right to patient autonomy requires that, when the individual is competent to give consent or refusal, freedom of choice in the widest sense must be guaranteed. Clearly, full disclosure of all the benefits and risks is critical and so-called 'therapeutic lies' and other forms of non-disclosure are an insult to patient autonomy. Commenting on UK medical practice, Brazier argues that 'the law relating to treatment pays little more than lip service to patient autonomy' (Brazier, 1992, p.92). Furthermore, in the area of human reproduction, for example, the right to information is essential to reproductive decision making. As Cook notes, 'The people's right to know applies both to their informed choice of medical care, as well as to their self-determination in all other matters of their lives that they are able to control and influence' (Cook, 1995, p.1011). Attention needs to be paid to the power imbalance between the patient and the doctor and the special vulnerability of patients in many circumstances. Moreover, the assessment of competency is fraught with human rights questions. It is not entirely clear that a doctor is the appropriate person to make this assessment and the role of the doctor in this process needs reappraisal. Also, in devising methods of assessing incompetence, processes such as advance directives and substituted decision making must be thoroughly addressed.

Important social and ethical consequences can flow from medical decisions. The information about the human condition being released by the Human Genome Project and other scientific advances presents enormous challenges to the future of the human race and the role of law (see Chapter 10 of the present volume). As McLean says, 'There can be few developments in medicine and science which have the capacity so fundamentally to alter our present and future lives as those emerging from the new genetics.' She adds that we cannot afford to ignore 'the impact that our new capacities will have on the actual providers of health care and on the patients whom they see' (McLean, 1996, p.41). Genetic information has wide ramifications for patients, medical practitioners and society as a whole. It is already challenging the confidentiality principles in the relationship between the doctor and the patient, particularly as doctors acquire access to information which affects not only the individual's health, economic and employment interests, but broad societal interests.

Recognition of the intersection between technical and non-technical aspects of medical decisions is an important step towards respecting human rights. Medical autonomy and discretionary authority may be an appropriate means of ensuring technical expertise, but the establishment of principles, guidelines and enforcement structures are necessary for the protection of the important non-technical or social, legal and ethical dimensions of medical decision making. Preparation for the future requires a balance to be achieved between the competing goals of public interest and human rights. Medicine and science offer many benefits and dangers to humankind and one of the challenges of the future is to capitalize fully on the benefits and to mitigate, if not avoid, the dangers.

Notes

1 This 'divisible' model of pregnancy was encouraged by the trimester construction established in *Roe* v. *Wade*, whereby the US Supreme Court balanced the competing interests of the pregnant woman and the fetus as a means of delineating a woman's right to an abortion and the state's interest in the developing fetus.

2 Charlesworth is citing Mischler *et al.* here. See E.G. Mischler *et al.* (eds), *Social Context of Health, Illness and Patient Care*, Cambridge: Cambridge University Press, 1981, p.239.

3 Some limits over medical practice have been laid down by the Australian High Court in *Rogers* v. *Whitaker* (1992) 175 CLR 479. In this case the court declined to permit the standard of medical care to be determined solely or even primarily by reference to medical practice based on a responsible body of medical opinion.

References

Brazier, M. (1992), *Medicine, Patients and the Law*, London: Penguin Books.

Charlesworth, M. (1993), *Bioethics in a Liberal Society*, Cambridge: Cambridge University Press.

Cook, Rebecca (1995), 'Human Rights and Reproductive Self-Determination', *The American University Law Review*, **44**, (4), April, pp.975–1475.

Dworkin, R. (1993), *Life's Dominion*, London: Harper Collins.

Freidson, E. (1994), *Professionalism Reborn*, Cambridge: Polity Press.

Katzman, Rothman, B. (1994), *The Tentative Pregnancy*, Pandora: London.

Kennedy, I. (1981), *The Unmasking of Medicine*, London: Allen & Unwin.

McLean, Sheila (1994), 'Mapping the Human Genome – Friend or Foe', *Social Science Medicine*, **39**, (9), pp.1221–27.

McLean, Sheila (1996), 'The New Genetics: A Challenge to Clinical Values', *Proceedings of Royal College of Physicians Edinburgh*, **26**, pp.41–50.

McLean, Sheila and Kerry Petersen (1996), 'Patient Status: The Foetus and the Pregnant Woman', *Australian Journal of Human Rights*, **2** (2), pp.229–41.

Mair, Jane (1996), 'Maternal/Foetal Conflict: Defined or Defused?', in Sheila McLean (ed.), *Contemporary Issues in Law, Medicine and Ethics*, Aldershot: Dartmouth, pp.79–97.

Mason, J.K. and R.A. McCall Smith (1994), *Law and Medical Ethics*, London: Butterworths.

Petersen, K. (1993), *Abortion Regimes*, Aldershot: Dartmouth.

Petersen, Kerry (1996), 'Private Decisions and Public Scrutiny: Sterilisation and Minors in Australia and England', in Sheila McLean (ed.), *Contemporary Issues in Law, Medicine and Ethics*, Aldershot: Dartmouth, pp.57–77.

Sherwin, S. (1992), *No Longer Patient*, Philadelphia: Temple University Press.

Singer, P. (1994), *Rethinking Life and Death*, Melbourne:The Free Press Publishing Company.

Cases

Airedale NHS Trust v. *Bland* [1993] 1 All ER 821.

Bolam v. *Friern Hospital Management Committee* [1957] 2 All ER 118.

F v. *West Berkshire HA* [1989] 2 All ER 547.

Gillick v. *West Norfolk and Wisbech AHA* [1986] 1 AC 112.
Law Hospital NHS Trust v. *The Lord Advocate and Others*, (transcript) 22 March 1996.
P and P (1994) FLC 92-462.
P and P (1995) FLC 92-615 (Full Court).
Paton v. *BPAS* [1979] 1 QB 276.
Re A C (1987)533 A 2d DC.
Re B (a minor) (wardship: sterilisation) [1988] AC 199.
Re C (Adult: Refusal of medical treatment) [1994] 1 All ER 819.
Re D (a minor) (wardship: sterilisation) [1976] 1 All ER 326.
Re Eve (1986) 31 DLR (4th) 1.
Re Jane (1989) FLC 92-007.
Re S (Adult: Refusal of medical treatment [1992] 4 All ER 671.
Re T (Adult: Refusal of medical treatment [1992] 1 All ER 649.
R v. *Arthur* (1981) The Times, 6 November, p1.
Roe v. *Wade* 410 US 113 (1973).
Rogers v. *Whitaker* (1992) 175 CLR 479.
Secretary, Department of Health and Community Services v. *JWB and SMB* [1992] 175 CLR 218.
Sidaway v. *Board of Governors of the Bethlem Royal Hospital and Maudsley Hospital* [1985] AC 871; [1985] 1 All ER 643 (HL).

Index

For Product Safety Concerns and Information please contact our EU representative GPSR@taylorandfrancis.com Taylor & Francis Verlag GmbH, Kaufingerstraße 24, 80331 München, Germany

Batch number: 10725802

Printed by Printforce, the Netherlands